教育部人文社会科学研究青年基金项目
"中美跨洋互动写作中的同伴互评研究"（项目编号：20YJC740049）赞助

新时代外国语言文学与文化研究系列丛书

An Analysis on Peer Review in
Sino-US Cross-Pacific
Exchange Writing

中美跨洋互动写作中的同伴互评研究

裘莹莹　左广明　著

图书在版编目(CIP)数据

中美跨洋互动写作中的同伴互评研究/裘莹莹,左广明著.—苏州:苏州大学出版社,2022.11
(新时代外国语言文学与文化研究系列丛书)
ISBN 978-7-5672-4071-1

Ⅰ.①中… Ⅱ.①裘… ②左… Ⅲ.①第二语言—写作—教学研究 Ⅳ.①H09

中国版本图书馆CIP数据核字(2022)第188727号

书　　名:	中美跨洋互动写作中的同伴互评研究
	ZHONGMEI KUAYANG HUDONG XIEZUO ZHONG DE TONGBAN HUPING YANJIU
著　　者:	裘莹莹　左广明
责任编辑:	万才兰
装帧设计:	吴　钰
出版发行:	苏州大学出版社(Soochow University Press)
社　　址:	苏州市十梓街1号　邮编: 215006
印　　刷:	广东虎彩云印刷有限公司
邮购热线:	0512-67480030
销售热线:	0512-67481020
开　　本:	710 mm×1 000 mm　1/16　印张: 16.75　字数: 275千
版　　次:	2022年11月第1版
印　　次:	2022年11月第1次
书　　号:	ISBN 978-7-5672-4071-1
定　　价:	56.00元

图书若有印装错误,本社负责调换
苏州大学出版社营销部　电话: 0512-67481020
苏州大学出版社网址　http://www.sudapress.com
苏州大学出版社邮箱　sdcbs@suda.edu.cn

总 序

　　淮阴工学院外国语学院的前身是1984年成立的淮阴工业专科学校英语教研组，迄今已有近40年的办学历史，现设有英语、商务英语、翻译和俄语4个本科专业，其中英语专业为省一流专业建设点，外国语言文学为校一级重点建设学科。

　　淮阴工学院外国语学院目前在校本科生总数为822人。现有教职工89人，其中教授5人、副教授33人、硕士生导师11人，博士（生）29人。拥有江苏省高校首批外语信息化教学示范基地、张纯如中外人文交流研究中心、语言文化研究中心、翻译研究中心、语音综合实验教学与研究中心、外语语言培训中心等教学科研机构。

　　近40年来，淮阴工学院外国语学院教职工秉承"为中华之崛起而读书"的校训，弘扬"明德尚学、自强不息"的淮工精神，聚焦重点，突出特色，深化内涵，围绕英汉语言对比、翻译理论与实践、英美文学、二语习得、俄罗斯语言文学等方向开展深入研究，并取得了丰硕成果。近5年来，外国语学院获批省一流课程1门、省在线课程1门、校在线课程8门；获省重点教材立项4部、校重点教材立项6部；教师共发表学术论文184篇，出版教材、著（译）作15部；先后承担教育部人文社科项目1项、省部级科研项目12项、市厅级项目77项，获市厅级科研教学奖励12项。

　　为迎接党的二十大胜利召开，立足新时代，担当新作为，淮阴工学院外国语学院进一步完善学科布局，出台一系列规章制度，繁荣学术氛围，以优异的学术成果向党的二十大献礼。我们决定推出"新时代外国语言文学与文化研究系列丛书"，展现淮阴工学院外国语学院学术研究最新成果，向学界汇报最新的研究发现，希望通过交流互鉴来促进学院的不断成长。

　　本套丛书呈现出以下三个特点：

一是学科覆盖领域丰富多元。丛书的学科研究涉及文学、语言学、翻译学等领域。在文学方面，有于敏博士的《互文重写：从中世纪浪漫传奇到〈哈利·波特〉》，尝试建构从经典文学到通俗文学的互文重写理论框架，以当代英国奇幻文学的经典作品为案例，讨论通俗文学中的文化传统承继与当下现实意义；郁敏副教授的《杰克·凯鲁亚克"垮掉"哲学研究》，从自由哲学、爱之哲学、救赎哲学与生态哲学四个方面探讨以杰克·凯鲁亚克为代表的美国"垮掉的一代"重精神生活轻物质主义、无所畏惧、勇于探索又心怀悲悯的"垮掉"哲学内涵。在语言学方面，有裴莹莹博士、左广明副教授的《中美跨洋互动写作中的同伴互评研究》，以网络同伴互动语料为研究对象，探讨中美同伴互评类型、互动行为、互动模式及其影响因素；张晓雯博士的《英汉日动结式结构的比较研究》，探讨英、汉、日三种语言动结式结构特征，以及三者之间的差异。在翻译学方面，有胡庭树博士的《翻译不确定性的哲学内涵及译学价值》，围绕蒯因的翻译不确定性论题展开相关研究，通过分析翻译中的意义、指称等不确定性问题来探讨翻译是如何可能的哲学问题；孙建光博士的《对话与融合：〈尤利西斯〉汉译研究》，以《尤利西斯》汉译本为研究对象，从宏观维度和微观维度对《尤利西斯》汉译进行描述性研究。这些作品既有理论探索，又有案例分析，形成了学理与实践的有机融合。

二是注重地方文化传播与译介。习近平总书记对建设大运河文化带做出重要指示：大运河是祖先留给我们的宝贵遗产，是流动的文化，要统筹保护好、传承好、利用好。大运河淮安段不仅历史底蕴深厚，而且发挥着水利航运、南水北调、防灾排涝等综合功能，素有"南船北马、九省通衢"之誉。淮安得名于1500多年前，取"淮水安澜"之意，其深厚的历史文化积淀造就了丰富的淮安文化。本套丛书中有专门译介出版淮安名人、淮扬美食文化、淮安古建文化、淮安戏剧文化等具有淮安特色的文化图书，力图做好地方文化的传播与译介，将数千年来淮安大地上形成的"城、人、事、景、食"等特色传统文化译介好、传播好，持续擦亮"伟人故里""运河之都""美食之都""文化名城"四张城市名片，做到文化传承薪火相传、代代守护，为淮安城市发展增添源源不断的文化动力。

三是国别与区域研究成效显著。国别与区域研究作为一门新兴的交叉学科，已成为交叉学科中的一级学科，为科学研究提供了全新的领域，未来将成为为国家服务的重要领域。外国语学院东南亚国家国情研究团队正积极开展菲律宾当代著名作家法兰西斯科·S.何塞的作品译介与研究，将先后出版《三个菲律宾女人》《法兰西斯科·S.何塞短篇小说》《树》等作品，通过译介菲律宾文学作品向广大读者呈现菲律宾的社会、经济、政治等全景式图景。俄语国家国情研究团队闫静博士的《新时代中俄关系对世界格局的影响》，聚焦百年未有之大变局的时代背景，分析探讨中俄关系的发展对维护两国在国际舞台上的国家利益以及维护世界和平的重要意义；刘星博士的《俄汉身势语对比研究》，以俄汉身势语为研究对象，在系统阐释身势语相关概念的基础上，从跨文化交际视角对俄汉语中具有代表性的不同类型身势语进行对比研究。外国语学院目前积极组织科研团队，聚焦于东南亚和俄语区国家研究，紧扣新文科建设要求，关注学科交叉，力争在新的角度、新的内容、新的视野、新的思想方面不断外延外语人在新时代的新使命、新作为，产出更多新成果。

术有专攻，学无止境。每位学者的研究难免有学术或者技术方面的不足，恳请同行能够不吝赐教。

2022 年 8 月于淮阴工学院品学楼 2 号楼

前　言

"英语写作跨洋互动"（Cross-Pacific Exchange in English Writing）项目是由广东外语外贸大学、苏州科技大学与美国宾夕法尼亚州立大学、宾夕法尼亚米勒斯维尔大学等高校合作开发的一种基于网络的同伴互评活动，旨在通过中美大学生的网上写作活动促进不同文化之间的交流。该项目的实施步骤如下：首先，中美大学生观看中、美影片各一部，在规定时间内完成相同话题和相同体裁的写作任务，并上传至写作平台。其次，同伴根据教师提供的反馈清单，分组进行网上互评，每个混合小组包括两名中国学生和两名美国学生。最后，写作者上传修改稿，并附上一份反思日志。这种跨国家、跨语言、跨文化的互动写作项目和模式，不仅是外语教学模式的新尝试，而且为教师、学生及其他研究者探讨二语写作研究与教学的可行性与有效性提供了新思路和新方法。

基于社会文化理论和认知互动理论，本书提出同伴互评的理论框架，对比中美同伴互评的类型和同伴互动行为的异同，分析混合小组同伴的互动模式及其影响因素，探索中美同伴互评体现的中西教育理念和文化思维异同。本书分为七章。第一章介绍研究内容、研究意义、语料与研究方法。第二章梳理同伴互评研究的多维视角，包括认知互动理论和社会文化理论。第三章构建研究的理论框架，包括同伴互评的界定、同伴互评的类型、同伴互动行为的编码和同伴互动模式的构建。第四章描述跨洋互动过程中同伴互评的特征，包括中美反馈者的反馈特征和中美写作者的回评特征，中美同伴互评类型的异同及其体现的文化思维方式。第五章分析中美跨洋互动写作中的同伴互动行为，包括中美大学生的修改行为、采纳行为、支架策略三种互动行为及它们生成的互动模式。第六章探讨二语写作中的中美同伴互动模式，并结合小组成员的在线讨论和写作者的反思日志，归纳互动模式的影响因素。第七章总结研究发现，阐述研究的理论意义和教学启示。

　　本书的意义在于在探索网络自然互动环境下（而非教学环境下），由中国英语学习者和美国母语者组成的同伴互评小组形成的同伴互评的类型、行为和互动模式；调查混合小组使用在线平台执行写作反馈任务时的交互动态，进一步拓宽合作写作研究的范围。鉴于同伴互评对学生学习和写作的促进作用，写作教学中的同伴互评研究成果丰硕。但现有文献中同伴反馈存在相关术语众多且所指不一致、分类重叠及识别方法耗时费力的问题。本书基于以往研究，重新界定同伴互评，确定同伴互评的编码框架，构建同伴互评的理论框架，为深入研究同伴反馈奠定理论基础。基于该理论框架，本书采用定量分析与定性分析相结合的研究方法，分析中美跨洋互动写作中的同伴互评。研究结果有助于教师制定同伴互评策略，优化同伴互动模式，以便最大限度地提高网上同伴互评的效果，增加学习者在合作写作中获得的学习机会。

　　在整个研究过程中，笔者作为观察员，了解项目实施的相关信息；下载学生的写作、在线讨论和反思日志；转写后续访谈的录音记录，撰写研究日志。在语料和数据搜集过程中，笔者得到了该跨洋互动写作项目的两位主持人，即广东外语外贸大学的郑超教授和美国宾夕法尼亚州立大学的游晓晔教授的大力支持，对此深表感谢。笔者还要感谢教育部人文社会科学研究青年基金项目的资助与本人所在单位的各种支持和鼓励，由此得以将该研究成果出版成书。

　　本书是笔者基于"英语写作跨洋互动"项目语料实施的中美同伴互评研究，限于水平，疏漏错讹之处在所难免，敬请专家、同行批评指正。

目 录

第一章 绪论 / 1

    1.1 研究内容 / 1

    1.2 研究意义 / 3

    1.3 语料与研究方法 / 4

        1.3.1 语料 / 4

        1.3.2 研究方法 / 6

    1.4 各章节简介 / 7

第二章 同伴互评研究的多维视角 / 9

    2.1 认知互动理论视角 / 9

        2.1.1 理论框架 / 9

        2.1.2 实证研究 / 11

    2.2 社会文化理论视角 / 19

        2.2.1 理论框架 / 19

        2.2.2 实证研究 / 21

    2.3 跨文化写作中的同伴互动研究 / 33

    2.4 结语 / 34

第三章 同伴互评的理论框架 / 37

    3.1 同伴互评的界定 / 37

        3.1.1 同伴互评的定义 / 37

        3.1.2 同伴互评的操作性定义 / 40

    3.2 同伴互评的类型 / 41

        3.2.1 同伴互评的分类 / 41

3.2.2 同伴互评类型的界定 / 55
3.3 同伴互动行为 / 66
　　3.3.1 语言功能的编码方案 / 66
　　3.3.2 作文修改的编码方案 / 69
　　3.3.3 支架策略的编码方案 / 72
3.4 同伴互动模式 / 74
　　3.4.1 同伴互动模式的定义 / 74
　　3.4.2 同伴互动模式的识别 / 75
3.5 结语 / 76

第四章 中美跨洋互动写作中同伴互评的特征 / 80

4.1 语料与研究问题 / 80
　　4.1.1 语料 / 80
　　4.1.2 研究问题 / 81
4.2 中美反馈者的反馈特征 / 82
　　4.2.1 中美同伴反馈的总体特征 / 82
　　4.2.2 中美同伴反馈的子类特征 / 85
4.3 中美写作者的回评特征 / 97
　　4.3.1 中美写作者回评的总体特征 / 97
　　4.3.2 中美写作者回评的子类特征 / 100
4.4 中美同伴互评类型的比较 / 112
　　4.4.1 中美同伴互评类型的共性分析 / 112
　　4.4.2 中美同伴互评类型的差异性分析 / 114
4.5 结语 / 130

第五章 中美跨洋互动写作中的同伴互动行为 / 132

5.1 语料与研究问题 / 132
5.2 中美同伴的互动行为 / 133
　　5.2.1 中美同伴的修改行为 / 133
　　5.2.2 中美同伴的采纳行为 / 136
　　5.2.3 中美写作组的支架策略 / 141

5.3 中美同伴互动行为的异同 / 149
    5.3.1 中美同伴互动行为的共性 / 149
    5.3.2 中美同伴互动行为的差异性 / 150

5.4 同伴互动模式的生成 / 151
    5.4.1 集体互动模式 / 153
    5.4.2 协作互动模式 / 155
    5.4.3 合作互动模式 / 158
    5.4.4 专家/新手互动模式 / 159

5.5 结语 / 164

第六章 二语写作中的中美同伴互动模式 / 166

6.1 语料与研究问题 / 166

6.2 中美同伴互动模式的生成 / 167
    6.2.1 中美同伴互动模式的识别 / 167
    6.2.2 中美同伴互动模式的特征 / 169

6.3 中美同伴互动模式的影响因素 / 169
    6.3.1 个体因素 / 170
    6.3.2 情境因素 / 174
    6.3.3 社会因素 / 178

6.4 结语 / 185

第七章 结论 / 187

7.1 研究发现 / 187
    7.1.1 中美同伴互评特征的比较分析 / 187
    7.1.2 中美同伴互动行为的比较分析 / 189
    7.1.3 二语写作中同伴互动模式的分析结果 / 191

7.2 研究启示 / 192
    7.2.1 理论启示 / 192
    7.2.2 教学启示 / 194

7.3 研究不足之处 / 195

7.4 对未来研究的建议 / 196

参考文献 / 197

附录 / 220

　　附录1：中国写作者的同伴反馈语料 / 220

　　附录2：美国写作者的同伴反馈语料 / 233

　　附录3：中国写作者后续访谈转录 / 242

　　附录4：第18轮跨洋互动写作项目活动说明（美国学生）/ 245

表格清单

表 3.1　反馈内容分类 / 50
表 3.2　反馈功能分类 / 54
表 3.3　语言功能的编码方案 / 67
表 3.4　作文修改的编码方案 / 71
表 3.5　支架策略的编码方案 / 73
表 4.1　中美大学生同伴反馈大类的总体分布 / 83
表 4.2　中国大学生同伴反馈大类的卡方检验 / 83
表 4.3　美国大学生同伴反馈大类的卡方检验 / 83
表 4.4　中美大学生同伴反馈大类的卡方检验 / 84
表 4.5　中美大学生同伴反馈子类的总体分布 / 86
表 4.6　中国大学生评价类反馈的卡方检验 / 91
表 4.7　中国大学生情感反馈的卡方检验 / 91
表 4.8　中国大学生验证性反馈的卡方检验 / 91
表 4.9　中国大学生指正性反馈的卡方检验 / 91
表 4.10　中国大学生同伴反馈子类的卡方检验 / 91
表 4.11　美国大学生评价类反馈的卡方检验 / 92
表 4.12　美国大学生情感反馈的卡方检验 / 93
表 4.13　美国大学生验证性反馈的卡方检验 / 93
表 4.14　美国大学生指正性反馈的卡方检验 / 93
表 4.15　美国大学生同伴反馈子类的卡方检验 / 93
表 4.16　中美大学生同伴反馈子类的卡方检验 / 95
表 4.17　中美大学生肯定性反馈的卡方检验 / 96
表 4.18　中美大学生重述的卡方检验 / 96
表 4.19　中美大学生信息性反馈的卡方检验 / 96
表 4.20　中美大学生情感反馈的卡方检验 / 97
表 4.21　中美大学生回评类型的总体分布 / 97

表 4.22　中国大学生回评类型的卡方检验 / 98
表 4.23　美国大学生回评类型的卡方检验 / 98
表 4.24　中美大学生回评类型的卡方检验 / 98
表 4.25　中美大学生回评子类的总体分布 / 100
表 4.26　中国大学生回评子类的卡方检验 / 103
表 4.27　美国大学生回评子类的卡方检验 / 104
表 4.28　中美大学生回评子类的卡方检验 / 105
表 4.29　中美大学生模糊性反馈的卡方检验 / 106
表 4.30　中美写作者视角的同伴反馈类型统计 / 106
表 5.1 　中国大学生作文修改的描述性统计 / 134
表 5.2 　美国大学生作文修改的描述性统计 / 135
表 5.3 　中国大学生采纳反馈的描述性统计 / 137
表 5.4 　美国大学生采纳反馈的描述性统计 / 139
表 6.1 　同伴互动小组语言功能的卡方检验 / 167
表 6.2 　同伴互动小组发起和响应功能的卡方检验 / 168
表 6.3 　中国大学生修改类型的卡方检验 / 169
表 6.4 　同伴互动小组互动模式的数据统计 / 169

插图清单

图 3.1　同伴反馈类型示意图 / 58
图 3.2　回评类型示意图 / 61
图 5.1　混合小组的同伴互动行为及模式 / 152
图 5.2　混合小组同伴互评的动态互动模型 / 164

第一章 绪 论

1.1 研究内容

迄今为止,写作研究已考查了母语和二语/外语课堂中与同伴反馈有关的各种问题,主要分为3个研究方向。一是同伴反馈对学生写作质量的影响。众多研究者认为反馈可以提高二语写作的质量,进而有助于二语习得;然而,对同伴反馈的效果仍然存有争议,并未达成共识。二语学习者必须以他们仍处于发展中的阅读和语言交流技能对同伴写作进行评论,并且二语学习者必须适应来自不同文化背景的同伴的沟通风格,并应对小组成员的不同工作态度和对团体规范的不同期望,二语环境中的同伴反馈可能极具挑战性。二是考察同伴反馈任务对学生的训练效果。在这些研究中,学生接受制定同伴反馈的培训,经过训练的同伴反馈会产生更多和更好的同伴反馈,提升同伴对话质量,增加学生在同伴反馈过程中的参与度和互动。三是调查同伴反馈的过程,重点关注学生互动和协商。学习是一种社交活动,社会互动对认知发展至关重要(Vygotsky, 1978)。基于学生在同伴互评期间的协作和互动交流,二语课堂上结对/小组写作任务环境中的互动和协作引起了教师与研究人员的注意。协作写作是一种鼓励在写作过程中进行交互的教学活动,已经被广泛应用于二语课堂。

互联网技术的发展提高了学习的便利性,使得基于网络的工具和在线同伴互评系统被广泛应用于在线学习,实现了不受时间和地点限制的学习互动。基于网络的同伴互评系统是专门设计用来支持写作评审和修改过程的,如SWoRD(Cho & Schunn, 2004)、Calibrated Peer Review(Russell, 2004)、MyReviewers(Moxley, 2012)、ELI(Hart-Davidson等,2010)、Peerceptiv(Schunn, 2017)等是北美高等教育机构开发的同伴互评系统。在线同伴互评系统的设计特点是参与者匿名互评，系统提供具体的评价维度表，写作者对同伴反馈进行回评，系统对反馈者的评分进行评估。（徐锦芬、朱茜，2019）该特点允许写作者以参与和互惠的方式撰写、查看与编辑内容。开放的评论系统、灵活的评论和响应结构使写作者能够在共同构建文本的过程中共同构建二语知识。（Hsu，2020）此外，异步协作写作功能提供了额外的反思时间，为二语学习者提供了更多对彼此的贡献做出更深层次的思考的机会（Storch，2012），让学习者专注于语言产出（Kessler，2009；Lee，2010）。现有研究也证实，在线讨论有利于知识构建和学习参与。（Huang等，2019）

在语言学习中，作为反馈的来源，同伴之间的相互评论和讨论已经被广泛应用于语言教育。（Hyland & Hyland，2006）现代教育使得学习者通过网络平台接触到多个反馈源（Diab，2016），特别是在线同伴互评系统的开发（如 Peerceptiv 互评系统、跨洋互动在线写作系统等），让母语者同伴反馈成为新的反馈源，丰富了同伴反馈的来源。网络交流互动不仅关注"地理上分散于各地的参与者建立的跨文化社区"（Thorne & Black，2007：138）中的语言，而且关注意义协商。在线互动满足当今语言学习者发展语言技能和跨文化交际能力的需求。（Guth & Helm，2010；Kramsch，2008；Thorne，2003）学习者从中体验到语言的多元性，接触到多种文化规范和价值观。在线同伴互评的参与者需要积极参与对话，与来自不同文化的同伴互动，感知同伴反馈的价值。（Guth & Helm，2010）在线书面反馈具有便利性和持久性的特点，可供反复阅读和思考；非本族语写作者不必依赖听力技能。在线学习环境为二语学习者提供了与英语母语者真实互动的机会。

因此，由母语者和二语学习者组成混合同伴反馈小组成为二语写作的一种趋势。与仅由母语者或二语学习者组成的同伴反馈小组相比，混合同伴反馈小组具有独特性，小组成员将不同的语言、文化及语用技能带入了同伴反馈任务。我们在很大程度上可以假定母语者具备同伴反馈所需的基本技能。二语学习者也仍然在开发他们的二语语言技能。尽管存在相当大的个体差异（如一些二语学习者在二语中具有母语或近乎母语的交际能力），但是混合同伴反馈小组中的这种情况与仅由母语者组成的小组或仅由二语学习者组成的小组的情况都不同：在由母语者组成的小组中，所有参与者已经获得了与同伴反馈相关的语言技能;在由二语学习者组成的小组中,所有参与者用来进行同伴反馈的语言技能都正处于发展中。

母语者和二语学习者的同伴互评值得进一步研究,同伴互评行为和互评模式的研究为跨洋互动写作中同伴反馈的实施提供了信息。虽然写作研究人员已经充分探讨了母语和二语环境下的同伴反馈,但是对网络自然互动环境下(而非教学环境下)混合小组互动的同伴反馈研究甚少。因此,本研究首先建立理论框架,然后探讨跨洋互动写作活动中中美同伴互评的特征和同伴互动模式及其影响因素。

1.2 研究意义

本研究选取广东外语外贸大学、苏州科技大学与美国宾夕法尼亚州立大学、宾夕法尼亚米勒斯维尔大学等大学合作的"英语写作跨洋互动"在线同伴反馈文本及母语者和二语学习者的在线讨论作为语料,从中美对比的角度出发,在认知互动理论和社会文化理论框架的指导下,运用语料库语言学的方法进行定量统计,对中美同伴互评类型和互动过程进行对比分析,具有以下意义。

第一,本研究构建了同伴互评理论框架,为深入研究同伴反馈奠定了理论基础。写作教学中的同伴反馈研究以书面同伴反馈研究居多,但现有文献中书面同伴反馈的相关术语众多且所指存在差异,存在分类重叠及识别方法耗时费力问题。本研究从行为、过程和结果3个视角重新定义同伴反馈;整合同伴反馈的分类以避免内容分类和功能分类重合,将书面同伴反馈分为肯定性反馈、指正性反馈和情感反馈3大类和25个子类;综合运用文献回顾和人工识别的方法,虽耗时长但是信度高。此外,本研究关注中美大学生的回评特征。基于Zhu(2001)的写作者评论功能的分类,本研究对回评进行分类,调查中美大学生如何回应同伴反馈,完善同伴互评理论框架。

第二,本研究确定了在线互动系统的编码框架,可以更全面、更充分地考察合作写作过程。尽管已有大量研究分析在线平台的学生互动,但是关于学习者如何协商写作任务以达到完善写作文本目的的结论仍不够明确,部分原因是缺乏用于分析在线互动系统的编码框架。以前的研究一直限于学习者的文本构建行为(如何共同构建写作文本),且没有统一的编码方案。为了全面了解合作写作过程，我们还需要追踪学生如何协商写作任务，共同完善写作文本。以前的研究很少探讨在线平台通过三个独特特征（评论、讨论和反思）进行合作的可能性。追踪学生对平台的使用情况有利于更充分地考察写作过程，包括联合任务协商、完善文本构建和反思写作过程。

第三，本研究考察中美跨洋互动写作中的同伴互动模式及其影响因素。随着基于网络的同伴互评系统的作用的增强，我们有必要调查学生在完成在线写作任务过程中如何协作，形成了哪些互动模式，解释形成特定的互动模式的原因。（Storch，2013）本研究探索同伴互评的互动模式，为探究在线同伴互动如何促进学习和写作的发展提供了新的线索。了解不同互动模式的特点及其影响因素，有助于教师制定策略，帮助学生形成有利于写作的互动模式，以最大限度地提高网上同伴反馈的效果，增加协作写作的学习机会。

第四，本研究描述了混合小组同伴互动的整体情况，拓宽了合作性写作研究的范围。鉴于同伴反馈是众多课程提供和收到写作反馈的重要渠道，我们有必要调查母语者和二语学习者如何使用同伴反馈。以往基于维基（Wiki）的协作写作的研究讨论了学生的修改类型（Arnold 等，2012；Kessler & Bikowski，2010），分析了小组成员的共同参与对协同写作的贡献（Li & Kim，2016），比较了协同写作与个人写作之间的准确性和流畅性的差异（Elola & Oskoz，2010）。对混合小组协作互动行为影响因素（Lee，2010）和互动模式（Li & Kim，2016）的研究值得进一步探索。此外，无论是面对面还是在计算机媒介背景下，对协同写作中同伴互动模式变化的研究都很少。目前尚无研究探讨中美跨洋互动写作项目中的同伴互评行为和互动模式。本研究调查了二语学习者和母语者组成的混合小组使用在线平台在自然语境下执行写作反馈任务时的交互动态，进一步拓宽了合作性写作研究的范围。

1.3　语料与研究方法

1.3.1　语料

随着网络科技的进步，基于网络的工具和在线同伴互评系统被广泛应用于课堂教学，目的是让学生参与同伴互评活动，提高他们的写作能力。

异步协作写作功能专注于语言产出（Kessler，2009；Lee，2010），提供额外的反思时间，为二语学习者提供了更多回顾彼此贡献的机会（Storch，2012）。

  本研究中的"英语写作跨洋互动"项目基于网络同伴互评系统，由国内高校与美国高校合作开发，旨在通过中美大学生的网上写作活动促进不同文化之间的交流。中美参与者中的美国学生为大二或大三学生，来自亚洲研究、中文、英语、哲学、国际金融、供应链管理等专业；中国学生均为来自国内几所重点大学的英语专业学生。在参与该项目之前，学习者们都已接受过议论文的写作训练。

  首先，在该项目实施过程中，中美参与者观看中、美影片各一部，之后在规定时间内完成相同话题和相同体裁的写作任务，并上传至写作平台。写作要求是分析两部电影所代表的中国文化和美国文化的任何方面（如妇女权益、社会和身体的流动性、个人成长与发展、成功和实现成功的方法等），以及使用的非语言策略（如摄像镜头、动作、角度、框架、光线、角色的服装、妆容、配饰、手势，等等）；将一两个文化方面或交际策略作为文章的重点（如气质、感伤、理性、义、礼、智、信、言，等等），用影片情节支撑论点。

  其次，中美学习者分组进行网上互评，围绕写作展开激烈的讨论，和同伴交流意见。每个小组成员包括两名中国学生和两名美国学生。教师提供反馈清单，清单内容包括以下几个方面：陈述对文章的总体反应和评论；找出文章的主题，指出文章内容是否与主题一致；陈述文章的读者视角，说明文章提供的细节是否满足读者需求；评价文章的组织性和一致性；点评文章的设计，说明网页的布局是否与文章的受众、体裁等一致；指出文章在语法、惯例等方面的错误；概括修改重点。

  最后，小组成员根据自己的需要和判断决定是否采用同伴反馈、是否做出相应的修改，进行在线互动协商后上交修改稿，并附上一份反思日志。反思的内容包括活动是否达到了自己对跨洋互动写作的期望，与美国同伴互动时印象最深的事情及原因（如在词汇选择、写作风格、思想表达、修辞偏好、文化习俗等方面的异同），通过活动是否增长了知识或提高了技能，参与活动的感受，等等。

  在活动结束后，跨洋互动写作项目的主持人游晓晔老师和一名硕士生用汉语分别对 5 位中国学生进行半结构式访谈。后续访谈（附录 3）包括 10 个指导性问题，涉及参与者对跨洋互动写作的态度，中国参与者对母语同伴反馈的期望，双方同伴反馈焦点的异同，参与者最有信心提出哪种类型的反馈，反馈时为什么注重组织、构思和主题句，等等。在访谈期间，两位采访者澄清了问题并在需要时询问了问题，重申并总结了信息，邀请受访者确认了自己对他们观点的理解。采访的顺利进行确保了学生修改报告的可理解性。

在语料收集、筛选过程中，本研究考虑到以下三个问题：第一，所建立的中美反馈文本语料库不能只在意规模的大小，而应结合研究目标进行筛选。第二，语料收集的标准可以不统一，可以根据研究目的，采取不同的抽样方法。选择语料时须保持主题、体裁等方面的一致，以避免主题不同和语域不对应等因素对研究结果造成的影响。例如，如果研究目的是对比同一体裁写作文本的中美同伴反馈的异同，对于有些体裁（如应用文），中国学生写作较少，则不能选取该类体裁。但是，如果研究目的是分析中美同伴反馈的类型，只需要选取既有美国同伴反馈又有中国同伴反馈的写作文本即可，不需要保持主题、体裁等方面的一致。第三，每位参与者的文章通常都由不止一位美国同伴和中国同伴评论，不论反馈者的人数多少，反馈文本和双方在线讨论结果都会被全部收集。应该指出的是，并非所有美国学生都在他们的中国同伴修改文章之前发表他们的评论。有些反馈者只在中国写作者完成第二稿之后提供了一些评价。但考虑到我们不仅要分析中美同伴反馈的类别，而且要分析双方的互动过程及反馈对写作者修改稿的影响，我们也收集了在第二稿之后提供的反馈。无论反馈者提供的反馈数量有多少，我们都会对提供给每个参与者的所有反馈进行一般性分析。所有语料均经过仔细的文本清洁处理后建档入库。基于上述三个问题，根据不同的研究主题，本研究选择了跨洋互动写作项目中的第 17 轮、第 18 轮、第 19 轮、第 20 轮语料，语料的具体介绍见相应的章节。

1.3.2 研究方法

本研究采用定量分析和定性分析相结合的方式，先对语料进行编码，之后结合 SPSS 软件进行推断性统计分析，最后结合反思日志和后续访谈对网络自然语境中中美学生的在线反馈和讨论进行描述性与推理性分析。

中美跨洋互动写作中同伴互评特征的研究方法具体如下：首先，进行定量分析。根据同伴反馈和回评编码方案,对同伴的反馈文本进行编码,定量统计同伴反馈类型及其子类的出现频次;进行独立样本曼惠特尼 U 检验(Mann-Whitney U Test),以确定中美同伴互评类型是否一致;根据同伴互评类型的出现频次,采用卡方检验(χ^2 Test)统计分析中美同伴反馈类型的分布情况。其次,进行定性分析。对中美同伴互评的类型和分布情况做具体的描述性分析;对中美学生的反思日志进行文本分析,从中美写作者的视角分析同伴的反馈类型,计算提及这些反馈类型的人数。最后,转写后续访谈并进行文本分析,三方验证中美同伴互评类型的异同,结合反思日志和后续访谈对中美跨洋互动写作中的同伴互评特征进行推理性分析。

中美同伴互动行为的研究方法具体如下:首先,分析在线评论记录,按照语言功能对每个思想单元进行编码,通过归纳推理得出语言功能的分类,然后将每个语言功能单元进一步分为发起(提出新想法)和做出回应(对其他成员的想法做出回应)。其次,编制分析网络写作环境中接受同伴反馈后中美文本修改的编码方案,利用 Microsoft Word 中"比较"和"合并"两个文档工具比较初稿和修改稿,查看中美学生做出哪些修改,计算其数量,以考察同伴在线交流共同构建书面文本的过程。通过分析在线讨论的同伴互评类型、反思日志和后续访谈,总结、归纳中美学生易采纳的反馈类型。再次,通过分析在线评论语言反映出的支架策略及学习者的反思日志,分析中美学生在网络交流过程中使用的支架策略。最后,统计语言功能、修改行为和支架策略这 3 种互动行为的出现频次,比较中美大学生在语言功能、修改行为、支架策略 3 个方面存在的共性和差异性。

中美同伴互动模式的研究方法具体如下:首先,基于前人的互动模式,从平等性和相互性两个维度识别中美同伴互动模式。其次,描述中美同伴互动模式的特征。最后,结合小组成员的在线讨论和写作者的反思日志,标记每个条目,比较条目之间的异同并进行分类,归纳互动模式的影响因素并进行推理性分析。

1.4 各章节简介

本书共由 7 章组成。

第一章为绪论,为研究提供一些背景资料,包括研究内容、研究意义、研究语料和研究方法。

第二章为同伴互评研究的多维视角,梳理同伴互评理论研究和实证研究的理论视角,包括认知互动理论和社会文化理论。

第三章为同伴互评的理论框架,包括同伴互评的界定、同伴互评的类型、同伴互动行为和同伴互动模式4个部分。此部分在综述以往同伴互评的定义后,提出适合本研究的同伴反馈和回评的操作定义;基于以往的编码方案,编制本研究的同伴反馈、互动行为和互动模式的编码方案与识别方法。

第四章描述中美跨洋互动写作中同伴互评的特征,从反馈者视角和写作者视角对收集到的数据进行分析,描述中美反馈者的反馈特征和中美写作者的回评特征,比较中美同伴互评类型的异同,进行推断性分析。

第五章分析中美跨洋互动写作中的同伴互动行为,从基于反馈的修改、对反馈的采纳和支架策略3个方面详细描述中方写作组和美方写作组的互动行为,对比中美互动的异同并分析原因。

第六章归纳二语写作中的中美同伴互动模式,从平等性和相互性两个维度识别中美同伴互动模式并进行描述性分析,结合小组成员的在线讨论和写作者的反思日志,探索互动模式的影响因素并进行推理性分析。

第七章为结论,总结研究发现,并与以往写作同伴反馈研究相比较,阐述研究的理论意义和教学启示,指出研究存在的不足,给未来的研究提出建议。

第二章 同伴互评研究的多维视角

同伴互评研究促进二语习得有多个理论依据，国内外对写作中的同伴互评研究成果颇丰。本章梳理了基于认知互动理论、社会文化理论视角的同伴互评研究，通过重点回顾跨洋互动写作中二语同伴反馈的文献，确定值得进一步探究的内容。

2.1 认知互动理论视角

2.1.1 理论框架

Long（1981）提出互动假说，认为不能将互动简单地看作将目标语单向输入给学习者内部习得机制的过程。相反，互动遵循"输入—互动—习得"模型的双向交流。也就是说，互动让多种要素的组合比单个因素更有效率。当学习者参与意义协商时，可理解性输入的有效性增强；为确保输入的可理解性，语言输入的本质可能会发生改变。

互动假说的提出与输入假说密切相关。Krashen（1985）认为，大量的可理解性输入对二语学习者是有必要的。若二语学习者的当前语言水平为 i，输入假设认为，当学习者可以理解比当前水平稍微领先的语言输入时，学习者在语言知识方面取得进步。Krashen 称这个过程为可理解性输入"$i+1$"，其中"$+1$"是语言习得的下一阶段。可理解性输入是引起语言能力提高的唯一机制，其产出对学习者的能力没有任何影响。（Krashen，1985）换言之，可理解性输入是二语习得的唯一必要充分条件。此外，Krashen 认为，只有在潜意识中习得语言才能形成语言能力，有意识地学习不是自发语言产出的源泉。他还认为，当学习者在交际中成功地表达自己时，就会自动达到适当的输入水平。（Krashen，1985：2）

然而，许多研究指出了假说中存在的问题，并表明仅有可理解性输入不足以实现二语习得。(Swain, 1995; Swain & Lapkin, 1998; 等等)虽然输入假设认为语言习得机制 (language acquisition device, 简称 LAD) 改进学习者的中介语系统是理所当然的，但是许多学者认为理解过程不同于产出过程。可理解性输入是否可以应用于整个语言系统（词汇、语音和句法）仍然是一个问题。当学习者在互动中协商输入和进行输出时，他们专注于可理解性输入部分，并以正确的语言形式表达自己。Krashen 声称，互动是促进可理解性输入的 3 种方法之一，其他 2 种为简化输入和语境。他认为，互动是获得可理解性输入的好方法，但它不是成功习得二语的充分条件。(Krashen, 1995) Long (1983) 认为，可理解性输入是语言学习的前提，交际障碍、困难或失败是提高理解能力和发展二语能力的驱动力。

协商 (negotiation) 是指为了成功交际而进行的沟通。(Richards 等, 1985) 二语研究中的"协商"，指母语者和非母语者为解决语言理解困难或进行语言修正而做出的互动性会话调整 (interactional adjustment)。(Long, 1985) "意义协商 (negotiation of meaning)，特别是由母语者或更有能力的对话者触发互动调整的意义协商，有助于习得，因为它以产出的方式将输入、学习者内在能力特别是选择性注意 (selective attention) 和输出联系起来。"(Long, 1996: 451-452) 因此，意义协商（确认检查、澄清请求和理解检查）是学习者获得可理解性输入的关键，意义协商的人际互动促进二语习得。(徐锦芬、舒静, 2020)

随着理论研究的深入，"协商"概念得以拓宽。Lyster & Ranta (1997) 提出形式协商 (negotiation of form)，指针对学习者话语中的形式错误，教师通过请求澄清、疑问式的重复等方式引起学习者注意或纠错的言语行为。针对语言形式进行的谈论、质疑或纠正被称为与语言有关的片断 (language-related episodes, LRES)。(Swain & Lapkin, 1998) 形式协商提供纠正性反馈 (corrective feedback)，如显性纠正、重述、澄清请求、元语言反馈、诱导等，让学习者注意到不符合语法的部分，进而修改输出、促进二语发展，为同伴学习或小组学习提供理论依据。(Long, 1996) 例如，当学习者的话语不被对话者理解时，他将诉诸各种交际策略以维持互动或寻找正确的解释，协商后对话者可以形成正确的语言形式。

在意义协商的过程中，对话者收到关于他的产出和语法的反馈。互动指导学习者彼此接收更多的输入并给予更多的输出。此外，若对话者停下来弄清楚他不明白的事，他将有更多的时间吸收输入，这可能会形成更好的理解和新语言形式的习得。因此，协商将学习者的注意力集中于目标语和正在听或写的语言之间的差异。互动也会引起学习者对未意识到的语言的未知部分的注意。同伴之间的意义协商和形式协商都能触发学习者的注意，使其意识到自己的语言与目标语之间的差距（Schmidt，1990），吸收正确的语言形式。在这个过程中，学习者可能会巩固或者重建中介语系统。(Swain，1985)

内容协商（content negotiation）由信息差或观点分歧引起。（Rulon & McCreary，1986）在内容协商过程中，学习者讨论信息的准确性，协商观点，产生新的内容，推动互动进程，但不会偏离会话"主流"（main flow）。（Rulon & McCreary，1986；徐锦芬、舒静，2020）内容协商包括确认检查、澄清请求、征求同意、显性求助和隐性求助。（赵雷，2015）内容协商过程增加了语言使用机会，同时也会增加意义协商和形式协商的使用，从而增加学习机会。形式协商使得学习者的言语输出更接近目标语的语言形式，而内容协商促使学习者在交流内容中提供更多的信息。van den Branden（1997）进一步区分了意义协商、形式协商和内容协商：学习者进行意义协商是为了达成共同理解，与交际问题有关；学习者进行形式协商为了推动产出更准确或更恰当的话语，与语言问题相关；内容协商推动学习者在话语内容上产出。

2.1.2 实证研究

同伴互动包括学习者协作和交流互动内容，调查同伴反馈过程的研究重点关注学习者的意义协商、形式协商和内容协商。这类研究考察同伴反馈期间产生的口头和/或书面反馈，探讨学习者如何感知反馈，以及他们的感知是否会影响随后的二语发展。研究者们通过分析话轮转换、行为，同伴对话的数量和功能，以及同伴评论所涉及的写作的不同方面，检测同伴互评。

2.1.2.1 意义协商

已有大量研究探讨哪些课堂活动可以让学习者从意义协商和修改输出

等互动调整中获得最大的收益。(Pica,1994) Foster & Ohta (2005) 讨论了识别协商互动的措施,并建议采用更严格的定义区分沟通问题的信号,以及表示感兴趣和鼓励的信号,记录和计算学习者完成互动课堂任务过程中协商行为(学习者的澄清请求、理解和确认检查)的发生率。结果表明,意义协商的发生率很低。在缺乏任何意义协商的互动过程中,学习者通过共同建构和提示,主动协助完成任务。在无沟通障碍的情况下,学习者在寻求和提供帮助,以及开始对自己的话语进行自我修复时表达了兴趣和鼓励。获得完全可理解的输入似乎比输出支持和友好的话语更重要。协商是一种会话过程,有助于学习者理解和表达二语。

在二语习得中,意义协商的实证研究内容主要包括意义协商和任务类型与水平结对的关系,以及二语学习者对互动协商的感知。第一,意义协商与任务类型的关系。Gass & Varonis (1985) 发现,单向信息和双向信息两种任务类型对结对小组的意义协商影响不明显。同伴互动是一个很好的获取所需信息的平台,是主要的互动类型。Duff (1986) 的调查显示,在封闭式问题导向任务中,学习者进行更多的意义协商;而 Nakahama 等人 (2001) 发现,学习者在封闭式图画信息沟通任务中协商更多。Doughty & Pica (1986) 考察了必做任务和选做任务两种任务类型后发现,必做任务比选做任务引发更多的意义协商;而 Foster (1998) 则发现任务类型对意义协商的数量没有显著影响。但是,Bryan (2005) 调查学习者在线聊天中的意义协商发现,任务类型影响意义协商的发生率,词汇问题引发大量的协商。

第二,意义协商与水平结对的关系。Yule & Macdonald (1990) 研究发现,在协商过程中,当低水平者是主要的信息提供者时,双方的意义协商较多;而当高水平者起主导作用时,双方的意义协商较少。而 Oliver (2002) 却发现,二语学习者结对的意义协商最多,母语者结对的意义协商最少,而母语者和二语学习者结对的意义协商的数量居中。

第三,二语学习者对互动协商的感知。Mackey 等 (2000) 以 10 名英语二语学习者和 7 名意大利外语学习者为研究对象,探讨二语/外语学习者在互动过程中感知反馈的方式,关注学习者在多大程度上确实认识或感知到通过互动提供的反馈,以及反馈的目标,即关于什么的反馈。研究基于任务的二元互动提供反馈,在任务完成后,采用刺激回忆法,让学习者观看互动录像带，反省在最初进行互动时的想法。结果表明，学习者收到的反馈集中在形态句法、词汇和语音形式上；学习者对词汇、语义和语音反馈的感知相对准确。意义协商很少涉及语法，形态句法反馈通常被重铸。此外，反馈的性质和内容可能会影响学习者的感知。

国内关于意义协商的相关研究较少。庞继贤、吴薇薇（2000）发现，在大学生小组活动中，必做任务比选做任务能引发更多的互动修正。赵国霞（2002）以互动理论为基础，研究课堂师生言语互动为学习者提供的语言、认知和情感环境，探讨课堂互动对学生的中介语使用和发展的影响。研究发现，师生言语互动未提供有利的语言、认知和情感环境，但是课堂互动对学生的中介语使用和发展产生了积极影响。汪清、谢元花（2011）考察了任务类型、水平结对和意义协商这3个变量之间的关系，研究结果显示，任务类型影响意义协商，且封闭式任务引发的意义协商较多，主要是关于词汇问题和内容问题的协商。水平差异大的结对不利于口语水平的提高。

2.1.2.2 形式协商

关于互动在二语习得中的作用的相关研究从学习者结对处理信息差转向了重铸（Long 等，1998；Braidi，2002）和全体参与者关注语言形式（Ellis 等，2001），这种互动通常由母语者或教师发起。这种转变使课堂小组合作（学习者之间的相互交流）转变为与更有能力的说话者（教师或母语者）合作，出现学习者的注意力从意义转向形式的情况。已有相关研究探讨了反馈、重铸和其他与语言相关的事件可能会将学习者的注意力转移到语言形式的方式上。（Swain，2000）

在同伴互评过程中，相关研究探讨双方如何进行形式协商，进而提高学习者的语言水平。Thonus（2004）通过分析母语者（1名写作教师和4名新生）在新生写作课上进行的6次小组写作会议的互动，为小组商讨形式的写作教学提供依据。小组会议的内容被转写，数据分析包括识别小组互动的过程，观察小组互动过程和写作过程之间的相似性，以及制定一个受众采集模型，用于说明学生写作发展的重要组成部分。分析结果表明：关于初稿的讨论往往以文本为中心；写作者谈论写作的进展，以阐明和拓展其作品；关注写作的讨论帮助学生从传统的演讲者角色转为面向读者的角色，了解他人如何看待世界，使自己的写作适应潜在观众的需要；

读者的评价性答复往往引起写作者的辩护。

Gere & Abbott（1985）从功能的视角考察跨年级写作组的语言行为，探讨话语方式和同伴反馈的语言功能之间的互动。受试者是9组母语者（2组五年级学生、4组八年级学生和3组高中生）。语料包括作业的副本、37个小组的会议录音的转写文本、小组的行为、学生的书面笔记和修改稿。小组会议的转写文本被编码成"1"，分为1 035个意义单元，并在3个维度（语言功能、注意区域和关注重点）被详细分类。具体来说，语言功能分为告知、指示和启发功能；注意区域是指写作或小组是否属于注意区域；关注重点包括过程、内容、形式、语境或表征。研究发现，高年级学生的写作文本更长，产生的意义单元更多。最常见的是意义单元关注告知功能，其次是指示功能的出现频率，揭示了学生在写作群体中所具备的语言能力。研究结果表明，学生能够完成任务并给予充足的同伴反馈，同伴反馈可以增强学生的读者意识。意义单位的数量和类型因话语模式不同而有所不同，这表明教师在写作任务上施加了约束，形成了写作群体的语言。

Dussias（2006）考察了西班牙语学习者和以西班牙语为母语的二语学习者在以计算机为媒介的沟通中的语言变化，特别研究了跨文化计算机介导的互动所带来的好处是否可以转移到面对面沟通上。二语为西班牙语的学习者被分配到实验组或对照组。实验小组的参与者以与西班牙语为母语的人士进行电脑媒介互动。对照组的学习者与其他具有相似熟练程度的西班牙语学习者进行网上交流。该研究考察了历时3个月的电子邮件和聊天室互动是否会带来更多的语言收益，通过检查OPI访谈的转录来评估语言方面的收获。访谈是在学习者进行网络互动之前，以及3个月后最后一次交流结束后进行的。结果显示，实验组中的学习者相对于对照组中的学习者来说强化了语言控制。母语者帮助二语学习者学习西班牙语一段时间后，二语学习者在性别的一致性、交流的流利性等方面都有了很大的提高。这表明母语者和非母语者在语言能力方面的远程协作互动是有益的。

Hu & Lam（2010）探讨了中国成人学生的第二语言学术写作教学中同伴反馈是否是一个有效的教学活动，具体而言，就是研究二语熟练程度、以前的同伴反馈经验、反馈偏好、基于文化的信念和实践等因素是否影响教学活动的有效性。受试者是来自中国的新加坡大学选修研究生学术写作班的 20 名英语二语学习者。数据来源包括学术写作作业的初稿、书面同伴反馈、作业修订稿、调查问卷和访谈。

该研究从 4 个方面进行编码，检测同伴反馈的有效性：第一，计算有效同伴建议（修改时采纳的以修改为目标的评论）的比例，即通过反馈类型（语言、内容和组织）和参与者小组的反馈类型来计算有效同伴建议的比例，使用公式"％有效建议＝（有效建议的数量/建议的总数）×100"。第二，计算在修改中采纳的有效建议的比例。修改中涉及的有效建议的比例根据类型（语言、内容和组织）及各个参与者和整个组的类型计算，使用公式"％采纳的有效建议＝（采纳有效建议数/有效建议总数）×100"。第三，考察根据同伴建议修改的二稿的质量。为了确定二稿是否比初稿质量高，并探讨二稿的完善是否与同伴建议相关，该研究进行了两种类型的数据分析。一是进行配对样本 t 检验以确定二稿的语言、内容和组织的分数及总分数是否明显提高。二是检测语言、内容和组织的得分及从初稿到二稿的总分数与有效同伴建议的数量和采纳率的相关性。第四，参与者对同伴反馈的有用性的评论评估。对同伴反馈的定量分析和对初稿的修改分析表明，初稿的重大修改与同伴反馈有关。以前的同伴反馈经验和反馈偏好两个变量并不影响同伴互评活动的有效性。

2.1.2.3　内容协商

二语习得环境中同伴互动的内容协商主要包括知识协商（negotiation of knowledge）和话题协商（negotiation of topic）。Nelson & Murphy（1992）从任务和社交两个维度描述二语写作小组活动。受试者是美国大学的中级 ESL 写作班的 4 名学生。该研究连续录制 6 个星期的写作过程，收集的数据包括录像、录像的转写、学生作文、学生对话和学生访谈，采用案例分析法分析 1 249 个反馈内容在语言、生活常识、生活个人知识、程序问题、格式问题 5 个方面的分布。研究发现，二语学习者反馈的意见大多关于语言（占意见总数的 72.7％），程序问题占意见总数的 12.2％，生活个人知识占意见总数的 9.3％，生活常识占意见总数的 3.1％，格式问题占意见总数的 2.0％，无法归类的意见占意见总数的 0.7％。语言讨论的比例之高说明学习者在讨论同伴文本时，以任务为导向。在讨论初期，学习者讨论程序问题较多（如话轮），一旦建立了程序规范，讨论程序性意见的数量就会减少。关于小组的社交维度（小组动态），写作群体的文献倾向于将写作群体互动理想化为写作者提供建设性的互助。但该研究表明，二语习得环境中同伴互动会遇到对小组工作的不同态度和对团体规范的不同期望的问题。该研究没有进一步探讨学生提供反馈时是处理哪些语言方面的信息。

Mendonca & Johnson（1994）总结了同伴互评过程中的协商类型，分析了同伴互评是否会影响协商性质，描述了ESL学生同伴反馈过程中的协商。受试者是12名选修写作课程的高级二语学习者。研究问题是ESL学生同伴反馈过程中有哪些类型的协商。教师提供了4个问题，即在同伴反馈之前和同伴确认：写作主题是什么？文章的中心思想是什么？文章中是否有不清楚之处？是否能对同伴的写作给出建议？首先，该研究确定了双向同伴互评的特定配置是否影响协商的性质，比较相同学术领域的双向同伴反馈的协商类型和不同学术领域的双向同伴反馈的协商类型的异同。其次，该研究收集、分析了学生初稿和修改稿并做定量分析，以确定书面文本的修改证据，对修改和未做修改部分做标记。最后，该研究进行了后期访谈以确定学生是否认为同伴反馈活动是有益的、如何利用同伴意见，以及是否使用同伴反馈以外的其他意见来源修改草稿。

研究发现，在同伴反馈过程中，除了内容的解释外，反馈者提出问题、提供解释、提出建议、重申同伴所写或所说和纠正语法错误的协商类型的数量都要多于写作者。反馈者承担了导师或教师的职责，而写作者似乎扮演了学生的角色。另外，比起同一研究领域，协商的一些特定模式更频繁地出现在不同的研究领域。来自不同研究领域的同伴以解释或理解检查请求的形式提出更多的问题，重述的类型略少，但是研究领域相同和不同的同伴的解释和建议协商类型相似。虽然学生接收同伴意见来修改他们的文章，但是在修改过程中有选择地吸收这些意见，自己决定文本的修改。后期访谈的结果支持学生修改行为，并证实总体上学生认为同伴反馈是有益的。这项研究的结果支持二语写作教学应包括同伴反馈的观点，并强调同伴反馈在写作中的价值。

在同伴群体中，互动往往与意义建构、意义协商或共同解决问题的活动相关联，并且不指定小组成员负责控制和指导互动，所有学生都有责任管理谈话并确定讨论的方向。（Mercer，1996；Gillies，2006）。抓住话题、从一个话题转移到另一个话题，以及恰当地引入新话题的能力是交际能力的核心。(Gan 等,2009) 例如,Tsui (2001) 观察到,学习者之间的互动有可能使学生进行真正的交流,并最终帮助他们提升话语能力,而不仅仅是句子层面的语言能力。最重要的是,同伴群体的本质排除了地位差异。(Fisher,1997)

Zhu (2001) 通过考察受试者的话轮转换行为、同伴反馈功能及双方的书面反馈,研究混合同伴反馈组的互动和反馈。语料包括来自3个混合同伴反馈组的11名同伴(8名英语母语者和3名非母语者)的同伴写作讨论内容的转写、写有学生书面评价的同伴反馈表。该研究分别从读者和写作者评论两个视角探讨口头同伴反馈的功能。分析结果表明,在写作的讨论过程中,特别是作为写作者,非母语者较少控制话轮和回应同伴反馈,不会澄清(解释意图或补充信息来帮助读者理解),产生较少的口头反馈类型;作为读者,非母语者提供的整体评论的数量与母语者相当,但是被打断时,很难继续话题或重新掌握话语权。母语者和非母语者都很少发挥启发功能,说明双方都没能有效发挥写作者的角色功能。

Gan 等 (2009) 探讨了在互动评估创新情境下,一组中学 ESL 学生如何适应和构建与评估任务相关的互动过程。该研究应用会话分析 (conversation analysis) 的原则,检查评估条件下小组讨论任务中话题讨论的组织。分析指出,不应受到先前理论假设的限制,而是应以参与者或成员的完成结果为导向,不依赖于预先确定的类别并将其强加于数据。会话分析不是从任何外部视角,而是从参与者如何互相展示他们对"正在发生的事情"理解的角度来揭示谈话的组织结构。(Hutchby & Wooffitt,1998)

该研究发现,在以同伴密集参与和积极参与为特征的小组轮流口头讨论情境中,学生能够发展和转移话题:一方面,确保成功完成分配的任务;另一方面,展示个人的贡献。参与者不断监控谈话内容与评估任务议程的相关性导致主题转换。参与者之间的主题协商表明:同伴小组讨论作为一种口头评估形式,有可能为学生提供机会,以让他们展示在口头交流中相互关联的"现实生活"互动能力。

小组评估任务中出现的意义协商知识,为课堂教学中双人/小组工作的组织和有效学习环境的创造提供了见解。学生须意识到,任何形式的二语/外语互动语篇都可以作为语言和会话能力的窗口。在测试情境中,分析协商中的话题组织，不仅可以帮助区分同伴之间的语言表现差异，还可以帮助识别推动话题的元素，话题是如何被协商或放弃的，以及同伴个人对话题协商的贡献。

之后的研究比较了学习者对3种协商类型的使用，以期为语言课堂互动教学提供借鉴。赵雷（2015）探讨了在基于任务的口语课堂中汉语的互动协商。通过课堂实录转写、课堂观察和统计分析发现，任务类型对意义、形式和内容3种协商类型数量的影响不显著，3种协商类型均以澄清请求和确认核查居多，学习者的形式协商意识亟须得到提高。该研究提出在基于任务的口语课堂中加强互动教学，以促进汉语学习。

徐锦芬、舒静（2020）以中国同伴课堂互动为语料，考察大学生的协商互动情况。研究发现，学习者互动以内容协商居多，以此推进话题；学习者互动也包括意义协商和形式协商，解决理解障碍和形式问题，提高目标语产出的可理解性和准确性。就协商的具体形式而言，内容协商以显性求助为主，意义协商以澄清请求为主，形式协商以显性及隐性求助和纠错为主。过半数的同伴互动协商未完成整个协商过程，大部分止于反馈。

互动被视为课堂教学的基本因素，因为课堂活动展示生动的人际互动过程。（Allwright，1984）在互动过程中，学习者努力产出可理解性输出，这成为其他对话者的输入来源。反馈有助于促进语言发展，特别是负面反馈（关于学习者不合语法的"话语"信息）会将学习者的注意力集中于语言形式和意义，并促使他们产出更易理解和更符合语法规则的语言形式。因此，从认知的角度来看，同伴互动主要被视为会话交换，在这种会话交换中，沟通的中断触发了意义协商。上述研究结果表明，相对于与母语人士的互动，学习者与其他学习者的互动更倾向于参与意义协商，在此期间，他们使用有利于二语发展的互动行为，如输入修改（Mayo & Pica，2000）和互动反馈（Adams，2007；Soler，2002）。除了这些互动行为外，学习者在与他人互动时，比与母语人士互动时更倾向于自我纠正（Buckwalter，2001；Sato，2007）。这种自我纠正被认为是"监控过程的明显表现"（Kormos，2006：123），以与纠正性反馈触发行为相同的方式促进二语加工。因此，如果产出实践被视为二语习得的必要条件，则同伴互动提供了最佳条件。（Sato & Lyster，2012）

Swain（1995，2000）认为，书面输出的需求鼓励学生深入处理语言，反思语言使用,并协作解决语言问题。在共同创作过程中,学生在写作的各个方面做出贡献(Storch, 2005),不仅考虑到语法和词汇,还关注语篇(Storch, 2002; Swain & Lapkin, 1998)。协同写作任务还为二语学习者提供了更多审阅和应用他们所学知识的机会。(Hirvela, 1999)在二语写作过程中,写作者通过同伴互动意识到自己的语言输出与目标语言的差距,根据同伴反馈调整和改进写作。互动理论重视根据反馈信息修改的写作文本。

2.2 社会文化理论视角

2.2.1 理论框架

社会文化理论认为,所有更高形式的学习和认知发展本质上都是社会性的(Vygotsky, 1978; Lantolf, 2000),知识是个人与社会互动的产物(Foster & Ohta, 2005)。人类通过中介方式(mediational means)发展认知,语言是一种重要的中介方式,对认知发展具有重要的作用(Swain, 2000)。学习作为一种社交和认知过程,是通过社会互动构建的。(Vygotsky, 1978)在社会互动中,通过他人调节或者中介活动,语言学习转变为自我调节,最终实现自主学习。也就是说,学习者的发展潜力是由他们与教师和同伴的互动关系共同构建的。在同伴互动过程中,学习者不断调节中介语,创造语言资源,习得语言。(Ellis, 2010)

社会文化理论强调社会互动在学习中的作用,关注语言在学习过程中作为中介工具的重要性。(Vygotsky, 1978)社会文化理论中指导同伴互动研究的两个关键概念是最近发展区(zone of proximal development)和支架(scaffolding)。为了阐释学习者如何通过与专家的互动发展认知,Vygotsky 提出了最近发展区,指"个体独立解决问题表现出来的实际水平与在他人的指导或是同伴的协助下解决问题时可以达到的潜在水平之间的差距"(Vygotsky, 1978: 85)。然而,考虑到二语学习中许多学习者是成人,且成人同伴不一定能提供帮助,Vygotsky 修改了最近发展区的定义以适应成人二语学习语境。(Ohta, 2001)修改后的最近发展区是指个体语言产出的实际发展水平与通过和教师或同伴合作达到的潜在发展水平之间的差距。

Vygotsky(1978)指出,合作使学习发生在最近发展区。最近发展区理论不仅可以构建新手和专家之间的互动，还可以构建没有专家参与的同伴互动或双向互动。同伴间能力的差异可以形成最近发展区，促进语言习得。换言之，相较于个人学习，来自知识渊博的同伴的帮助可以改善个人表现。

支架是"使孩子或新手能够解决问题，执行任务或实现超出其独立努力目标的辅助过程"（Wood 等，1976：90）。Vygotsky（1978）认为，从心理学角度来看，人类认知能力的发展主要基于互动学习和合作，教师起"支架"的作用，即促进作用，而不是主导作用。能力较强的学习者通过外化和表达知识获益，而能力较弱的学习者从能力较强的同伴处获得支持。在互动过程中，学习水平高的学生可以给学习水平低的同伴构建认知的最近发展区。支架不仅可以帮助儿童或新手完成手头的任务，还可以提供信息；当信息内化后，儿童或新手可以独立完成任务。成人或专家通过有益的、有组织的互动来帮助儿童或新手，从而促进儿童或新手在最近发展区的发展。

之后，支架的概念从成年或儿童互动扩展到同伴互动，同伴反馈可以潜在地帮助学习者通过意义协商和思想交流获得语言知识和学术写作技巧，从而改进他们的学术书面文本（Donato，1994；Hu & Lam，2010；Ohta，2000；Yu & Lee，2016a、2016b）。学习者既是专家又是新手，在结对活动或小组活动中相互提供支架。通过与同伴的互动交流，学习者发掘自己的潜力，建立自身的知识结构。在二语写作中，同伴反馈可以被理解为个体学习中的同伴互助、合作及协商，是基于最近发展区产出和完善写作文本、提高写作水平的学习活动。同伴反馈可以构成社会认知学习活动，有助于探索监管、支架、最近发展区等概念（Lantolf，2000；Villamil & de Guerrero，2006；Vygotsky，1978、1986）。作为一种相互学习的过程/活动，同伴反馈的接收者和提供者得到的好处包括创建一个支持性的社会互动环境，使学生在其中接受和提供社会支持和同伴支架（Hu & Lam，2010）；相互学习发生在一个递归的和具有社会建设性的过程中，通过同伴反馈实现意义创造和知识转化（Berg，1999；Susser，1994；Zamel，1983）；反馈提供者和接受者在其最近发展区提供有利的教学环境，从他人调节（在他人的帮助下执行）阶段发展到自我调节（独立解决问题）阶段（Villamil & de Guerrero，2006）。

2.2.2 实证研究

社会文化理论指导二语写作研究，为检验学习者的互动和合作提供理论视角（de Guerrero & Villamil，2000；Donato，1994；Li & Zhu，2017a、2017b；Storch，2004）。作为重要的同伴互动行为之一，同伴反馈是提高二语写作教学效果的有效教学活动（Min，2006；Yu & Lee，2014；Zhao，2014）。同伴反馈研究调查学生的同伴互动，关注各种问题，包括互动模式和群体动态（Li & Kim，2016；Zhu，2001）、文化问题（Hu & Lam，2010；Nelson & Carson，2006）、学生立场（Lockhart & Ng，1995；Zhu & Mitchell，2012）、动机和目标（Yu & Lee，2014；Zhu & Mitchell，2012）、EFL 学生同伴反馈策略（Yu & Lee，2016b）等。

同伴反馈研究涉及两个根本的问题：第一，同伴互评活动对学习者（写作者和反馈者）有何帮助？第二，同伴互评过程中的学习者如何互动和协商？学者们针对这两个问题进行了一系列的实证研究。

2.2.2.1 同伴互评对学习者的影响

写作研究者和教师们最关心的是同伴互评活动是否能帮助学习者撰写更好的论文，即写作者能否根据同伴的意见修改自己的文本，反馈者是否在提供同伴反馈的过程中获益。下面分别从写作者和反馈者两个视角回顾不同的同伴互评类型的作用。

国内外研究同伴互评对写作者影响的成果颇丰。本研究主要回顾不同类型的同伴互评对写作者修改行为和写作质量的影响。例如，Paulus（1999）分析了反馈和修订过程对学生写作质量的影响。受试者是某公立大学选修写作课程的 11 名大一国际学生。该研究基于课堂，根据每篇作文修改的类型和来源分析学生对作文的修改，然后进一步评估初稿和三稿以确定修订是否可以提高写作质量。这包括两个研究问题：一是在实行多稿制、过程写作法的课堂，同伴反馈和教师反馈如何影响学生修改。二是进行的多稿修改是否可以提高课堂写作的整体质量。收集的数据包括反馈和三次文稿。研究进行重复测量 t 检验以确定初稿到三稿是否有显著改善；为确定改变的数量和/或类型之间是否存在显著相关性，还进行相关性检验。研究结果显示，学生最常见的修改类型是意义保留的修改，即改写或重新阐述文本中的概念。尽管表面修改的比例很高，但是学生也能进行一些整体性修改。同伴反馈和教师反馈对学生的修改稿质量都有影响，并且因同伴反馈和教师反馈而做出的修改更多是意义层面的修订。研究指出，不仅要分析学生的修改稿有哪些改变，还要分析这些改变对文章整体改进有何影响。

Tseng & Tsai（2007）探索了高中在线同伴互评的效果和有效性，并分析了各类同伴反馈对学生的影响。受试者是通过在线同伴评估活动学习电脑课程的184名十年级学生。来自同伴和专家评估的研究数据表明，同伴评定的分数与专家标准高度相关，这表明，高中同伴评估可以被认为是一种有效的评估方法。考察同伴反馈类型与其后续表现之间的关系发现，加强型同伴反馈有助于学生制订更好的计划，但是说教型和纠正型同伴反馈可能对改善计划起不了积极的作用。建议型反馈在同伴互动的前期发挥重要作用，但是在互动的后期对学习帮助不大。

Nelson & Schunn（2009）考察了同伴反馈特征、中介变量水平和反馈实施率之间的相关性。受试者是美国大学的历史类主题的新手写作者。数据来源包括评论者提供的关于如何改进论文的评论，写作者提供的关于同伴反馈是否有助于修订的评论，以及每篇论文初稿和终稿之间的不同。该研究根据已有文献首先推测出5种反馈特征（摘要、具体性、解释、范围、情感反馈）与问题/解决方案的潜在内部调节变量及问题或解决方案协议有关，从而影响反馈实施的最终结果。研究分析了来自同伴互评的1 073个反馈单元后发现，同伴反馈特征、中介变量水平和反馈实施率之间有一定的相关性。首先，在反馈特征和实施反馈的关系方面，反馈特征中只有解决方案与反馈实施有显著关系，获得解决方案的写作者比未获得解决方案的写作者做出修改的可能性多10%；其他变量对反馈的实施未产生积极影响。虽然这些因素与实施没有显著的直接联系，但这并不一定意味着这些因素与实施无关；这些因素可以与相关的调解变量直接相关，与实施间接相关。其次，在潜在内部调节变量和实施反馈的关系方面，是否赞同解决方案与反馈实施无显著相关性，对解决方案的理解与反馈实施也无显著相关性。理解与反馈实施有一定关系，如果写作者理解问题，那么实施反馈的可能性提高23%。最后，在反馈特征和理解的关系方面，摘要、问题识别、解决方案提供及定位有望增强理解，但是解释的增加和范围的扩大会减弱理解。总结（反馈层面的分析）、提供解决方案及定位

（分段层面的分析）与问题理解显著相关。如果反馈中包括摘要，那么写作者理解该问题的可能性提高 16%；如果反馈提供解决方案，则可能性提高 14%；如果提供问题和/或解决方案的位置，则可能性提高 24%。在问题解释和解决方案的解释两者之中，问题解释与问题的理解显著相关。对问题的总结、解决、定位和解释可能是影响问题理解的独立因素，因为这些反馈特征互相无显著相关性。

邵名莉（2009）探讨了同伴评价在英语专业写作教学中的可行性和有效性。研究结果表明：学生认可同伴评价的方式，对同伴评价持积极肯定的态度；学生被证明具备评价他人作文的能力，他们的评分和教师的评分具有很高的一致性；同伴评价使学生作文在内容、结构和语言上都有很大的改进。因此，只要设计合理、操作严谨，同伴评价可以作为一种有效的评价方式，融入写作教学，促进英语专业的学习。

Cho & MacArthur（2010）研究了学习者如何根据同伴反馈修改文本，并且通过分析组别和反馈类型对修改类型的影响及修改类型对写作水平的影响，确定修改是否提高写作质量。受试者是 28 名选修心理学课程的大学生，他们参加为期 12 周的心理学研究方法的写作课。该研究有 3 个研究问题：在 3 组实验条件下（单个专家反馈 SE、单个同伴反馈 SP 和多个同伴反馈 MP），学习者有哪些修改类型？针对不同的反馈类型，学习者会产生哪些修改类型？不同的修改类型对写作水平有何影响？

研究者们采用多变量回归分析检测自变量反馈类型的频率（指示性、非指示性和表扬）和因变量修改类型（简单、复杂、拓展内容、新内容和结构）之间的关系，以及自变量修改类型、组别和因变量写作质量之间的关系。之后，采用一元回归分析检测自变量非指令性反馈与因变量复杂修改和新内容修改之间的关系，并利用 Microsoft Word 自带功能"比较"，对比初稿和终稿的差异。研究结果表明，SE 组学生比 SP 组学生有更多的简单修改，但是关于新内容的修改并不显著；MP 组学生的修改注重澄清和阐释内容；非指令性反馈和复杂修改有关，与拓展性内容修改无关，与新内容的修改有关；澄清、阐释内容的修改和增加新内容的修改会提高写作质量；复杂修改能提高写作水平，但是通过拓展内容和新内容不能预测质量的提高。MP 组收到的反馈最多，包括所有反馈类型。非指令性反馈预测复杂修改，MP 组的修改比其他组更复杂，复杂修改与质量提高有关。

Cheng 等（2015）探讨了同伴反馈内容在提高本科生写作表现中的作用，并进一步检测了同伴反馈在 3 轮同伴互评过程中对学习的渐进性影响。具体研究问题如下：情感、认知和元认知同伴反馈的内容为大学生提供了哪些信息？在 3 轮反馈活动中，3 种反馈类型出现频率的差异有哪些？3 种类型的反馈对大学生的写作水平有何影响？将 3 轮反馈中共 705 个同伴反馈消息作为研究数据，对反馈内容进行编码分析，计算反馈类型的出现频次。研究方法包括相关性分析和方差分析。对同伴等级评定和教师等级评定进行相关性分析，检测同伴等级评定的信度；对反馈类型进行方差分析，检测 3 轮反馈中 3 种反馈类型对学生表现的渐进性作用。研究结果显示，在初始阶段，认知反馈（具体的建议、概念和改进方法）出现频率高；在之后的阶段，情感反馈（赞扬）出现更多；然而，这种积极影响在活动的最后阶段减少。同伴等级评定与教师等级评定显著相关，学生参与在线同伴评估次数越多，同伴评估技能越好。重复测量结果显示，学生的分数在知识的深度、主题的合理性、概念运用的正确率、报告的创新性和整体水平上都有显著提高。方差分析结果显示，在第 1 轮到第 2 轮反馈过程中，相对于情感反馈和元认知反馈，认知反馈在提高学生写作水平方面的作用更显著。在第 2 轮到第 3 轮反馈过程中，反馈的作用不明显，但是认知反馈对学生整体写作水平提高仍起到一定作用。

Leijen（2017）考察了反馈的类型和特征，及其对后续修改的影响，以便更好地了解二语写作者如何进行同伴反馈活动。受试者是爱沙尼亚大学参加英语学术写作课程的 43 名英语二语学习者，收集的数据包括同伴对文本的不同部分（介绍、正文、结论）的反馈意见和写作文本（二稿、三稿和终稿）。回归分析显示，反馈类型中的替换和反馈特征中的再现是修订的重要预测因素。由于提供了关于如何修改文本的明确建议，替换可能是最简单的修订方式。再现可能是预测学习的比较好的特征，因为再现可能与意义协商密切相关，这在语言学习环境中更为常见。修改时理由类反馈与其他反馈发生正面和负面互动；理由与替换相结合增加了修改的机会；然而，理由结合区域（局部）和观点（文本）却减少了修改的机会。

上述研究表明，不同类型的同伴互评对学生修改行为和写作质量产生不同程度的积极影响。但是，同伴反馈在课堂实践中也遇到一些挑战。高歌（2010）研究发现，在同伴反馈活动中，不同的分组类型会影响到活动效果，以及学生对活动有效性的态度。在学生写作提高程度方面，无论是高水平学生小组、低水平小组还是混合小组，同伴反馈都是有效果的。但是低水平小组的效果不如其他两组，由于他们自身英语写作能力较弱，虽然他们可以指出组员写作中的一些问题，但是无法给予进一步的建议。高水平小组的活动效果也不错，但成员之间需要更多的信任。杨苗（2006）发现，教师反馈更容易被学生接纳，更能提高作文修改质量，而同伴反馈则能激发学生进行更高程度的自主学习和互动。孟晓（2009）、杨丽娟等（2013）、周一书（2013）都肯定了同伴反馈在学习者作文修改中的积极作用，但强调同伴反馈不能代替教师反馈，倡导使用多种反馈方式。翁克山和李青（2013）分析了 ACMC（非即时计算机辅助通信）环境下同伴互评手法的评判水平、互评的有效性及两者对写作质量的影响，发现经过同伴互评的修改稿相较于初稿，在写作质量上有一定提高，但学生采用的互评手法评判水平偏低；初稿接收同伴评价单元较多，最终被用于修改初稿的单元却很少；被用于修改初稿的单元大多属于低评判水平互评手法的单元，对学生写作的表面修改有促进作用，但对整体修改水平没有明显提升。刘永厚（2015）证实"小组同伴反馈＋教师反馈"的模式比单一教师反馈模式的教学效果更好，能更加显著地提高实验班学生的写作水平。

　　已有的关于在线同伴反馈是否有助于修改稿件的研究，结果不一致甚至相互矛盾，我们有必要进一步探索在线 ESL 同伴反馈的效果。Guardado & Shi（2007）以 22 名来自西加拿大大学的且将英语作为第二语言的学生为研究对象，以受试者收到的电子反馈、初稿、修改稿及后续访谈为研究语料，旨在回答以下研究问题：写作者收到了什么类型的在线同伴反馈？写作者在修改稿中采纳同伴反馈了吗？如果采纳了，他们是如何看待这种经历的？写作者在修改稿中忽视同伴反馈了吗？如果忽视了，他们怎么看待这样的经历呢？首先将反馈内容进行编码，然后利用 Microsoft Word 的"比较"和"合并文档"工具比较受试者的初稿和修改稿，突出添加和删除部分，确定是否为由同伴反馈引起的修改。受试者的访谈意见用于解释受试者在修改中采纳或忽略在线同伴反馈意见的经历。研究表明，电子反馈解决了纸张携带不便的问题，同时保留了一些传统书面反馈的优点，如纯文本环境有利于学生有条不紊地评论，而且匿名的方式有益于同伴做出批判性评论。然而,参与的(以英语为第二语言)学生对同伴反馈总体上没有信心。有些人无视同伴要求表达意义和澄清意图的反馈,将在线同伴反馈变为单向沟通过程,未处理的同伴反馈比例很高。同伴反馈应与教师面对面讨论相结合,澄清有疑问的评论,以最大限度地发挥在线同伴反馈的作用。

同伴互评对写作者影响的研究主要集中在接受同伴反馈的优点,即同伴互评改变写作者的写作文本,提高写作质量方面,但较少关注反馈者提供同伴反馈时得到的学习益处和被激活的机制。(Topping,2010)然而,最近的一些实证研究表明,学生可以通过向同伴提供反馈来提高他们的写作水平和文本修改水平。Lundstrom & Baker(2009)探讨了哪种同伴反馈(给予或接受同伴反馈)更有利于提高学生的写作水平。受试者是英语学院的9个写作班的91名学生。在整个学期的课程中,给予反馈小组审查匿名文本但不接受同伴反馈;而接受反馈小组只接受反馈,不评论他人的写作。收集学期初和学期末的写作文本并将其作为研究数据,分析结果表明,提供反馈比仅仅接受同伴反馈更有利于提高ESL学生的写作水平。语言水平较低的反馈者在写作的整体方面(如内容和组织)比在局部方面(如语法、词汇和技巧)取得的进步略大。该研究结果被Cho & MacArthur(2010)证实,他们将61名以英语为母语的本科生分成3组:反馈组、阅读组和无活动组。反馈组在阅读同伴的论文后给予反馈,阅读组在阅读同伴的论文后不给予反馈,而无活动组没有任何预写活动。预写活动结束后,反馈组的写作质量高于阅读组和无活动组,从而证实了给予反馈的价值,表明了同伴反馈在支持学习中的潜在作用。

Cho & Cho(2011)探讨了在同伴互评的环境下,学生如何通过评审同伴初稿提高自身学习水平。物理入门课程的母语本科学生参加了这项研究,作为他们课程活动的一部分。受试者采用SWoRD系统撰写技术类研究文章,审查3个或4个同伴的初稿并修改自己的初稿。研究从评价和范围两个维度对3 889个评论片段进行编码后发现:在评价维度上,反馈者做出的关于缺点的评论要多于关于优点的评论,反馈者更多地是检测和解释同伴初稿存在的问题,而不是指出优点;在范围维度上,反馈者给予的宏观意义上的评论要多于微观意义上和表面特征上的评论。识别同伴初稿的弱点时,反馈者提供的宏观意义上和微观意义的评论数量相当;反馈者做出的评论关注微观意义上的缺点和宏观意义上的优点，有关微观意义上的缺点和宏观意义上的优点的评论都可以提高反馈者的写作水平。此外，反馈者原本的写作技巧和同伴初稿的质量影响所给出的评论类型。

Lu & Law（2012）既考察了同伴反馈对写作者写作质量的影响，也检测了反馈行为对反馈者写作质量的影响。受试者是 181 名香港公立中学的学生，他们通过在线系统 iLap 参与同伴评估。研究问题主要包括同伴评级行为对反馈者和写作者终稿质量的影响，不同反馈类型（认知反馈和情感反馈）对反馈者和写作者的写作质量的影响。研究采用方差分析、多级类间相关性分析、多元回归分析等定量分析研究方法。

该研究检测了学习者评定等级和接受等级评定的经历，并且从不同的认知和情感维度对同伴反馈进行编码，然后用方差分析检测学生写作的得分是否存在显著差异，用多级类间相关性分析考察不同班级（任课教师不同）之间有无显著性差异，用多元回归分析检测在线评估活动和学习成效之间的关系。方差分析和多级类间相关性分析结果表明：实验前学生写作水平无显著差异；班级变量无显著差异，即班级任课教师不是影响研究差异的因素。多元回归分析的控制变量为两门课程的期末成绩，以及写作者和反馈者的评级与反馈措施；自变量为给予和得到的分数，同伴给予的建议、解释、识别问题、语言方面问题及批评和赞扬等情感反馈的数量。

研究结果显示，认知反馈中的识别问题反馈出现频率最高，提出建议的反馈次之，阐释和语言反馈最少；认知反馈（识别问题和提供建议）对反馈者产生的效果更明显，但是情感反馈（赞扬）对写作者的作用更大；反馈对反馈者的作用要大于被反馈者，同伴反馈对较差的学生帮助不大。换言之，反馈者提供的识别问题和提出建议的反馈是反馈者自身水平的重要预测因素，积极的情感反馈与写作者的表现有关。反馈与写作水平之间有个中间步骤——反馈实施，反馈对于写作者的间接作用是通过理解协调的，水平低的学生对反馈的理解有限，因此反馈对水平低的写作者的作用不明显。同伴评级对写作表现无积极作用。

Huisman 等（2018）研究了接受或提供同伴反馈是否更有利于本科生的写作表现。结果表明，在学术写作背景下，接受反馈的学生从初稿到终稿总体上都有进步。同时，反馈者也提高了他们的写作水平，这种提高体现在文本的各个方面（如内容、结构、风格）。

除了进行实证研究外,研究者们还通过探索学生的自我报告来拓展调查范围,自我报告的内容包括对给予和接受同伴反馈的价值的信念与感知。例如,Ludemann & McMakin(2014)对新西兰一所大学的 37 名本科生进行了 Likert 量表问卷调查。总的来说,学生们表示审核同伴论文比接受同伴反馈更有利于提高他们自己的写作水平。这一发现与 Nicol 等(2014)及 White & Kirby(2005)的研究结果一致。在 Hislop & Stracke(2017)进行的研究中,一年级英语学术课程的参与者表示,审核同伴论文能使他们学习新的想法和不同的观点,更加意识到自己的写作弱点,并提升自己的写作技能。Yu(2019)探讨了研究生是否从提供反馈中获得认知和学习经验。该研究利用多种数据来源,包括论文初稿(原始稿、修订稿和定稿)、书面同伴反馈、半结构化访谈和回忆激发,调查了 7 名硕士生如何及在多大程度上受益于向他们的同伴提供反馈。数据分析揭示了学生通过提供同伴反馈获得的益处:提高对论文/论文文体的认识,提高学术写作技巧,通过寻求外部帮助成为更有技巧的学习者,以及成为一个更具反思精神和批判精神的学术写作者。

尽管上面讨论的结果表明为同伴提供反馈可以提高学生写作水平,但其他研究展示了相互矛盾的结果(Rosalia,2010;Trautmannn,2006)。总体而言,同伴反馈活动对写作者有益。同伴互评(接受反馈和给予反馈)对学习者的写作质量和写作水平提升起着积极的作用,学习者可以从中获得潜在的学习机会。然而,我们需要更多的定量和定性研究来考察同伴互评提高学习者写作水平的潜力,特别是在二语学术论文写作环境中。(Zhang 等,2018)

2.2.2.2 同伴互评中的互动模式

除了关注同伴互评过程中的反馈类型和互动行为外,研究者们还关注合作写作中的群体动态和互动模式。下面回顾同伴互动模式对学习者的影响。

基于 Damon & Phelps(1989)的研究,Storch(2002)与 ESL 大学生进行了一个协同写作项目,发现持有合作立场的合作伙伴(协同型和专家/新手)在随后的个人写作中比其他两种合作伙伴(主导型/主导型、主导性/被动型)采纳更多的意见,实现更多的知识转化。

在该框架基础上,学者们提出一些在线同伴互动模式(Arnold 等,

2012；Bradley 等，2010；Li，2013；Li & Kim，2016；Li & Zhu，2017a、2017b；Hsu，2020）。例如，Li & Zhu（2013）研究了维基讨论记录，并辅以维基页面和历史记录，得出了 3 种不同的 EFL（以英语为外语）小组进行维基写作的互动模式：集体贡献/相互支持、权威/应答、主导/撤回。该研究发现，和面对面的互动一样，以维基为媒介的互动影响学生的写作表现和学习经历：访谈中前两种模式的小组比第三种模式的小组报告更多的学习机会。

着眼于通过写作变化功能来扩展对小群体文本共构的分析，即学生在维基中共同产出联合文本的写作/修改行为（Mak & Coniam，2008），Li（2013）的研究重点是递归维基编写/修订过程，以集体贡献/相互支持小组为重点，确定了各种类型的写作变更功能（添加、删除、改写、重新排序和更正），并且从小组成员的文字贡献角度进一步研究了平等和相互性，包括写作变更功能的频率计数和对变更的区分。这些研究提供了特定的分析程序，以识别维基介导的写作中的相互作用模式。

Bradley 等（2010）利用维基的历史记录，确定了 EFL 学生构建维基作业时的 3 种不同的互动模式：缺少可视互动（一人发布全部文本）、合作（个人以平行的方式工作）和协作（大家互相交流意见并且共同撰写论文）。同样，在 Arnold 等（2012）的研究中，二外是德语的学生在维基小组写作项目中表现出合作和协作模式。有趣的是，当学生对语言使用进行正式修订时，会出现更多的协作模式，而当他们进行内容更改时会出现更多的合作模式。

Li & Kim（2016）指出，已有研究关注基于维基的协作写作过程中的群体互动，但很少有研究探讨学生执行多个维基写作任务时的互动模式的变化。该研究调查了两个 ESL 团体在完成两个协作写作任务期间的互动，这两个协作写作任务在一所美国大学的学术英语课程中使用了 Wikispaces 网站。该研究检查了在任务协商期间执行的语言功能，在文本共建期间执行的更改功能、支架策略及跨任务的互动模式。数据包括维基模块、访谈和反思论文。分析表明，在同一维基空间中执行相同任务的两个 ESL 小组制定了截然不同的互动动态模式，并且这些模式在每个小组内的两个任务之间发生了变化。该研究参考小组内支架的流动性讨论互动模式的动态特征。

Li & Zhu（2017b）在学术英语课程中进行了一个基于维基的异步协作写作项目，扩展 Storch（2002）的互动模式并开发了一个更系统的编码框架，分析了 4 个小组的在线互动并推导出同伴互动模式。该研究通过分析小组成员的"平等"和"相互性"两个维度，以及语言功能、写作变化功能和共同写作中出现的支架现象，总结了两个小组的同伴互动模式。研究发现，A 组在任务一中展示了集体模式，但在任务二中切换为主动/撤回模式。相比之下，B 组在任务一中展示了主导/防御模式，但在任务二中切换为协作模式。该研究基于社会文化理论、从在访谈和反思论文中获得的参与者主位视角，结合维基话语，解释小组内部的动态互动，揭示了动态目标、灵活的主体性和社会构建的情感 3 个社会文化因素影响互动模式的形成。研究发现，在异步网络环境中表现出合作立场的群体（集体和专家/新手）在修辞结构、连贯性和语言准确性方面产生了最高的写作质量，加强了社会文化理论在探索和解释在线写作环境下的同伴互动中的作用。

上述研究主要集中于不同任务类型对基于网络的异步二语协作写作的影响，发现任务类型影响着协作模式和最终的协作工作。此外，任务复杂性对互动模式也有影响。基于 Robinson（2001）对任务复杂性的界定，Hsu（2020）对比了 26 名大学英语学习者如何结对完成具有不同复杂度的写作任务，探讨任务复杂性如何影响基于网络的异步二语协作写作中的交互模式。结果表明，在基于网络的异步二语协作写作过程中，任务复杂性对互动模式的影响有限；互动模式在不同任务之间保持一致，且主要的互动模式是权威/撤回。

不同的同伴互动模式对学生修改行为和写作质量产生不一样的影响。Liu & Sadler（2003）讨论了利用计算机中介通信（computer-mediated communication，简称 CMC）研究同伴反馈活动的效果和学生初稿的修改程度。该研究调查二语写作中同伴评论和互动模式（新技术和传统）的差异是否会导致同伴评论在分布（整体和局部）、类型（评估、澄清、建议和改变）和性质（修改导向和非修改导向）方面的不同，以及这些不同对学生修改的影响。研究问题主要有 3 个：CMC 的异步注释模式（Word 编辑）与传统注释模式（笔和纸）的区别会导致同伴评论在分布、类型和评论的性质方面存在差异吗？CMC 的同步交互模式（multiple dimension object-oriented，简称 MOO）与传统的同步交互模式（面对面）是否也会导致出现上述差异？学生在多大程度上根据传统与新技术的互动模式和同伴评论修改论文？受试者是 48 名第二学期选修写作课的大一新生。对照组（传统课堂）的所有受试者是非英语母语者。实验组（新技术课堂）的受试者中有两个组是非英语母语者。该研究选择 8 名非英语母语者（每班 1 组 4 人）的数据，做深入的数据分析。研究数据包括两个部分：一是学期开始时收集的学生个人信息表，记录学生的人口统计信息和他们对同伴反馈与课堂信息技术使用的态度；二是 3 个与该课程相关的数据，即每位学生的 3 篇初稿、同伴对初稿的意见和 2 份后续问卷（对学生的非正式访谈及课堂同伴反馈互动的转写）。

该研究的分析和解释侧重于同伴评论在整体层面（关于观点的展开、读者和目的、文章组织的反馈）和局部层面（关于措辞、语法和标点符号的反馈）的分配情况，关注每个层面评论的 4 种类型，即评价（对写作特征好/坏的评论）、澄清（解释和辩护的探查）、建议（指出改变的方向）和改变（提供具体修改建议），以及聚焦于每种类型和每个层面评论的性质。研究结果表明，新技术组的评论总数、以修改为导向的评论的百分比及最终修改的总数都大于传统组。但是，在基于修改导向的评论所做出的修订百分比方面，传统组要明显高于新技术组（41% vs 27%）。因此，尽管新技术组确实做了大量修改，但评论的有效性不高。对互动模式的深入观察表明，虽然新技术组的受试者发现 MOO 互动更有吸引力，但是因为同伴反馈中存在跨文化交际不可或缺的非语言交际特征，面对面交流比 MOO 交流更有效。鉴于评论模式（Word 编辑 vs 笔和纸）和互动模式（MOO vs 面对面）的差异，研究者们建议在二语写作课堂同伴反馈活动中，综合运用电子同伴反馈模式中的 Word 编辑和传统的同伴反馈模式中的面对面互动。

随着活动理论（Activity Theory，简称 AT，社会文化理论的一个分支）在二语教育和二语写作领域的兴起（Lantolf & Thorne，2006；Lee，2014），使用 AT 作为分析方法来理解同伴反馈中的策略使用，可以获得很多信息。基于该理论，Yu & Lee（2016a）探讨了 4 位中国英语学习者的同伴反馈策略，收集了同伴反馈会议的视频记录、半结构化访谈、刺激回忆和学生的写作草稿等数据。经过分析发现，参与活动和有所合作的英语学习者在同伴反馈中主要采用了 5 种策略：使用母语（普通话）（人工）、采用二语写作标准（规则）、采用小组活动规则（规则）、向教师寻求帮助（社区）和扮演不同角色（分工）。该研究结果表明，学生作为活动的主体，使用策略促进群体互动，以及同伴反馈是一种社会中介活动。

国内关于同伴互动模式的研究主要来自徐锦芬老师的研究团队。寇金南（2016）在任务用时、对话内容和对话发起方式3个方面，探讨了大学英语课堂小组互动模式。研究发现，合作型和专家/新手型完成任务用时最多；专家/新手型产出的与任务有关的对话最多，发起对话的比例较高；主导/被动型和轮流型产出的与语言无关的对话较多；合作型和轮流型发起对话数量比较平均。徐锦芬 & 寇金南（2017）通过课堂观察、录音和访谈等方法定量研究非英语专业大二学生的小组互动模式，发现中国大学英语课堂小组的同伴互动模式有合作型、轮流型、主导/被动型和专家/新手型4种，任务类型都不影响小组互动的相互性、话轮长度、比例和互动模式，但是影响话轮数量。此后，研究者重点关注任务类型对大学英语课堂小组互动的影响，徐锦芬 & 寇金南（2018）通过定量和定性相结合的方法，考察整体听写任务、拼图任务和观点交流任务3种任务类型对大学英语课堂小组互动的影响。研究发现，平等性维度、任务类型影响学习者产出的话轮数量，不影响话轮平均长度和短话轮比例；相互性维度、任务类型对小组互动没有影响。访谈显示，参与者对3种任务类型有不同的偏好，但是这些偏好不影响互动表现。

总之，社会文化理论认为学生是学习的主体，而不是反馈的被动接受者（Lantolf & Pavlenko，2001）；纠正性反馈不仅处于宏观层面的社会文化和社会政治语境中（Goldstein，2006），还处于互动语境中，可以作为支架，帮助学习者更独立地使用目标形式。（Aljaafreh & Lantolf，1994）通过口头讨论和协商，学生们可以向同伴解释为什么会对写作形式进行评论，而不是只读书面评论。在口头协商过程中，学生们可以修改他们在阅读同伴写作时所做的书面评论，使其更加明确、准确，以期对同伴有所帮助。同伴的书面反馈与口头反馈之间存在差异，同伴互评需要综合口头反馈和书面反馈。同伴在提供口头反馈意见的过程中，可以与写作者进一步协商，向写作者解释他们的书面反馈，提供更多细节来澄清评论的信息，达到主体间性。因此，在同伴互评过程中，书面和口头反馈的结合对于提高 ESL 课程中同伴反馈的质量至关重要。

2.3 跨文化写作中的同伴互动研究

现代化教育技术的发展使得英语母语者的同伴反馈成为可能，由母语者和二语学习者组成混合同伴反馈小组成为二语写作的一种趋势。目前，国外关于混合小组的研究主要关注互动和反馈对二语学习者的写作技能与文化意识的影响。例如，Lee & Markey（2014）报道了一个二语学习者（西班牙语者）和母语者的远程协作项目，学生在一个学期内使用推特、博客和播客进行互动交流。该研究通过定性和定量数据收集，探索了 Web 2.0 的应用如何促进了互动交流，以及数字技术的使用如何影响了学生对跨文化学习和同伴反馈的看法。调查结果显示，学生将在线交流视为与母语者进行跨文化交流的最佳方式。通过社交活动，学生不仅获得了文化知识，而且更加意识到自己对本国文化的信仰和态度。此外，关于有形和无形文化主题的讨论为学生增强对文化规范和实践的认识提供了机会。同伴反馈帮助学习者增加词汇知识，防止出现语言僵化，使语言更地道。该研究表明，分配足够的时间完成每项任务并对网上贡献做出个人承诺，对于成功进行跨文化交流至关重要。

Angelova & Zhao（2016）探索了 CMC 工具的潜力，以促进二语习得和发展 ESL 教学技能与文化意识。该研究描述了中国学生和美国学生的在线协作项目。他们使用讨论板和电子邮件进行沟通，学习语法并培养文化意识。该研究对 23 名来自 ESL 教学计划的美国学生与 26 名中国一年级英语专业学生进行配对，分析中国学生对美国生活和文化的介绍性论文中的语法错误，指导二语学习者选择语法结构。针对性指导介绍了特定的语法点，并通过文本描述美国文化的不同方面。中国学生使用讨论板、电子邮件及 Skype 与美国同伴交流，并在项目结束时写第二篇关于同一话题的文章，由美国学生分析其中的语法错误。研究结果表明，这两个群体在 3 个方面有所受益：辅导英语为非母语者提高教学技能，培养跨文化意识，提高非母语者的语言技能。这项研究表明，CMC 可以用来帮助来自不同国家和不同项目的学生提高他们在研究领域内的技能，同时培养他们的跨文化意识。

国内关于二语写作中中美同伴互动的研究主要集中于对"跨洋互动"的研究。例如，许春燕等（2017）基于动态系统理论，对"跨洋互动在线英语写作"课程的中国学习者的二语写作的语言特征进行了实证研究，发现中国学习者写作语言的复杂度和流利度普遍得到提高，但准确度普遍下降。每个写作文本的语言复杂度、准确度和流利度呈现出不同的发展趋势。写作成绩以流利度和准确度的贡献权重最大。许春燕、张军（2018）探索了跨洋互动写作过程中二语学习者与母语者组成的混合小组中互动合作的学习方式对二语学习者写作的影响。该研究结果显示，二语学习者的英语书面语具有以下特征：词汇复杂度具有显著性变化，句法复杂度和语言准确度动态复杂变化，意义协商并不能提高学生写作的各项指标水平。对同伴反馈进行分类发现，对词汇的反馈的效果最直接、最显著。刘立新、游晓晔（2018）将跨文化修辞学的理念应用于跨洋互动写作活动，发现中美学习者会对主题构思、篇章结构和语言形式进行互动协商，这个过程中"小文化"资源会影响意义的建构，写作规范可以得到协商。结合英语作为通用语的背景，跨洋互动写作活动可以有效提升二语学习者对英语写作规范非本质主义的认识。伍志伟（2018）从宏观视角综述了二语写作跨洋互动所取得的研究成果，发现了现有研究与实践的问题，展望了未来研究的方向。裴莹莹等（2019）对比中美同伴反馈类型的分布和出现频率，发现中美同伴的总体反馈类型并无明显差异，均为指正性反馈数量最多，肯定性反馈次之，情感反馈最少；但是中美同伴反馈出现频次存在显著性差异。结合学习者的反思日志，研究发现中美同伴反馈的差异主要体现为批判与读者友好、权威对话与平等对话、静态文本与动态话语 3 个方面。此外，薛红果（2011）研究了美国同伴的网上反馈对中国学生英语写作能力的影响，发现美国同伴的反馈能够帮助中国学生重视修改过程，提高他们的写作构建能力。

2.4 结语

跨洋互动写作超出课堂教学环境，在中美学生之间构建起一个学习社区，同伴在网上互评作文的互动过程中，积极地构建学习上的最近发展区；非母语学生认识到自己与母语者之间的差距，通过书面反馈搭建支架，反思二语写作。互动及可理解的输入，可以促进二语习得的发展。因为母语者或更流利的对话者的互动修改或反馈而产生的可理解输入，进一步提高了非母语学习者的写作水平，促进二语习得。

同伴互评是一个合作项目，须依情况决定是否采用（如果学习者能够自我纠正，就不需要反馈），同伴互评只提供学习者纠正错误所需要的帮助。同伴互评是灵活的，适用于社会/情景语境和学习者个人。同伴互评须考虑到学习者的情感需求，必须由学习者而不是教师来决定是否采纳专家的反馈。学习者的吸收和修改是有益的，是走向自我调节的第一步。如果同伴互评能够使参与者共同构建学习者的最近发展区，则是成功的互评活动。

综观基于两种理论视角的同伴互评研究，二语同伴反馈过程中的互动和反馈，解决了与同伴话语的语言功能、学生写作、读者立场、群体动态等有关的问题。英语母语同伴反馈和非母语同伴反馈的研究已经在同伴反馈的5个方面取得了丰硕的成果，即小组如何运作，学生如何进行同伴反馈和对同伴写作发表评论，成功的同伴小组的特征有哪些，影响同伴互动的因素有哪些，以及同伴反馈培训的作用有哪些。然而，大多数研究集中在专门由母语者或二语学习者组成的反应小组，探究了口头同伴反馈的功能、二语写作的语言特征、互动合作的学习方式对二语学习者写作的影响，以及应用跨文化修辞学的理念分析混合小组同伴反馈的互动协商等方面。虽然部分研究已经关注合作写作中的群体动态，但是对混合小组中的二语学习者和母语者的同伴互评与同伴互动的研究较少。

国内关于同伴互评的研究以实证研究居多，缺少对反馈语言、内容、功能等同伴反馈类型的理论研究。因此，本研究将对同伴互评的类型做进一步的理论研究，以期为同伴互评的更深层研究奠定理论基础。关于同伴互评的实证研究，从研究对象来看，目前的同伴互评研究主要将母语者或者二语学习者作为研究对象，针对由母语者和二语学习者组成的混合小组的研究较少且多为个案研究，我们有必要借助语料库的方法对比母语者和二语学习者的同伴反馈类型及互动模式的异同。从研究问题来看，目前的研究主要集中于同伴反馈是否可以提高写作质量、哪种反馈类型更能有效提高写作水平，即关注同伴反馈的有效性，对同伴反馈的互动行为和互动模式的关注不够，尤其是跨洋互动写作中混合小组的互动。从研究方法来看，以往的研究综合运用了文本分析、访谈、问卷调查和统计分析法，较少使用语料库研究方法，而借助语料库对同伴反馈进行大量的统计和分析值得关注。

认知互动理论和社会文化理论为研究混合小组写作中的同伴互动奠定了理论基础，为理解和解释网络环境中混合小组的互动和协作的性质提供了宝贵的视角。在同伴反馈过程中，二语写作者通过同伴互动意识到自己的语言输出与目标语言（母语者的反馈）之间的差距，构建学习上的最近发展区，通过书面反馈搭建支架，反思二语写作。在同伴互动协商过程中，二语学习者与母语者触发互动调整的意义协商，将输入、学习者内在能力（特别是选择性注意）和输出联系起来。本研究对同伴互评进行界定和分类，以期为同伴互评的更深层次的研究奠定理论基础；借助语料库方法对比跨洋互动写作混合小组中母语者和二语学习者的同伴反馈类型及互动模式的异同。

第三章 同伴互评的理论框架

本章讲述同伴互评的理论框架,具体包括同伴互评界定、同伴互评类型、同伴互动行为和同伴互动模式 4 个部分的内容。以下在综述以往的同伴互评定义后,提出适合本研究的同伴反馈和回评的操作定义;基于以往的编码方案,编制本研究的同伴互评、互动行为和互动模式的编码方案与识别方法。

3.1 同伴互评的界定

3.1.1 同伴互评的定义

同伴互评(peer review),作为过程写作法的一个重要教育措施,是相较于教师反馈的另一个反馈来源,是"一种协作活动,涉及学生对彼此写作的阅读、批评和反馈;在写作过程中,双方互为'支架',改进即时文本,提高写作能力"(Hu,2005:321—322)。

同伴互评有若干相近术语,如同伴反馈、同伴评估、同伴反应、同伴编辑和同伴修订等。首先是同伴反馈(peer feedback)。"反馈"这一术语源于控制论,指作为输入信号、回应系统的控制器的输出(Wiene,1954)。计算机辅助教学认为,反馈是指学生在回应学习任务之后由计算机提供的任何消息或信息,反馈可以是关于结果的信息(knowledge of result)、关于正确与否的信息、关于正确与否的详细解释、赞美的语句或指出正确与否的动画图形(animated graphic)或听觉信号(auditory signal)。(Wager & Wager,1985)但是,这些定义给出的反馈没有包含后期反馈信息(post-response information)和让学习者将其实际结果(actual outcome)与期望结果(desired outcome)进行比较的信息(该类信息被实验研究者称为信息反馈)。信息反馈（informative feedback）是指由外部信息源提供的所有后期反应刺激（post-response stimuli），通知学习者调节或控制该学习任务的下一次尝试。

之后，反馈这一概念被引入教学领域，成为有效教学的基本原则与重要要素，成为教学及学习评估过程的一个组成部分（Collies 等，2001）。教学中的反馈是"提供给学习者的所有后期反应信息，告知其学习或表现的实际状态（actual state of learning or performance）"（Narciss，2008：127），是可以帮助学习者确认、添加、重写、调整或重构记忆中信息的信息，该信息可以是专业知识、元认知知识、关于自身和任务的信念，或认知策略（Wiene & Butler，1994），是施动者（agent）提供的关于他人的表现或者个人理解的信息，是表现的"结果"（consequence of performance），包括来自教师或家长的纠正信息或赞美、来自同伴的替代策略、来自书本的用于澄清想法的信息或学习者自己的正确反应（Hattie & Timperley，2007）。

反馈应用于写作教学中，是指"反馈者针对写作者的产出提供的信息，为写作者修改文章提供建议"（Keh，1990：294）。反馈者对写作的反馈是给写作者提供的输入、给写作者提供的信息（如评语、问题和建议），以供其对文本做出修改。"输入"可以是帮助写作者获得写作想法的任何方式或者途径。它们可以是写作策略，如头脑风暴、快速写作、聚类和采访，也可以是针对特定类型或特定主题的写作范文，还可以是词汇拓展，如与特定主题相关的词汇介绍。从 Keh 的定义看，反馈包含首次写作之前和之后提供的相关信息，或者说包括反馈和前馈。

反馈者可以是任何目标文本的读者。例如，教师作为学生作文的读者可以给学生提供反馈。教师反馈是指教师对论文进行的实质性评论，为学生提供读者反应、改进方法并给出合理的分数。（Hyland，2003）学生作为同伴作文的读者也可以给同伴提供反馈，这种反馈被称为同伴反馈。作为反馈形式的一种，同伴反馈的概念以反馈的定义为基础，明确反馈行为的施动者是写作者的同伴。

在教学中，同伴反馈是指"将学习者作为信息和互动来源，并承担通常由受过正式培训的教师、评阅者或编辑者担任的角色和职责，在写作过程中，对同伴草稿进行书面或口头形式评改"（Liu & Hansen，2002：1）。

同伴反馈是一种"协作写作方法"(Chong,2010:53),学生受益于同伴的反馈和同伴输入的多样性。

其次是同伴评估(peer assessment)。同伴评估是指学生自己批判地审查其他同学的写作并根据相关的标准提供反馈的过程。这个过程可能是单一的活动,也可能是学生为日益完善的文稿提供反馈的一系列说明。(Falchikov,1986)但是,也有学者认为,同伴评估"仅指学生依据相关标准评估彼此的工作和提供反馈,不仅有益于反馈的接收者,还是为了评估者的自身发展"(van den Berg 等,2006:342)。与之前定义相比,该定义侧重于写作标准,以及提供和接收同伴反馈的双重学习效果。

评估与反馈作为二语写作教学的重要组成部分,影响教与学的认知行为,对写作控制系统的优化也起到重要作用。二语写作的评价侧重于不同的判分机制,如形成性评价和计算机辅助评价;反馈的重点是给予写作者意见和建议的不同形式,如教师反馈和同伴反馈。有学者区分了同伴反馈和同伴评估,指出同伴反馈是一个沟通过程,在这过程中学习者针对同伴的表现进行对话;而同伴评估则是学习者根据相关标准对同伴的表现打分(Liu & Carless,2006)。具体来说,同伴反馈是没有成绩的详细评论,同伴评估包括有评论或没有评论的成绩。Gielen & de Wever(2015)提出了同伴反馈和同伴评估之间存在更为一般的关系,认为同伴反馈是同伴评估的一种重要教学实践,其目的是缩小当前表现和预期表现之间的差距。

最后是同伴反应(peer response)。同伴反应的本质是"学生向其他学生提供关于初稿的反馈,以便学生写作者可以获得更广泛的读者意识,并努力完善他们的作品"(Nelson & Murphy,1993:135)。有学者认为,同伴互评与同伴反馈和同伴反应相似,都是学生从同伴那里接收的有关他们写作的反馈。(Richards & Schmidt,2010)其实每个术语意味着反馈的特定角度,可以被看作给定反馈的连续体和不同焦点。例如,同伴反应可能出现在反馈过程的早期,聚焦于内容(如文本组织和论据呈现);同伴编辑则出现于草稿完成的最后阶段,侧重于形式(如语法、词汇和标点符号)(Keh,1990)。由此可见,不同的术语之间有重叠之处,也有各自不同的内涵。这种状况不利于同伴互评的理论研究,也影响对相关研究结果的比较和归纳。

此外,在线同伴互评不是单向的反馈活动,而是一个多向的、动态的协作过程；回评在跨文化互动写作中具有重要意义。回评指写作者对同伴反馈给予回应，阐释同伴反馈的作用。（Nelson & Schunn，2009；高瑛等，2019；解冰等，2020）

3.1.2 同伴互评的操作性定义

本研究以在线平台的电子书面同伴互评及母语者和二语学习者的在线讨论为研究对象，检测网络环境下混合同伴小组的互评类型、互动行为和由此形成的互动模式。本研究的同伴互评既包括同伴对彼此写作的反馈，也包括写作者接收到同伴反馈后做出的回应。

以往文献对于同伴反馈的定义显示，可以从行为、过程和结果3个方面对写作中的反馈进行定义。

首先，反馈是一种行为。反馈是评论者对写作者的输入，向写作者提供信息（如评语、问题和建议）以供其修订（Keh，1990）；反馈是一种协作活动，涉及学生对彼此写作的阅读、批评和反馈（Hu，2005）；反馈也是写作过程中反馈者对写作初稿进行的书面或口头形式的评改（Liu & Hansen，2002）。由此可见，反馈是一种输出行为、协作行为和评改行为。

其次，反馈是一个过程。反馈提供关于写作者学习或表现的信息及其互动协商的过程（于书林、Lee，2013）；反馈是一个沟通过程，在这个过程中，学习者基于写作者的表现与写作者进行对话（Liu & Carless，2006）；反馈既可以是单一的活动，也可以是学习者为不断完善写作文本提供的一系列活动（Falchikov，1986）。因此，反馈包含写作之前和之后提供信息的整个过程，即包括反馈和前馈。

最后，反馈是一种结果。反馈是关于结果的信息、关于正确与否的信息、关于正确与否的详细解释及赞美的语句或指出正确与否的信号（Wager & Wager，1985），是帮助学习者确认、添加、重写、调整或重构记忆中信息的信息（Wiene & Butler，1994），是提供给学习者以告知其学习或表现的实际状态的信息（Narciss，2008），是反馈者提供的关于他人的表现或者本人理解的信息（Hattie & Timperley，2007）。这说明反馈是一种提供与写作相关的各种信息的结果。

同伴是指具有同等能力或资历、相同年龄或社会地位的人。参与"英语写作跨洋互动"的学习者是国内大学英语专业本科生和美国大学的大二或大三学生。他们年龄相近、学习资历相似,是跨洋互动写作活动的同伴。

本研究将同伴反馈定义为反馈者针为具有同等年龄或身份的写作者,就其写作提出的各类评价信息及情感回应。评价信息包括给对方提供的关于写作整体和局部的评价、关于未来的建议或者与写作主题相关的信息。该类信息可以帮助写作者确认、增减、纠正或者重写写作内容,以缩短当前写作水平和预期写作水平之间的差距。

回评指跨洋互动写作中写作者收到同伴反馈之后做出的回应,包括阐释同伴反馈的作用和/或写作者对同伴反馈的接受度,这是从写作者视角做出的反馈。此类反馈包括对同伴做出的评价、建议及对其他相关信息的回复和态度,该类信息可以帮助写作者确认和澄清相关信息。

本研究以中美大学生的在线互评、在线讨论、反思日志和后续访谈为研究对象,采用"同伴互评"这一术语,比以往研究中的同伴互评范围更广。本研究的同伴互评既包括学生对彼此写作的阅读、批评和反馈(Hu,2005)(同伴反馈),也涵盖写作者接收到同伴反馈之后做出的回应(回评)。

3.2 同伴互评的类型

3.2.1 同伴互评的分类

相关文献表明,反馈信息的质量是由反馈的模态、内容和功能决定的(Narciss,2008;Shute,2008)。Narciss & Huth(2004)指出,至少有以下3个方面可以影响反馈的性质和质量:① 与教学目标相关的功能,如促进对信息处理的认知,加强正确回应或维持激励功能;② 与反馈内容相关的语义方面;③ 与反馈的呈现相关的形式和技术方面,如频率、时长、模式、数量和形式。在以往的文献中,研究者们从模态、内容和功能3个方面对同伴互评的类型进行了分类,并提出了多种同伴互评的分类体系。

3.2.1.1 同伴互评的模态

在过去的20年里,反馈研究的不断深入与发展产生了多元反馈模态,如书面与口头反馈、写作研讨会、口头会议或计算机反馈等(Hyland &

Hyland，2006）。同伴反馈同样有多种模态。

首先，根据呈现方式，同伴反馈可以分为口头反馈、书面反馈、电子反馈和计算机自动反馈与评估 4 种类型。口头反馈是指反馈者用口头话语的形式向写作者陈述反馈信息。书面反馈是指反馈者以书面文字的形式呈现反馈信息，并提供给写作者。王颖、李振阳（2012）将电子反馈定义为以计算机为中介传递的教师或同伴反馈，或者是计算机自动反馈和评估。Ene & Upton（2014）将电子反馈定义为借助计算机，由教师或者学生同伴产生并电子传递给学生的反馈。网络为二语学习者提供了与目标语和母语同伴在网上交流、接收母语同伴反馈的机会，这种互动和交流帮助学习者获得比自身水平高的语言学习支架。计算机自动反馈与评估是指自动写作评价提供从现有的评价和纠错数据库中提取的自动计算得出的反馈。这类反馈节省师生的时间，让教师有更多时间进行教学和科研，让学生在较短的时间内获得详细的反馈意见，但是此类反馈侧重于作文的表层问题，对于能否应用于不同体裁作文的评估需要再验证。

其次，根据反馈的次数，同伴反馈可以分为单次反馈和多次反馈。单次反馈只提供单次尝试的机会，即学习者对项目做出反应，收到一次反馈，没有机会再次做出反应；多次反馈提供在反馈后多次尝试的机会，又分为同步阐释反馈（所有信息被包含在一个步骤中）和序列阐释反馈（累积地或逐步地进行）两种类型（Narciss，2008）。

最后，根据提供反馈的人数，同伴反馈分为单个同伴反馈和小组同伴反馈（刘永厚，2015）。综合反馈的形式（呈现方式、次数和人数），同伴反馈可以分为多种形式，如书面单次/多次同伴反馈、口头单次/多次同伴反馈、在线即时/延时同伴反馈、单模态单个同伴反馈和多模态小组同伴反馈等多种同伴反馈类型。

3.2.1.2 同伴互评的内容

以往有不少关于同伴互评内容的理论研究。这些研究表明，同伴互评的效能在很大程度上取决于其内容（Cho & MacArthur，2010）。有效的反馈内容应提供两种类型的信息，即验证和阐释（Narciss，2008），最好两者都包括（Mason & Bruning，2001）。

基于反馈内容进行分类的研究大体上可以分为 4 类。第一类是从语言、内容、组织和形式等方面对同伴反馈进行分类。例如，Nelson &

Murphy（1992）将反馈分为语言问题、生活一般知识、生活个人知识、程序问题和格式问题。语言研究包含所有的语言问题，包括词序、组织、衔接手段和写作者意图。生活一般知识是指围绕课堂之外的生活话题的学生评论，即背景知识，包括与外部世界信息相关的评论。例如，一个学生对另一个学生关于环境绿色和平组织的文章感兴趣，并问道"How can someone become a member? How long has this organization existed?"[①] 另外，当学生的评论是生活一般知识和语言研究的混合时，若该组学生的写作讨论做出实质性的贡献，则评论被编码为语言研究。例如，在之前引用的关于环境绿色和平组织的讨论中，如果学生建议写作者在写作中加入关于如何成为环境绿色和平组织成员的信息，而不是简单地询问自己想了解的环境绿色和平组织的信息，那么评论将被编码为语言问题。生活个人知识包括学生的评论，解决个人关于世界的知识和感受问题，包括个人传记、情感表露，以及选择的内容和自己的个人感受、想法和意见之间的联系。例如，在一篇文章中，一个学生描述了种植盆栽的过程。在同伴反应小组会话期间，另一个学生说"I know what a Bonsai is because I once had a Bonsai tree … I love the Bonsai."。此类评论被编码为生活个人知识。程序问题涉及团体的管理，如实施话轮活动、澄清手头的任务、保存记录和监控团体行为。例如，"Which one（of us）is going to talk first？""Just let me say what I think and then you can say what you think."等意群被编码为程序问题。格式是指书面材料的布局或外观。例如，首行缩进两格、增大行间距等被编码为格式问题。

Sommers & Lawrence（1992）认为，同伴反馈具体有3种内容表达形式：① 使用规避语（如"可能""有点""我不确定"）；② 使用表明自己陈述的标记（如"我认为""我想"）；③ 没有使用上述表明自己陈述的标记（如"你没有论点"）。

Cho 等（2006）基于反馈内容的表达方式，将反馈分为6种类型：指令性、非指令性、表扬型、批评型、摘要型和与任务无关型。指令性反馈对写作文本的具体方面给出具体的建议，如"In clearly understanding the

---

[①] 本研究举例均选自语料。为真实体现跨洋互动写作中参与者的表现，仅对举例中的拼写、标点符号、语法错误进行适度修改，尽量保证语料原貌。

arguments, I had some trouble. To improve this problem, try to introduce the topics you are going to discuss in your introduction for the reader to connect each point and understand the significance of each argument."。非指令性反馈不会针对写作文本的细节给出反馈，不提出修改的建议，如"There were several grammatical and spelling errors that at times made it difficult for me to follow the paper."。表扬型反馈对文本或其中一部分做出积极的评价，包括令人鼓舞的评论，如"The writing was very catchy and once I started reading the introduction, I just wanted to read even more. Therefore, the introduction is good because it sets the tone of the whole paper, making it very insightful and attention getting."。批评型反馈对文本或其中一部分做出消极的评价，并指出欠缺之处，不提出改进意见，如"The intro leaves me wondering what the paper is going to be about. At first, the grammatical errors overwhelm the paper, but after putting the pieces together, it is hard to tell if the paper is talking about visual perception, evolution."。摘要型反馈总结论文或其中一部分的要点，如"The main points of your paper involve visual perception, the retina, cognitive system, top-down and bottom-up processing, visual data, reading text, and how visual perception affects our everyday lives."。与任务无关型反馈不属于上述任何一种分类，可能是不明确的观点或没有评论的打分。

Hu & Lam (2010) 从语言、内容和组织3个方面对同伴反馈进行分类。与语言相关的反馈解决语法（如时态和词序的错误）、词汇（如措辞不当和搭配错误）或用法（如拼写和标点错误）问题。与内容相关的反馈涉及文本中包括的信息和想法的充分性与相关性，如"I agree with you that adapting to studying helps to save time for leisure. However, the reason for lower study pressure is not clearly stated."。与组织相关的反馈是关于信息和想法的发展与组织，如"You really need to get a conclusion to this part based on what you have said. Just a conclusion for discussion …"。

第二类研究的反馈内容聚焦于写作文本的整体和局部特征或者表面特征、微观意义和宏观意义。例如，McGroarty & Zhu (1997) 将同伴反馈分为整体的、局部的和评价的意见。整体反馈涉及思想、受众和目的的发展及文本的组织，局部反馈涉及诸如文字、语法和标点符号的复制编辑方法，评价反馈是指学生对同伴写作的总体评价。

Cho & Cho（2011）从评价和范围两个维度对同伴评论进行分类。首先，评价维度指出同伴初稿的优缺点。如果反馈者指出了同伴初稿好的方面，或者解释为什么好，那么该评论被编码为优点评论；如果反馈者指出了同伴初稿的写作问题，对问题类型进行分类，阐释为什么需要修改，或者指出如何修改，那么该评论被编码为弱点评论；如果反馈者的赞美只是出于礼貌且主要是为了指出写作问题（如"It is good, but ..."），那么该评论也被编码为弱点评论。其次，在范围方面，同伴评论分为3类：表面特征、微观意义和宏观意义。表面特征是指评论内容涉及写作技巧，如拼写、标点符号、语法或风格。另外，评论语句无关写作的意义也被认作表面特征。微观意义主要涉及一个段落的内容，宏观意义涉及多个段落的内容。如果评论表示对写作内容（焦点、论证、有效性和组织）赞成或不赞成，则既可属于微观意义也可属于宏观意义。焦点是指考虑到读者的同时确保写作有明确的目的，论证是用充分的解释和足够的论据支持主要观点，有效性涉及主要观点的精确度，组织涉及句子和段落的顺序与顺畅性。所有不属于上述类别的被编码为"其他"。

第三类研究中反馈内容关注写作文本的情感、认知和元认知特征。例如，Nelson & Schunn（2009）将反馈分为认知反馈和情感反馈两类。其中，认知反馈又分为摘要性反馈、具体性反馈、解释性反馈和范围性反馈4种类型。摘要型反馈是指总结性陈述，将关于特定行为的信息压缩并重组为块，这些陈述关注范围较广（如正确答案、所采取的行动或讨论的主题/主张）。具体性反馈是指反馈中包含详细的信息；反馈的具体性在从结果反馈（行为正确与否）到高度具体（明确识别问题、指出位置和提供解决方案）的连续体过程中不断变化。具体性反馈包括问题识别、提供解决方案及定位。识别问题即批评，提供解决方案是指明确提供处理问题的方法，定位是指精确指出问题和/或解决方案所在位置。解释型反馈是指提供动机或澄清反馈目的。例如，评论者建议"Delete the second paragraph on the third page"，但没有做出解释，写作者可能不会接受该建议，因为他不知修改的必要性。范围型反馈所指的是从局部到整体的连续体：局部层面的聚焦面更窄（如关注表面特征），而整体层面是对表现或产出的整体检查。例如，"You used the incorrect form of 'there' on Page 3. You need to use 'their'."是局部反馈，而"All of your arguments need more support."是整体反馈。情感反馈针对写作质量，分为表达赞美、批评和使用非语言表达（如面部表情、手势和声调）等3种形式。反馈中的情感语言包括赞美和用于批评/建议的缓和性语言。赞美和缓和性语言相似，但是缓和性语言也包括批评，通常是为了让批评的伤害性更小。例如，"The examples you provide make the concepts described clearer."是赞美，而"Your main points are very clear, but you should add examples."属于缓和性语言。

Lu & Law（2012）在 Nelson & Schunn（2009）的分类基础上，将同伴反馈分为情感反馈和认知反馈两种类型。情感反馈分为正面反馈（赞扬）和负面反馈（批评）。认知反馈分为识别问题、建议、解释和对语言的评论。识别问题的反馈是指对文章的具体问题或具体方面的评论（如"You don't have enough survey questions!"）。建议类反馈是指处理文章中的问题的方法（如"The topic is too broad. You should narrow down the topic."）。解释类反馈是对所提出的问题或建议的阐述〔如"Your project lacks of reliable evidence. If you don't collect people's opinion, how can you know it（subway）is convenient?"〕。关于语言的反馈是对总体写作的评论（如"Your writing is too colloquial."）。

Cheng 等（2015）从情感、认知和元认知3个方面对同伴反馈的内容进行分析。情感维度包括两个类别：支持（A1）评论和反对（A2）评论。显示赞美或支持的想法的消息（如"The topic is interesting, and the report is well-written."）被列为 A1 类，只表示负面感受的消息（如"This job sucks."）被列为 A2 类。认知维度包括3个类别：直接纠正（C1）、个人意见（C2）和指导（C3）。侧重于正确性的同伴反馈信息属于类别 C1（如"You are not allowed to copy data from the Internet."），表示一般性意见的反馈信息被列为类别 C2（如"I think the information and relevant graphics in this report are insufficient."），对修改给予明确指导的反馈信息属于类别 C3（如"You can add personal comments to complete the writing."或"You can add subtitles to emphasize the main idea of each paragraph."）。元认知维度包括两个类别：评估（M1）和反思（M2）。验证报告中的知识、技能或选择策略的同伴反馈信息被列为M1类（如"Compared with other reports on the topic of eagles, the framework of your work is vague, and the interpretation made me bored."），批评或要求对方彻底反思的同伴反馈信息属于M2类（如"Things easily get mildewed in our county. Since the phenomenon is associated with our life, it is suggested that you introduce how to prevent it."）。此外，与情感、认知和元认知反馈无关的消息都被列入类别IR中。

  Luo（2016）将同伴反馈分为纠正反馈、认知反馈和情感反馈。纠正反馈指出演示文稿的问题（如"Text is very hard to see on this slide."）。认知反馈是指对演示主题提供很长的解释或反思的反馈（如"I don't mind Wiki, but it should be monitored … but since its a non-profit organization no one will get paid."）。情感反馈是指以表扬或赞美的形式表达的鼓励和激励性的反馈（如"It's very creative."）。此外，该研究将建设性反馈单独列出，包括批评、质疑和建议3种类型。批评是指明显的负面评论（如"There are a couple of problems with viewing the text on some of the slides. I don't think I would ever use this in my class."）。质疑是指以问题形式出现的疑问、忧虑和询问（如"Would the best use for a Wiki be one that is isolated to a certain class or even school?"）。建议是指为改进所给予的意见（如"It would be easier on the eyes if the text were not black."）。

  第四类研究沿用了简单反馈和复杂反馈的分类方式。例如，Shute（2008）按照反馈的复杂度将反馈分为无反馈、验证、正确反应、再试一次、差错举报和阐释6类。无反馈是指反馈者向学习者提出问题并要求其回答的反馈，不涉及学习者反应的正确与否。验证性反馈又称结果信息（knowledge of result，简称KR），告知学习者回答正确与否。正确反应反馈（knowledge of the correct response，简称KCR）告知学习者具体问题的正确答案，不包括其他信息；再试一次（repeat-until-correct）反馈告知学习者有错误，允许学习者再一次或多次回答同一个问题；差错举报反馈（location of mistakes，简称LM）突出解决方案中的错误，但是不提供正确答案；阐释型反馈包括提供对正确答案的具体解释，允许学习者回顾教学过程，也可能呈现正确答案。阐释型反馈再细分为属性隔离、话题相关、回应相关、暗示、错误相关和信息指导 6 类。属性隔离是指反馈的信息呈现目标概念或技巧的重要属性；话题相关是指反馈为学习者提供与当前讨论主题相关的信息；回应相关是指反馈关注学习者的具体反应，描述对错的原因，但是不进行正式的错误分析；暗示是指反馈为学习者指引正确的方向（如暗示下一步怎么做或给出样例或指示），但不直接提供正确答案；错误相关是指反馈对学习者的具体错误进行分析和诊断；信息指导是最详细的反馈，包括验证反馈、指出错误（不提供正确答案）和关于下一步的策略暗示。

Narciss（2008）指出，反馈信息的内容包括两种类型：评价类和信息类。评价类与学习结果相关，表明已达到的水平（如判断对错、正确的百分比和与学习标准的距离）。信息类是与主题、任务、错误或解决方案相关的附加信息。

Gielen & de Wever（2015）采纳 Narciss（2008）提出的反馈分类方式（验证型和阐释型），将反馈信息的内容进一步细分为验证型、阐释型和一般型 3 类。验证型反馈是一个二分法的判断，验证之前的表现是对还是错，是否依据最初的标准（如"Your limitations are not included in the abstract.""Well-written!"）。阐释型反馈包含帮助纠错的相关信息，分为信息性和启发性阐释两种类型，分别指对之前的表现提供同伴反馈和关于未来改进的建议（Hattie & Timperley, 2007）。对同伴的表现做出的告知、判断、确认和证实等反馈，属于信息性阐释；对未来的表现做出的建议、激活、意见等反馈，属于启发性阐释（如"Your limitations are lacking, so please try to include them in your final version.""I like it because you use your own words."）。一般型反馈只是一般性陈述，既不验证也不阐释（如"This week, I'm providing feedback on your second abstract."）。

之后，该研究分别从同伴反馈类型、验证类型和焦点、阐释类型和焦点等方面具体分析反馈内容。首先，将验证分为正面、负面和中立 3 种类型。正面验证是指确认评价性陈述是正面的（如"The intention of the study is well-formulated!"），负面验证是指确认评价性陈述是负面的

(如"I cannot find your limitations in the draft！"），中立验证是指确认评价性陈述是中立的（如"In your abstract, you refer to the methodology."）。验证焦点分为一般抽象、一般标准、具体标准和语言4种类型。一般抽象验证是指确认反馈是否是对整体文章给出一般细节，但没提及特定标准的评价性陈述（如"All necessary components are included in your draft version."），一般标准验证是指确认反馈是否是对特定标准给出具体细节或者表述特定标准正确/出现与否的评价性陈述（如"The problem statement and research purpose are present."），具体标准验证是指确认反馈是否是对关于过去表现中满足特定标准的程度提供进一步具体细节的评价性陈述（如"The introduction summarizes perfectly the intention of the research by mentioning the research purpose before stating the actual context of the research."），语言验证是指确认反馈是否是对动词、翻译、代词、拼写、语法及句子构造和布局等语言特征的评价性陈述（如"There are some little spelling mistakes in your conclusion."）。其次，将阐释分为信息性和启发性两种类型。信息性阐释是对写作文本的信息性陈述，目的是更详细地评价，不是激发学生改写文章（如"Your intro is well-formulated! ... Particularly, I like how your abstract deals with the shift from the intention of the study towards the problem statement."）；启发性阐释是对写作文本的启发性陈述，目的是激发学生改写文章（如"In your final version, you should integrate the limitations, which you can find on Page 9."）。阐释焦点也分为一般抽象、一般标准、具体标准和语言4种类型。一般抽象阐释是对整体文章给出一般细节，但没提及特定标准的阐释性陈述（如"I believe you can still improve the quality of your abstract."）；一般标准阐释是对特定标准的最小细节提供一般性阐述，表达特定标准是否正确或是否存在的阐释性陈述（如"Maybe you should try to merge more the intention of the research and the problem statement."）；具体标准阐释是对关于过去表现中满足特定标准的程度提供进一步具体细节的阐释性陈述（如"I would add the number of participants and more details about the context in the methodology section."）；语言阐释是指确认反馈是否是对动词、翻译、代词、拼写、语法及句子构造和布局等语言特征的阐释性陈述（如"Once you finish, please check spelling mistakes.")。

基于对上述文献的梳理,本研究总结、归纳了反馈内容的分类,具体见表 3.1。

表 3.1 反馈内容分类

研究者及时间	反馈内容分类
Cho 等,2006	指令性、非指令性、表扬、批评、摘要、其他
Shute,2008	无反馈、验证、正确反应、再试一次、差错举报、阐释
Narciss,2008	与任务约束相关的信息、与概念相关的信息、与错误相关的信息、与程序相关的信息、与元认知相关的信息
Nelson & Schunn,2009	认知、摘要、具体、解释、范围
	情感、赞美、批评、非言语表达
Hu & Lam,2010	语言、内容、组织
Cho & Cho,2011	评价、优点、缺点
	范围、表面、微观、宏观
Lu & Law,2012	情感、正面、负面
	认知、识别问题、建议、解释、对语言的评论
Gielen & de Wever,2015	验证、阐释、一般
Cheng 等,2015	情感、支持、反对
	认知、直接纠正、个人意见、指导
	元认知、评估、反思
Luo,2016	纠正、认知、情感

3.2.1.3 同伴反馈的功能

教学中的反馈有两个功能:一是激励学习者,二是提供关于学习者反应正确与否的信息(Wager & Wager,1985)。反馈的激励功能是多变的、因人而异的。反馈的信息功能体现在以下两个方面:一是告知学习者回应是准确的或正确的;二是如果学习者回答错误,给予纠正或允许自我纠正。Wager & Wager(1985)主要关注纠正反馈或针对特定学生的反馈信息,认为反馈的纠正作用是其最重要的功能,对学习影响最大。虽然对纠正反馈的研究仍没有定论,但它从未被证明是有害的。

Stanley(1992)总结出读者评论的 7 个作用(指出、建议、协同、宣布、反应、启发和提问)和写作者评论的 3 个作用(回应、引发和宣布)。

Zhu（2001）对 Stanley（1992）的编码方案进行了适当修改，增加了一些类别（如阐释、缓和语气、确认和辩护），修改了部分类别的定义（如宣布、反应和启发），删除了两个类别（写作者视角的合作和宣布）。该研究的评论分类具体说明和实例如下：

首先，读者评论具有 10 个功能：指出、建议、宣布、反应、启发、提问、阐释、缓和语气、确认和辩护。具体而言，指出功能是指读者回应时指向文本的特定部分（如"Like right here, you say the elderly should not be sent to the nursing home."）；建议功能是指读者提出一般或具体的建议（如"Give a picture about their lives."）；宣布功能是指读者浏览写作者的文章时识别问题或说明他们对文章的反应（如"You mentioned something about atmosphere, and then it kind of got lost."）；反应功能是指读者通过提供评价意见回应文章或回应其他读者的评论（如"I thought it was very well-written."）；启发功能是指读者明确地引导写作者或其他组员给出反馈，反馈可以集中于特定的文章也可以针对同伴反馈的过程（如读者 A 问读者 B"What do you have to say?"）；提问功能是指读者向写作者或其他参与者提出问题（如"What are their values?"）；阐释功能是指读者通过举例说明之前的评论（如"Like maybe why you like that one better than some other one or something?"）；缓和语气功能是指读者使用"I don't know."等来减轻批判的语气；确认功能是指读者肯定写作者或另一位读者对其评论的理解或表明自己赞同写作者或其他读者的意见，回应同伴的评论"I thought we didn't have to talk about others' learning styles."；辩护功能是指读者通过说明理由进行辩护〔如用"I thought he (the instructor) was talking about learning styles, teaching styles, how you adapt." 回应同伴评论"I thought we didn't have to talk about others' learning styles."〕。

其次，写作者评论具有 3 个功能：回应、启发和澄清。回应功能是指写作者对读者的评论做出反应（如"Alright, I see what you are saying."），启发功能是指写作者明确地引出反馈（如"What did you guys think?"），澄清功能是指写作者解释意图或用附加信息帮助读者理解（如"We were in this place, and my mom and I had a deal."）。

Sommers & Lawrence（1992）认为同伴反馈的作用是以特定方式传

达意义，包括提出问题和简洁或详细陈述两种方式。其中，问题的提出方式有 3 种：澄清或信息类、建议或意见类、反问类。例如，"Are you going to put that in as your main idea? Or are you going to put that at the end?"属于澄清或信息类问题提出方式；"I think maybe you need some quotes to specify what you're trying to prove … some quote from him to back up your central idea?"属于给出建议或意见类型；"Do you know what I'm saying?"属于反问。陈述的方式有 9 种：观察、提出建议或意见、阐述意见、对回答者赞同、对回答者不赞同、对写作者赞同、对写作者不赞同、欣赏和道歉。例如，"I just thought you needed a central focus to it."属于观察；"I think what you should do is put these two sentences together, and then that would solve the problem."属于提出建议；"Show how he's really different. Show how he's different, really different from the stereotypical. That he seems like that but he's really not, when you talk to him or whatever."属于阐述意见；"I agree with them on the central idea."属于对回答者赞同；"I don't know. I don't think you should give that view at all."属于对回答者不赞同；"Yeah. It's good."属于对写作者赞同；"No, you have a good paper."属于对写作者不赞同；"Sounds good."属于欣赏；"I just didn't seem to get the meaning. Sorry."属于道歉。总之，该研究将同伴反馈的作用分为 3 种问题提出方式和 9 种陈述方式。

  Mendonca & Johnson（1994）提出同伴评论具有提问、解释、内容解释、建议和语法纠错 5 种功能。提问反馈分为要求解释和理解核实两个子类：要求解释是指反馈者想要获取写作者所说内容或者关于论文中不清楚内容的（如一个未知的术语或一个想法）进一步解释，这个请求可以是一个明确的问句，也可以是一个陈述句（说明不清楚的内容）；理解核实是指写作者向反馈者确认他们是否已经理解文章中的术语或想法的含义，还包括写作者和反馈者彼此确认是否已互相理解所述内容。解释反馈包括对文本中不明确点的解释、意见解释和内容解释 3 个子类：对不明确点的解释是指写作者向反馈者解释不清楚的术语或想法的含义；意见解释是指反馈者或写作者解释他们认为给定的术语/想法清晰或不清晰的原因，以及应不应该在文章中使用；内容解释是指写作者向反馈者解释文章的主题。内容解释是指反馈者或写作者重新陈述（总结或复述）所写/所说内容，以表达对论文部分的理解或重读。建议是指反馈者或写作者关于改变论文的用词、内容和组织的建议。语法纠错是指反馈者或写作者纠正文章的语法结构错误，与主谓一致、动词时态、单复数等相关。

Tseng & Tsai（2007）提出4种同伴反馈类型：加强型、说教型、纠正型和建议型。加强型反馈是指对写作中正确或合适之处给予积极的肯定的反馈，这种反馈有时发生在学生需要鼓励而不需要知道具体原因的情况下；说教型反馈是指当写作者犯错误或提供的信息不充分时，同伴以说教的语气提供长段解释的反馈，以便指导写作者走上正轨；纠正型反馈直接指出写作计划或信息的不正确，以有效地减少写作中不正确的设计或信息；建议型反馈是指当学生的写作计划不完整时，同伴给予间接性的建议、提示，但不直接指出问题，这种反馈被认为是一种支架，可以以提示、停顿或语音中的上升语调的形式，重新定向学生的思维。

Narciss（2008）提出了反馈的3大功能：认知、元认知和激励功能。首先，认知功能包括提供信息、补充、纠正、区分和重组功能。信息功能是指在错误的数量、位置和类型或原因未知的情况下提供信息；补充功能是为缺乏与内容相关的、程序性或策略性知识引起的错误提供关于缺失知识的信息；纠正功能是指由于错误内容或错误的程序性或策略性因素而造成错误时，提供可用于纠正错误因素的信息；区分功能是指由于与内容相关的、程序性或策略性知识因素不精确而造成错误时，提供澄清不精确要素的信息；重组功能是指内容、程序性或策略性因素之间的错误联系，提供可用于重构这些不正确因素的功能。其次，元认知功能包括信息、说明、纠正和指导功能。信息功能是指在元认知策略或其使用条件未知的情况下，提供关于元认知策略的信息；说明功能是指反馈为监管目标提供标准或指定使用特定解决方案策略或元认知策略的条件；纠正功能是指在使用元认知策略时出现错误，反馈提供纠正错误策略的信息；指导功能是指鼓励学习者对监测（评估）或评估自己的解决策略（或其他行为）的适用性形成自己的标准。最后，激励功能包括鼓励、简化任务、增强自我效能和再归因功能。鼓励功能是指反馈呈现任务处理的结果；简化任务功能是指反馈为克服任务困难提供信息；增强自我效能功能是指即便出现错误或困难，反馈提供的信息也可以成功地帮助学习者完成任务；再归因功能是指反馈提供有助于掌握经验的信息，与个人原因有关。

Li & Zhu (2013) 将反馈语言分为承认、赞同、不赞同、阐释、启发、问候、辩解、提问、请求、说明和建议 11 种功能。承认功能是指承认或赞扬他人的想法、评论、有用性和能力（如"Nice job!"）；赞同功能是指表达对他人观点的同意（如"I agree with you."）；不赞同功能是指表达对他人观点的不同意（如"—We should focus on one company because we should narrow the topic. Focus on Apple. —Apple could be just an example, and I think it will be too narrow."）；阐释功能是指扩展或解释自己或他人的写作想法（如"There is one more subtopic I come up with…"）；启发功能是指邀请或征求组员的意见和评论（如"How you think about that?"）；问候功能是指和组员打招呼；辩解功能是指说明理由证明自己的想法或意见（如"We can choose Coca-Cola as our target. Because it owns wide-range consumers, and its successful development experience has made it standing over 100 years."）；问题功能是指对不清楚的问题进行提问（如"What is the difference of Wiki comparing to Google Docs?"）；请求功能是指直接要求或请求（如"Please respond and add something."）；说明功能是指陈述某人的观点或者说明之前小组已经讨论的内容，发布内容或共享信息（如"As I knew, Starbucks has cooperated with three local companies in China."）；建议功能是指对书写内容、结构和格式提供建议（如"We can just discuss benefits for outsourcing, what the reason for it is … something like that."）。

根据以上文献综述，本研究总结、归纳了反馈功能的分类，具体见表 3.2。

表 3.2 反馈功能分类

研究者及时间	反馈内容分类
Wager & Wager, 1985	纠正、激励
Stanley, 1992	读者、指出、建议、协同、宣布、反应
	写作者、启发、提问
	提问、回应、启发、宣布
Mendonca & Johnson, 1994	读者、解释、内容解释、建议、语法纠错

续表

研究者及时间	反馈内容分类
Zhu, 2001	写作者、指出、建议、宣布、反应、启发
	提问、阐释、确认、辩护、缓和语气
	回应、启发、澄清
Tseng & Tsai, 2007	强化、说教、纠正、建议
Narciss, 2008	元认知、信息、说明、纠正、指导
	认知、信息、补充、纠正、区分、重组
	激励、鼓励、简化任务、增强自我效能、再归因
Nelson & Schunn, 2009	激励、强化、信息
Li & Zhu, 2013	承认、赞同、不赞同、阐释、启发、问候
	辩解、提问、请求、说明、建议

3.2.2 同伴互评类型的界定

3.2.2.1 同伴反馈的类型

本研究对以往研究的编码方案进行了适当修改，重新命名了两个类别（肯定性反馈和指正性反馈）；增加了三个子类（移情、讨论邀请和谦辞）；修改了部分类别的定义和范畴（如评价类反馈、情感反馈和信息性反馈），将以往的一些子类单独列为一类（如重述和提出问题），引用了两个口语反馈类型（理解核实和解释需求）。本研究的编码方案具有以下 4 个特点。

首先，基于 Cho & Cho（2011）的评价维度和 Narciss（2008）的评价类反馈，本研究的编码方案将评价类反馈定义为指出同伴初稿的优缺点的信息，以及与主题、任务、错误或解决方案相关的附加信息。本编码方案中的情感反馈完全不同于以往研究中的情感反馈，这里的情感反馈只表达与文本具体内容无关的情感信息，包括学习者之间的问候、祝愿和感谢等。

其次，本研究首次提出指正性反馈和肯定性反馈这两个术语。指正具有指出错误或提出问题以便改正或解决问题之意。因此，指正含有学习者指出同伴的错误/缺点，对写作文本或者反馈文本进行点评、指导的含义；指正性反馈包括同伴识别学习者的问题、提出建议或者提供与写作主题相关的信息等内容。肯定性反馈不同于以往研究中的情感反馈（既包括正面反馈也包含负面反馈),相当于以往研究中的正面反馈。本编码方案采用 Gielen & de Wever (2015) 提出的验证性反馈,验证同伴的写作表现是否依据最初的标准,是对还是错,是一个二分法的判断。验证性反馈包括肯定性反馈和否定性反馈,体现反馈者对写作文本的态度和观点。

再次,本编码方案将以往研究中的定位、直接纠错和错误分析分类都并入重述类反馈,使得编码方案的大类更加简洁,比 Lu & Law (2012) 研究中的识别问题类反馈的分类更加具体、明确。提出问题反馈采纳了 Mendonca & Johnson (1994) 研究中的提问反馈分类,不仅包括以问题形式出现的疑问、忧虑和询问,还包括以陈述句形式出现的对写作文本中观点或信息的确认或者对进一步解释论文中不清楚内容的请求。虽然作为意义协商中的两种形式,理解核实和解释要求多用于口头反馈,但是本语料中书面反馈的多轮互动正是意义协商的过程,也会呈现这两种反馈类型。信息性反馈指反馈者提供的与主题相关的附加信息或者对写作文本的理解或重读,以及反馈者对主题的理解。该类反馈的范围要明显小于 Narciss (2008) 的信息类反馈,属于与概念相关信息的反馈的一部分,但是完全不同于 Gielen & de Wever (2015) 的信息性阐释。信息性反馈增加了总述这一类型,总述是写作中的常见句式,反馈者在输出意见时,以写作者的身份简要地介绍即将给予的评价。建设性反馈与 Luo (2016) 研究中的建设性反馈不完全相同,因"建设性"不应包括否定词,因此,本研究将该研究分类中的批评和质疑列入否定性反馈,并增加了反馈者对自己给出的建议进行解释的部分(意见解释)。

最后,本编码方案增加了移情类反馈。从本质上说,移情是设身处地从他人的视角看待问题的一种意识或行为(项茂英,2003)。教学中的移情是指教师观察和识别学生的外在表现,感受和理解学生的内心想法和行为动机。在 CMC 中,移情是显而易见的,文本 CMC 的独特功能,如选择性的印象、减少的抑制、及时的信息建设、反馈和编辑,可以促成更有利的互动(Bargh 等,2002)。因此,CMC 中匿名性和距离的增加可能反而促成了更多的移情联系(Preece,1998)。尤其是 CMC 可以在共享经验、主题或兴趣方面,提供在其他情况下完全不可能的移情关系,如在线支持社区(Caplan & Turner,2007)。本研究将移情概念应用到 CMC 的写作反馈的分类中,描述反馈者通过写作文本感知和识别写作者的情绪与想法，设身处地为写作者着想，表达自己对写作观点、语言和动机等内容的理解。反馈中的移情、谦辞、问候、祝愿和感谢等都体现了反馈中的情感因素，是交流沟通过程中的基本礼节，被归为情感反馈。

总的来说，本研究将同伴反馈分为评价类反馈和情感反馈两种类型。评价类反馈被定义为指出同伴初稿的优缺点的信息（验证性反馈），以及与主题、任务、错误或解决方案相关的附加信息（指正性反馈）。情感反馈是指不涉及文本内容的、表达情感的信息。这两种反馈类型既能体现反馈的激励功能，又能表达反馈的信息内容。这两种反馈类型可以细分为整体肯定、局部肯定、批评、质疑、直接纠错、定位、错误分析、理解核实、解释需求、内容解释、回应、总述、信息补充、建议、意见解释、讨论邀请、谦辞、移情、问候、祝愿和感谢 21 个子类。同伴反馈的类型见图 3.1。

具体而言，同伴反馈分为评价类反馈和情感反馈两种类型。评价类反馈是指反馈者指出同伴初稿的优缺点的信息和与主题、任务、错误或解决方案相关的附加信息，如"I like how you related the movies back to Emma Watson's speeches at the UN and the World Economic Forum. I agree that these characters show toughness—just as tough as men!"。情感反馈是指反馈者提出的不涉及文本内容的、表达情感的信息，如"Thanks for sharing. If you have any questions about my comments, contact me."。

评价类反馈分为验证性反馈和指正性反馈；情感反馈包括讨论邀请、谦辞、移情、问候、祝愿和感谢 6 类。验证性反馈是指反馈者对同伴的写作表现是否依据最初的标准的判断，即是对还是错，如"I really liked this response. It was very descriptive and elaborate, and it is made quite clear what you think about the subject."。指正性反馈是指反馈者为对方提供的关于当前表现与期望表现之间差距的信息，既包括反馈者识别作者的问题，提出建议或者提供与写作主题相关的信息等内容，也包括作者期待得到反馈者指导的诉求，如"However, I saw a few syntax errors that might stand some improvement."。讨论邀请是指写作者邀请同伴对自己的写作给出建议或者对某个话题进行讨论，如"I'm curious about what you think each ending says about the movie."。谦辞是反馈者表示谦虚或谦恭的语句，如"Of course it's my personal point of view. I don't dare to

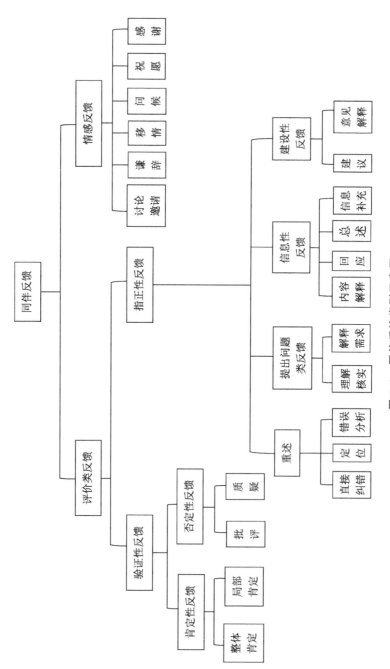

图 3.1 同伴反馈类型示意图

say that I have the correct understanding of what the films tried to display."。移情是指反馈者仔细地观察写作者的文本,准确地理解和把握写作者的写作动机和目的,站在同伴的角度思考问题,用亲身经历指出问题,以及识别和体验写作者的情绪,表达对写作者行为的理解,如"When I was writing my paper, I was really struggling to keep it near the word limit, so I definitely understand why you did not elaborate on these observations more specifically."。问候是反馈者在正式评价之前或之后的打招呼和送祝福或者向对方表达节日的问候,如"It's the day before Thanksgiving Day, and I wish you a happy and joyful holiday!"。祝愿形容反馈者对写作者的写作表达一种迫切的意愿或者良好的愿望,激励写作者取得更大的进步,如"Best wishes to your progress!"。感谢是指学习者表达对同伴给予反馈的谢意,如"Thank you for your feedback on my essay! I appreciate your input."。

验证性反馈分为肯定性反馈和否定性反馈。肯定性反馈是指反馈者对同伴的写作文本给予积极的、肯定的评价,如表扬、赞同和鼓励,以及给出支持写作者的理由和原因,如"I did not notice any errors of language or grammar in your essay. It is well-written!"。否定性反馈是指反馈者对同伴的写作文本给予消极的、否定的评价,如批评和质疑,以及给出支持写作者的理由和原因,如"By the way, I disagree with the author that American citizens understand the legal system any better than Chinese citizens do. While I agree with the author's conclusion, I do not feel that it is supported by the source material."。肯定性反馈分为整体肯定和局部肯定两种类型。整体肯定是指反馈者对写作文本的总体质量给出肯定性评论,但没有给出具体的支持理由和原因,如"Generally speaking, I do like the point of this argument. It is a great work indeed."。局部肯定是指反馈者对写作文本的具体问题或具体方面给出肯定性评论,并给出支持的理由和原因,如"Your essay flows really well, and you are a really capable of expressing your thoughts in a structured way."。否定性反馈分为批评和质疑两种类型。批评是指反馈者对同伴的写作文本给予否定的、消极的评价(不赞同或反对),如"However, the paper does not clearly state the similarities and differences; rather, it just summarizes the films，which is not the objective of the assignment.". 质疑是指以问题形式出现的疑问、忧虑和询问，如 "How do you think we can be more vocal about situations like human trafficking and prison farms in order to prevent this cycle of waiting?"。

指正性反馈分为重述、提出问题类反馈、信息性反馈和建设性反馈 4 种类型。重述是指反馈者改写同伴的词汇或句子，以便让同伴将"地道的"版本和自己的版本进行比较，如 "Great structure, although you omitted the thesis echo in the conclusion." 重述包括定位，即精确指出问题和/或解决方案所在位置，如 "In Para. 2, the word 'emit' and 'left out' seem to be contradictory."；直接纠错，即直接指出问题所在，并给出正确形式，如 "I would also add a second copula ('to be' verb) in the latter part of this sentence, reading ... and is not afraid to fight for it."；错误分析，即反馈者对同伴的具体错误进行分析和诊断，如 "You said that 'From beginning to end ...'. But the truth is that ... because ..."。提出问题类反馈是指反馈者向写作者或其他参与者提出问题，如 "Does it suggest anything about the theme?"。提出问题分为理解核实，指反馈者确认是否已经理解文章中的术语或想法的含义，也包括同伴彼此确认是否已互相理解所述内容，如 "As a reader, I would say that the focus statement of your essay is ... Is this statement correct?"；解释需求，即反馈者想要获取写作者所表达内容或者关于论文中不清楚内容的进一步解释，如 "But I am curious about why you mention the faith Qiuju holds in the 5th paragraph."。信息性反馈是指学习者提供的与主题相关的附加信息或者对写作文本的重读，如 "I didn't know these terms (ethos, logos and pathos) much before, so I googled them. And I found a very interesting cartoon on YouTube about how does a child use ethos, logos, and pathos to persuade his mom to order pizza."。信息性反馈进一步细分为内容解释，指反馈者或写作者重新陈述（总结或复述）所写或所说内容，重读文本，以及反馈者提供的关于写作主题的具体理解，如 "Your main idea is that people should follow the way of the universe to put the right effort in our concrete goals, so that we can finally acquire what we desire."；回应，指反馈者对写作文本的具体内容或写作者观点的反应，

既不明确支持也不反对，如"While I found it very interesting and like knowing your stance on the movie ..."；信息补充，反馈者为同伴提供与当前讨论主题相关的信息，如"Recently, I've learned about some views on anti-feminism. Those anti-feminists ..."；总述，指反馈者概括性地描述将要或已经阐述的内容，如"Structural commentary aside, there are a few remarks I'd like to make."。建设性反馈是指学习者提供的合理的且通常是帮助性的评估意见，如"A thesis statement to introduce what themes you will be discussing would make your introduction much stronger."。建设性反馈进一步细分为建议和意见解释。建议是指反馈者为改进文本给予同伴的意见，如"One thing I would have changed about the focus of your essay is make it a little more clear and cohesive as a statement of your ultimate purpose."。意见解释指反馈者解释或澄清自己对同伴写作所给出的建议，如"I think that a thesis statement or an addition to the first paragraph could bring the topics of Erin and Qiuju to the beginning, which may help tie the beginning and end of the passage together."。

3.2.2.2 回评的类型

在跨洋互动写作中，反馈者和写作者进行了大量的互动交流，因此我们也有必要认识回评类型。基于 Zhu（2001）的写作者评论功能的分类，本研究将回评分为接受性反馈、模糊性反馈和不接受性反馈 3 个大类。接受性反馈是指写作者赞同和接受反馈者的评价，分为整体接受和局部接受 2 个子类。模糊性反馈是指写作者未直接表明对反馈者评价的态度，分为澄清、辩护、答疑、解决方案、回应、经验求教和反思 7 种类型。不接受性反馈是指写作者不赞成或拒绝接受反馈者的评价。回评的分类见图 3.2。

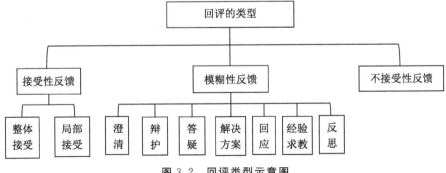

图 3.2 回评类型示意图

本研究在回评的分类中增加了反思性反馈类型。反思实践就是反思自己的行为，从而不断学习的过程。反思是人类重新获得经验、慎重思考和评估经验的重要活动，正是这种经验在学习中起着重要的作用（Boud 等，1985）。反思是指实践者对行动、信念或知识做积极的、慎重的思考，是一种间接认识。反思是经验的循环模式和从经历中获取的教训的自觉运用，是将理论和实践结合起来的重要途径。反思实践是基于实践的专业学习的重要工具，在这个过程中，反思者从自己的专业经验中学习，而不是从正式学习或知识转移中学习。当学习者重新思考或复述事件时，可以对事件、情绪和想法等进行分类，并将过去行为的预期目的与行为的结果进行比较。在写作互评过程中，写作者收到反馈者的评论后，有意识地看待反馈者的经验、观点和反馈行为，并将其分类；同时反思自己的观点、行为和反应，将反馈者的评论和观点与自己的进行比较，并利用这些信息来增加知识，达到更高层次的理解。鉴于反思在教学过程中尤其是反馈实践中的重要作用，本研究提出反思性反馈类型，用于描述写作者根据反馈者的评论内容，对自身写作或者语言学习等做出的评价。

接受性反馈中的整体接受是指写作者笼统地赞同反馈者的评价，但是没有给出具体的理由和原因，如"I agree that some of my ideas could definitely be expanded upon now that I am looking back on what you mentioned."。局部接受是指写作者具体指出接受反馈者的哪些评论，给出赞同的理由和原因，如"The grammatical errors that you pointed out do need to be paid more attention to make them more fluent and easier to understand."。

模糊性反馈中的澄清是指写作者解释意图或提供额外的信息，以帮助读者了解所写的内容，或举例解释自己的观点，如"I'd like to say something about 'strong voice' which you had mentioned. Perhaps it's because of the writing style. We're required to write something like a review of these two movies, and I think the personal opinions are quite important in this kind of writing."。辩护是指写作者说明理由证明自己的想法或意见是正确的，如"At the end of your comments, you suggested that 'surprising' is better than 'amazing'. So I looked them up in the dictionary and found that there is a little difference between the two words.

The difference is that 'surprising' emphasizes 'beyond expectation' while 'amazing' is often used to describe inspiring awe, admiration or wonder."。答疑是指写作者回答反馈者提出的问题或者针对反馈者的质疑做出解释，如"The cause of the suppression of women's rights, at least from my point of view, is quite complicated. I would like to exemplify this based on these two movies which reflects two different contexts at certain periods."。回应是指写作者对反馈者的评价给予回复，既不明确赞同也不反对，如"Thank you for pointing out that the people on the bus may have just been trying not to offend the local people. When you say this …"。解决方案是指写作者接受反馈者的建议后，自己给出解决办法，如"And I think I should change my thesis statement and compare the cinematography of the two genres of film unbiased."。经验求教是指写作者激发反馈者就某一话题发表观点，话题可以针对同伴反馈的过程或关注写作文本内容的特定部分，如"So, I wonder that how you learn the fixed phrases in English. Do you learn by reading and reciting or do you have any other specific method? I eagerly hope you can share your experience with me."。反思是指写作者根据反馈者的评论内容，对自己的写作或者语言学习等做出评价，如"As for the expressions in English, I'm usually quite confused about how to manipulate them correctly. It seems to be the weakest part in my writing …"。

3.2.2.3 同伴互评类型的识别

我们从局外人的角度观察两轮写作和反馈活动。在整个研究过程中，我们是观察员：撰写研究日志，以便在整个研究期间保持研究活动的简洁记录；记录和下载涉及项目实施各个方面的具体信息；查看学生的写作、讨论和修改报告；转写后续访谈的录音记录。然而，我们的观察、案例选择和数据解释的偏向是基于自身对互动理论的兴趣，以及对同伴反馈的关注，以期探索中美大学生跨洋互动写作过程中同伴反馈的异同及双方合作写作的动态过程。

Jeffrey（2015）使用内容分析方法来研究反馈评论，认为任何预先存在的编码方案或先验设计的新方案都不太可能适合一组新的数据，并且根据数据呈现的编码方案更可能产出精确的表述。因此，编码较耗时，我们在编码期间通常需要回顾评论、重新编码，以便适应编码方案中的新修改。基于以往研究的编码方案，本研究提出分别从反馈者（同伴反馈）和写作者（回评）两个视角识别同伴互评类型，将其分为肯定性反馈、指正性反馈和情感反馈 3 种类型。编码方案的设计分为以下 3 个阶段。

（1）编码方案的预先测试

若要对同伴反馈类型进行编码分类，需要先对比、分析已有研究中同伴反馈的编码系统，再建立适合本研究的同伴反馈文本的编码方案。在回顾了反馈评估和科学教育文献后，我们未发现可以解释本研究所期望的特定水平的所有同伴反馈类型的现成编码系统。因此，我们创建了自己的编码系统。在搜索了众多文章和写作书籍的同伴反馈"类别"的详细清单之后，经过半年的编译，我们构建了最初的编码方案。

我们尝试对一批语料进行编码，之后对类别进行了预先测试并做出改进。编码员接受了我们的培训，进行合作编码，以更全面地开发、凝练和修改同伴反馈类别。在两个月的培训和实践过程中，我们分析了不属于收集的语料的同伴反馈的一些分类。在这个分析过程中，我们意识到需要对一些类别进行整合。例如，以往有些研究将同伴反馈按内容和功能进行分类，但是按内容的分类与按功能的分类存在诸多重叠现象，因此我们整合学者们对于反馈内容和反馈功能的分类，避免以往分类的重叠部分。另外，以往出现在口语反馈中的理解核实和解释要求，也出现在本研究的中美双方在线意义协商中，因此编码方案增加了这两个类别。同样的，以往研究侧重于关注教师反馈中的移情，却未提及同伴反馈中的移情，我们在编码过程中发现了移情性反馈。

Gielen & de Wever（2015）指出，内容分析包括 3 个重要内容：分析单元的选择、编码方案的选择和编码信度的确定。在预测阶段，研究者制定了一套编码规则，以保证编码的一致性和准确性。编码规则主要是关于分析单元的选择。分析单元是为了定义如何将同伴反馈内容划分为片段。基于研究目的，只提及文本某一个方面的反馈被划分为一个反馈单元，因为"句子或复合句的一部分更可能包含一个单一的概念、表达或陈述"（Strijbos 等，2006：37）。如果一个反馈包括多个信息，如拼写错误和具体背景信息等，则该反馈被切分为两个反馈信息。这种情况大多出现在错误分析类型中，如"I believe you developed your essay in the correct way.

However, your analysis seems to focus mostly on the Chinese movie and points that were made in that movie, missing some of the important aspects of the American movie.",该反馈可以被切分为 4 个反馈单元,包括 1 个整体肯定性反馈(I believe you developed your essay in the correct way)和 3 个错误分析(错误分析 1 "However, your analysis seems to focus mostly on the Chinese movie"、错误分析 2 "and points that were made in that movie" 和错误分析 3 "missing some of the important aspects of the American movie")。

具体来说,本研究遵循以下 4 个编码规则:

编码规则 1:如果一个句子或者一个复合句的一部分本身没有意义,不论编码分类的意义如何,该句子或者该复合句中的这部分都不被看作分析单元,如 "I think a better word choice would be that—'it was a surprising fact rather than an amazing fact'."。该反馈中第一个从句不需要编码,该反馈计为一个反馈信息。

编码规则 2:如果标点符号或者 and 这个词的前后句子有意义,那么标点符号或者 and 就是分割复合句单元的标记,如 "Overall, your essay is very well-written and points out very important topics."。这个反馈中,and 连接两个反馈信息,计为两个分析单元。

编码规则 3:如果反馈内容可以同属于两种反馈类型,须根据定义再进行确定,每个反馈内容只可以归属为一种反馈类型。例如,"I would agree with this viewpoint, as in the movie Erin was seeking redemption for her community as she had always wanted to give back to the world, while Qiuju was seeking redemption for her husband, maintaining the family's values through her pursuit of justice." 中的 "我赞同这个观点" 属于肯定性反馈,后面的几句可以作为解释反馈者赞同的原因,被归为局部肯定性反馈;但是 "影片中,Erin 一直在为她的社区寻求救赎,因为她一直想回报世界;而秋菊则在寻求对丈夫的救赎,通过追求正义来维护家庭的价值观" 是反馈者对影片的理解,被归为内容解释类反馈更恰当。

编码规则 4:回评中的澄清和答疑须被区分开。澄清是针对反馈者对写作文本中的信息或者观点不清楚或者不理解之处提供解释或额外的信息;而答疑是针对反馈者的质疑或者新提出问题做出的解释或者回答。例如，"Speaking about lawyers and lawsuits in China, I think people are getting more and more used to lawsuits and lawyers. As far as I know, law is a competitive major in China, because many people can simply sense how much money they can make as long as they can become an lawyers."属于澄清；而"Back to your question：Actually, I had given little thought to how Erin tries to engage with the local so as to win the trust of them and why she seems to be more helpful than the other lawyers."属于答疑。

(2) 互评类型的识别

在对同伴反馈类型进行预测之后，经多次讨论和修改，所有同伴反馈标注单位最终被归入以上 10 个类别。每一种反馈类型的顺序并不代表它们的重要性：有意义的大类中的子类被排序，但是其中子类的序列是随机的。

(3) 编码培训

为了保证编码过程中评价者间的信度。我们对另外两位二语习得专业的硕士研究生进行了培训，介绍了切分程序的规则和特例。三位编码者同时进行初步编码，之后进行案例编码实践。一位编码者对反馈类型进行编码后，其他两位编码者随机抽取其中的 25% 进行复评。评判者间的信度 Kappa 值为 82.1%，说明编码者具有很高的一致性。编码者对每个有争议的分类进行讨论，直到达成协议为止。

3.3 同伴互动行为

同伴互动行为是指同伴在互动过程中实施的语言功能、修改功能和支架策略。(Li & Kim, 2016; Leijen, 2017; Li & Zhu, 2017b; Hsu, 2020) 基于以往研究，3 种互动行为的编码方案如下。

3.3.1 语言功能的编码方案

协同写作任务为二语学习者以互动和协作的方式发展写作技能提供了机会。(Storch, 2005) 这种协作过程可以通过联合的建设性互动提高二语写作水平，为学习者提供辩论、协商和修改目标语言知识的机会（Castaneda & Cho, 2013; Parker & Chao, 2007），对语言进行深度加工，反思语言的使用，共同构建语言问题的解决方案（Swain, 1995; Swain & Lapkin, 1998）。

Li & Zhu（2017b）将语言功能分为 11 种，即承认、同意、不同意、阐述、引出、问候、辩护、提问、请求、陈述和建议，并且将每一个语言功能分为发起和响应。基于该分类，本研究根据语料特点做出相应的调整，精简类型。因为每一条评论以"问候"开头或结尾（问候团队成员），包含"承认"（承认或赞扬他人的想法、评论、帮助和能力）的内容、不具有对比和比较的意义，所以删除承认和问候两种语言功能。整合"请求"和"建议"，在"建议"功能中加入"请求"的内容。调整"陈述"和"阐述"的内容，"陈述"包括说出观点和分享信息，而"阐述"指阐释观点和解释理由，加入了"辩护"。将"提问"中表示质疑的部分归入"不同意"，将表示疑问的部分归入"建议"。因此，本研究中的语言功能分为陈述、阐述、建议、同意、不同意和引出 6 种类型。语言功能的编码方案详见表 3.3。

表 3.3 语言功能的编码方案

语言功能类型	描述	举例
陈述	陈述自己的观点和小组之前讨论过的观点；张贴、书写内容或分享资讯	The article talks about the performance of the two protagonists' self-consciousness and collective unconsciousness, and the question of what we should do when the two conflict, which also leads to our thinking.
阐述	阐释和扩展自己或他人关于写作的想法；和/或解释自己的观点或评论	Here I want to share with you the idea of collective unconscious. Collective unconscious refers to structures of the unconscious mind which are shared among beings of the same species. Namely, sometimes human beings have a consistent attitude and recognition that are populated by instincts towards something. We can see collective unconscious in the two movies from many details. For example ...
建议	对写作内容、结构、格式等提出建议或要求	However, there is a problem in the article. Perhaps we do not know much about the words "self-consciousness" and "collective unconsciousness", and the discussion in the article is somewhat empty and difficult to understand. So you can explain the two words for us, and it might be better to use the examples in the films to prove it.

续表

语言功能类型	描述	举例
同意	赞同他人的观点	Your essay has a very interesting analysis! I like the reflection on self-awareness and collective unconsciousness. I agree that these movies show self-awareness and the collective unconsciousness of their different countries and communities. I think this essay does a great job of explaining how difficult it is to overcome hardships, but overcoming hardships is possible.
不同意	不赞同他人的观点	In the character analysis, you think that Wang Cailing epitomizes the pursuit of personal goals by millions of people in developed cities. On this aspect, I don't quite agree because in the film Wang Cailing is actually a music teacher in a small city and wants to live in a developed city to realize her dream. So I think Wang Cailing should be the epitome of many people in small cities pursuing to live in big cities and realize their dreams.
引出	邀请或引出小组同伴的意见、评论等	How to make a direct exposition between artistic techniques and feminism, and do you have any good angles or ideas on this issue? Or do you have any better thoughts for us to learn from?

每一个语言功能的两种类别	描述	举例
发起	提出新想法	But I wonder if you think these two aspects are logically related to the topic? If so, what is the logical connection? And can you specify how they relate to the old and the new?
响应	对他人的想法做出回应	For one thing, I think your suggestion of adding topic sentences is valuable. Our article is indeed lacking in this respect, and there is no way to find the central meaning of every paragraph we want to express at a glance.

我们和两位语言学专业硕士生独立编码了两组历史记录的25%，编码者间的信度Kappa值为84.3%，分歧通过讨论得到解决。然后我们按

照相同的步骤编码剩余的数据。最后，计算每个类别的作文修改的出现频率。

3.3.2 作文修改的编码方案

相关研究关注学生的在线讨论和修改行为。Mak & Coniam（2008）确定了4类中小学ESL学生在编写学校小册子时参与的写作修改功能：增加想法、扩展想法、重新组织思想、纠正错误。Kost（2011）在一项关于德语与外语大学生合作写作的研究中，发现了意义的变化（如添加、删除和替换）和形式的变化（如对拼写、标点符号、词序和词汇的修改等）。

Li（2013）研究了一小部分中国英语学习者的合作写作过程，并确定了5种写作变化：添加、删除、改写、重新排序和修正。该研究通过每种类型的写作变化，从两个子类型角度分析了团队成员在协作维基写作过程中的相互参与：自发修改和他人修改。在此研究基础上，Li & Kim（2016）将写作文本的变化分为5种，即添加、删除、改写、重新排序和更正，并且将每一个写作修改分为自发修改和他人修改。

基于该分类，本研究修改了"重新排序"的定义，将其定义为重新构思文章的组织和结构或移动文本内容位置的行为。本研究调整了改写和更正两个分类，将词汇选择的修正划分到改写中，而将语法的修正划分到更正类别中。因为词汇的选择是指现有词汇意义的不同表达方式（可能是写作者认为的更准确、更精确或者更地道的表达方式），而不是简单的单词修改。例如，在"The amount the village chief (head) needs to offer is not a matter to her and her family."中，将head改为chief是为了使表述更地道，属于改写类作文修改方式；而在"For instance, Qiuju was then dispirited by her husband's argument that it was no use to seeking (seek) the so-called justice and that she should stay at home for the sake of her pregnancy."中，将seek改为seeking是因为语法问题，属于更正类作文修改方式。

本研究将每一个写作修改也区分为自发修改和他人修改两种，但是重新定义了自发修改和他人修改。如果反馈者没有具体指出存在的问题，只是宽泛地指出存在一些问题，那么写作者通过学习他人作品发现自己存在的问题并做出相应的修改属于写作者自我间接习得，被归为自发修改。例如，在"However, it is not difficult to find some hints revealing the fact that the situation of legal knowledge popularization (inadequate popularization of legal knowledge) was quite worrying."中，改写后的句子更简洁，写作者学习了美国学生的文本，认为对方的语言简洁、精确，这个改写不是反馈者直接提出的修改建议，而是写作者间接习得的。写作者的反思日志也证实了此类修改不是反馈者直接提出的，而是写作者自行修改的，如"When I read the passages from America, I could feel the different ways of expression between Chinese students and native speakers. Generally speaking, their languages are more concise and accurate. I deleted lots of redundant words and modified the directions, so the essay was shorter than before."。这个改写属于自发修改。有时反馈者虽然没有具体指出存在的问题，写作者却直接将反馈者或者他人的用法借用到修改稿中，这种修改属于他人修改。例如，在"There are so many differences between stories of Qiuju and Erin Brockovich, but what impresses me most is that both of the female (heroines) protagonists are infinitively tough."中，写作者更改了用词，反馈者并没有指出这个问题，但是反馈者在评论中使用了这个词（"Your essay is great! I also focused on some similarities between the two female protagonists in these movies so I enjoyed reading about the ideas that you shared."），写作者将词汇 female 直接借用到自己的修改稿中，这种修改属于他人修改。

接着，本研究通过使用 Microsoft Word 中"比较"和"合并"两个文档工具比较初稿和修改稿，追溯写作者的修改。该工具强调添加和删除两种作文修改，我们仔细逐个查看突出显示的单词，以确定修改部分属于改写、重新排序还是更正，然后根据同伴在线讨论内容和写作者的反思日志识别修改是属于他人修改（根据同伴评论修订）还是自发修改。我们进行作文修改编码时，对局部修改部分以出现次数进行统计，如将"First of all"改为"On one hand"统计为一个作文修改；在删除"For example, Erin's son wanted his mother's accompany. Even under the same society and the same culture, actions with the expression of moral sense vary from person to person."部分，虽然这是两句，但是一起出现，也被统计为一个作文修改。作文修改的编码方案详见表 3.4。

表 3.4　作文修改的编码方案

作文修改类型	描述	举例
添加	以不同形式为不同层次的现有内容提供新内容或添加信息	In order to avoid making silly mistakes, we should also take some good advice that doesn't go against our will. （画线部分是添加的内容）
删除	去掉文本现有的信息	I was deeply touched by the toughness and conviction of these two characters (as women who served as two significant proofs that women can never be disparaged).
改写	用另一种方式表达现有的想法	And as a result, we would live a happy life with the dignity internally and externally. 改为：I really appreciate the value of human dignity, without which one cannot live for an hour happily.
重新排序	重新构思文章的组织和结构或移动文本内容的位置	The discussion above is helpful for us to consider the relation between our behavior and morality and the potential conflicts between our own morality and that in others, between the public morality and our individual morality. （该句由最后一段调整到倒数第二段）
更正	纠正或试图纠正语法、标点符号和拼写错误	They may might not live a decent life, but they have had many virtues in common; they are were strong-minded, courageous and fighting for what they believed (believe) in against all the odds.

每一个作文修改的两种类别	描述	举例
自发修改	写作文本的修改由写作者自己发现和实施	In real life, we need someone like Qiuju and Erin to make evil and corrupt pay for what they did and demonstrate social justice, rather than be deterred by power and leave the matter take its own course.
他人修改	写作文本的修改由其他人发现和提出	Cultural context, in general and individually, has marked importance within the ability of both women's rhetoric to be understood and accepted by their respective audiences. Although I have been shown how social might play a larger role than I originally presumed thanks to comments, I still believe in general that the most important elements within both these movies are societal and cultural context. （增加总结段落） 反馈者：The ending is little bit abrupt. It will be better if there is a conclusion paragraph.

我们和两位外部研究人员独立编码了两组历史记录的 25%，编码者间的信度 Kappa 值为 87.6%，分歧通过讨论得到解决。然后我们按照相同的步骤编码剩余的数据。最后，计算每个类别的作文修改的出现频率。

此外，了解哪些反馈易于被接受、被理解和被采纳是进行有效反馈的重要组成部分，也是形成良好的协作关系的前提。本研究通过检查在线交流、学习者的反思日志和后续访谈来确定哪些反馈类型易于被接受、被理解和被采纳。在本研究中，如果写作者在在线讨论、反思日志和后续访谈中直接或间接地表达对同伴反馈的赞同或支持，那么该类同伴反馈属于"易于被接受、被理解和被采纳的"反馈；如果写作者的修改稿中因同伴反馈而出现了"他人修改"的作文修改，该类同伴反馈也属于"易于被接受、被理解和被采纳的"反馈。只有与实施或未实施以上 3 类反馈（接受、理解和采纳）相关的数据才被编码。本研究的同伴反馈和回评编码方案，以及写作者的反思日志提及的易于被接受或者不易于被接受的反馈类型，丰富了我们对采纳类型的分析。

3.3.3 支架策略的编码方案

成功的支架互动体现出良好的合作关系，所以本研究了考察同伴在线讨论是否使用了支架策略。在这项研究中，支架被定义为帮助小组成员完成完善写作文本任务的协助。在线评论的记录按照情节编码，即形成参与者讨论写作问题和任务程序的话语单位。(de Guerrero & Villamil，2000) 只有与支架策略使用与否相关的数据才被编码。基于支架的人际性质，本研究的讨论以小组互动（至少一对一的互动）过程中的支架策略为分析单位，而不是区分每个小组成员采用的支架策略。

基于 Li & Kim（2016）制定的支架策略，本研究构建了 5 种支架策略，分别是情感涉入、应急响应、指导、主体间性和启发兴趣；本研究中因未出现过"方向维持"策略，删除了该类策略。

情感摄入是指那些向小组成员表达温暖，在项目中给予小组成员关怀的语句。应急响应是指对小组同伴行为做出的解释及对同伴行为做出的回应。指导策略是小组成员以权威的语气教育同伴，指出存在的问题。主体间性是指小组成员参与共同的任务，对情况有共同的理解，并且保持一致。例如，小组成员提出增加主题句的建议（指导策略）。

激发兴趣策略是指引起小组成员对完成写作任务的兴趣，通常以制造新话题的方式出现。支架策略的编码方案详见表3.5。

表3.5 支架策略的编码方案

支架策略	描述	举例
情感摄入	向小组成员传达温暖，在互动过程中给予小组成员关怀	Thank you so much for your feedback on my confusion of idiomatic expression!
应急响应	解释小组同伴的行为并做出适当的回应	反馈者：For me, structure is a problem because sometimes when I write, some other ideas pop up in my head, and I also want to put them in my essay. But sometimes those ideas seem to be irrelevant, so I don't know how to conclude them in the first and then the last paragraph or connect them naturally between paragraphs either. 写作者：I find that for me when this happens, I pick my top five or so key ideas to work with and forget the rest (as hard as that is!). It helps me find a focus and prioritize.
指导	以权威的语气教育对方	Your introduction has to be as eloquent and well-planned as your essay topics and transitions. You should smoothly go into your discussion but not really. Your introduction should not have much information, but towards the end of the intro you need to have enough information so that the reader gets a good idea of your main objective.
主体间性	小组成员参与共同的任务，对情况有共同的理解，并且保持一致	反馈者：I think that a thesis statement or an addition to the first paragraph could bring the topics of Erin and Qiuju to the beginning, which may help tie the beginning and end of the passage together. I do think for grammar change, it could say ×××has not graduated from a law college. I think that is technically correct, but has sounds much more natural. 写作者：I do think there is something improper in the structure while I did not find it myself. The thesis statement is not clear, and the topic of "the value of human dignity" has not been solidly supported by clear details. So I would accept your advice and rewrite it accordingly.

续表

支架策略	描述	举例
激发兴趣	引起小组成员对此任务的兴趣	Since the topic I chose is about women and their rising status, I am interested in the situation in America. I am looking forward to your sharing, and then we can have a comparison according to my knowledge about China.

按照上述编码方案，我们和两位语言学专业硕士生独立编码了两组历史记录的 25%，编码者间的信度 Kappa 值如下：语言功能 0.84、修改功能 0.87、吸收率 0.83、支架策略 0.85。分歧通过讨论得到解决。之后我们按照相同的步骤编码剩余的数据。

3.4 同伴互动模式

3.4.1 同伴互动模式的定义

Damon & Phelps（1989）和 Storch（2002）的研究为同伴互动模式的构建提供了可操作性的定义和概念。Damon & Phelps（1989）最早提出同伴互动模式的两个维度：相互性和平等性。相互性是指团队成员对彼此贡献的参与程度。平等性是指小组成员的贡献水平和对写作任务方向的控制程度。高度平等的特点使小组成员之间的贡献平衡，小组成员之间的相互指导使写作任务顺利完成。两位学者区分了 3 种同伴互动模式：同伴辅导（低平等，可变的相互性）、合作学习（高平等，可变的相互性）和同伴协作（高平等，高相互性）。

Storch（2002、2012）基于 Donato（1994）的研究，通过从字数/轮数和语言功能等方面分析同伴谈话记录，将平等性和相互性概念应用于协作写作任务中的结对互动。平等是指同伴之间对任务方向的控制、分配和贡献程度相等。相互性是指同伴彼此之间的贡献，体现在语言的确认、修复、解释等功能上。基于对平等性和相互性的整体评估，Storch（2002）确定了 4 种不同的二元互动模式：合作（高平等和高相互性）、专家/新手（低平等和高相互性）、主导/主导（高平等和低相互性）和主导/被动（低平等和低相互性）。这 4 种同伴互动模式是互动模式研究最常用的框架。该研究发现，表现出合作倾向的学生，即合作和专家/

新手互动模式的学生，比表现出主导/主导或主导/被动模式的学生展现出更多的学习场景。

Li & Zhu (2013) 总结出集体贡献/相互支持、权威/应答和主导/撤回 3 种互动模式。Li & Zhu (2017a、2017b) 归纳出集体（高平等性、高相互性）、专家/新手（中低平等性、高相互性）、主导/防守（低平等性、低相互性）和合作（高平等性、低相互性）4 种互动模式。Hsu (2020) 提出 5 种不同的互动模式：协作、主导/主导、权威/退缩、合作和专家/新手。中国大学英语课堂小组的同伴互动模式有合作型、轮流型、主导/被动型和专家/新手型 4 种类型（寇金南，2016；徐锦芬 & 寇金南，2017）。

3.4.2 同伴互动模式的识别

基于 Storch (2002) 的互动模式，首先，本研究从平等性和相互性两个维度识别同伴互动模式。因中美同伴结对小组数量不同，本研究对数据进行了标准化处理，处理方式为"原始反馈频次/小组数×100"。采用 Li & Kim (2016)、Li & Zhu (2017b) 和 Hsu (2020) 的编码方案，平等性的识别方法是检验在线平台的历史记录中显示的语言中介功能（陈述、同意、不同意、建议、阐述、启发），统计各组成员的语言中介的数量。小组中写作者和同伴贡献的语言数量平衡则表示高平等，不平衡则表示低平等。通过检查发起和回应语言功能的比例关系，比较自发修改和他人修改两种修改方式的比例，对相互性进行识别。高频率地使用响应语言功能和他人修改功能属于高相互性，反之则是低相互性。其次，基于上述数据和前人互动模式分类，识别中美同伴互动模式并进行描述性分析。最后，结合小组成员的在线讨论和写作者的反思日志，标记每个条目，比较条目之间的相似点和差异性以生成类别，归纳互动模式生成的影响因素并进行推理性分析。

影响因素部分借鉴 Unlu & Wharton (2015) 的研究方法，不仅记录分析结果，还反思观察到的实践并在其语境下理解。除了分析反馈文本外，本研究还分析了学习者的反思日志和后续访谈。从探索反馈实践的总体思路开始，用数据凸显研究的具体焦点。为了尽量避免先入为主，本研究根据数据自下而上地生成分析类别，并得出一个解释性框架来解释观察到的现象。收集数据后，从数据中推导分析代码和类别，使用不断比较的方法，通过数据收集和分析的步骤逐步发展理论。在整个过程中，使用了手动分析。我们通过打印数据版本，并确保定期阅读所有的副本，进行人工编码。

首先，观察在线讨论的数据。先简单阅读，进行开放编码，然后逐步细化代码，找到围绕反馈实践和写作讨论出现的关键主题，并得出一组稳定的类别以说明观察到的反馈互动的主要特征。在这个过程中，采用连续备忘和不断比较的方法，在抽象过程中归纳相似性和差异性。

其次，聚焦于反思日志和后续访谈的数据。使用上一步中反馈文本分析数据产生的主题来指导反思日志的数据分析；将反思日志和后续访谈插入分析过程，搜索和分析反思日志和后续访谈中阐明了关系模式主题的那些部分。为了选择反思日志摘录进行编码，本研究修改了 Unlu & Wharton（2015）的方法，将反思日志中讨论内容主题的变化作为切断点。先选择阐明关系模式主题的摘录，再使用类似于反馈文本分类的方法对它们进行编码；标记每个摘录，然后比较摘录标签之间的异同以生成概念，并比较概念标签之间的相似性和差异性以生成类别。接着，分析可能影响网络自然语境中反馈互动关系模式的因素。

最后，形成理论编码。将前两个阶段的分析类别相互关联，使用不断比较的方法，将分析范畴联系起来，以解释自然语境中混合小组同伴反馈互动带来的结果。

按照上述编码方案，我们和一名语言学专业硕士生独立编码了数据的 25%，语言功能的信度 Kappa 值为 0.85，修改功能的信度 Kappa 值为 0.86，分歧通过讨论得到解决。之后笔者按照相同的步骤编码剩余的数据。接着，两人分析平等性和相互性，识别同伴互动模式。另一名语言学专业教师验证了互动模式，同意率为 87%，分歧通过讨论解决。

3.5 结语

本章是指导同伴互评研究的理论框架。从对同伴反馈定义的梳理可以发现，尽管目前相关研究成果颇丰，但学界对于同伴反馈的定义、分类和识别存在重叠和不一致的现象。与同伴反馈有关的术语众多（如同伴评估、同伴编辑、同伴反馈、同伴反应、同伴互评和同伴修订等）；国内学者的译法各异，如同伴反馈、同伴互评、同侪互评、同侪反馈等。虽然每个术语所指范围不同，体现了反馈的特定角度，是给定反馈的连续体和不同焦点，但是这种状况不利于反馈的理论研究，也影响相关研究结果的比较和归纳。

不同的研究对同伴反馈内容的分类不同，体现出子类划分的不同和侧重点的不同。我们分析以往研究对同伴反馈内容和功能的分类后发现：学者们将表达支持/反对同伴写作文本的评论单独列为一类，如评价反馈、情感反馈和验证反馈；对同伴反馈内容分类的研究较多且比较系统，对功能分类的研究较少且系统性不强；同伴反馈按内容的分类与按功能的分类存在诸多重叠现象，如表扬、批评、鼓励等反馈。而且，不论是同伴反馈内容的分类还是功能的分类，都体现出反馈的两大方面：激励和提供信息。因此，本研究认为，有必要整合学者们对于反馈内容和反馈功能的分类，避免以往分类的重叠。

在归纳、总结文献中同伴反馈的定义和分类的基础上，本章对同伴反馈和回评进行了界定。同伴反馈是指反馈者为具有同等年龄或身份的写作者就其写作提出的各类评价信息及做出的其他情感回应。回评指写作者接收到同伴反馈之后做出的回应，包括对同伴的评价、建议及提供的其他相关信息的回复和态度；该类信息可以帮助写作者确认和澄清相关信息或者表达对反馈者的感谢及继续交流的愿望。接着，基于以往的编码方案制订了适合本研究的同伴互评编码方案。

本研究将同伴反馈分为评价类反馈和情感反馈 2 个大类，将回评分为接受性反馈、模糊性反馈和不接受性反馈 3 个大类，并详细、具体地阐述了分类方法。同伴反馈的评价类反馈分为验证性反馈和指正性反馈 2 个子类；验证性反馈分为肯定性反馈和否定性反馈 2 个子类；指正性反馈分为重述、提出问题、信息性和建设性 4 个子类。情感反馈分为讨论邀请、谦辞、移情、问候、祝愿和感谢 6 个子类。

在归纳、总结文献中同伴反馈的定义和分类的基础上，本章对同伴反馈和回评进行了界定，将同伴反馈分为 2 个大类和 21 个子类，将回评分为 3 个大类和 10 个子类。这些分类为第四章具体研究中美同伴互评类型奠定了基础。

本研究提出的同伴互评分类方法具有以下特点：首先，整合以往学者们对于反馈内容和反馈功能的分类，解决两种分类的重叠问题；修改部分类别的定义和范畴并删除一些类别，解决以往分类中子类界限模糊的问题；将以往的一些子类单独列为一类，使得方案更加细化、操作性更强。以往研究侧重于关注教师反馈中的移情，忽视了同伴反馈中的移情，本研究加入了移情类反馈。其次，本研究提出的同伴反馈编码方案的大类更具概括性。与写作内容、观点和方法有关的信息全部被归入评价类反馈，剩下的不涉及文本内容的、表达情感的都属于情感反馈。随着语言教学对情感因素的重视，本研究对以往研究中的情感因素进行了具体区分。最后，本研究首次提出回评，用来指写作者收到反馈者评论后的反应和态度。反思是基于实践的专业学习的重要工具，因此，本研究将反思纳入同伴互评的实践活动中。

总的来说，本研究的编码方案整合了以往研究中反馈的内容和功能分类，解决了两种分类重合现象较多的问题；为了更加清晰地呈现反馈文本的性质和功能，本研究的编码方案的分类更加具体、细致。另外，本研究分别从反馈者和写作者两个视角对同伴互评进行分析，使得同伴互评类型的分析更全面。

本研究对同伴互动行为进行了界定，将其分为3个大类和16个子类。本研究基于以往的编码方案制订了合适的同伴互动行为编码方案，其中语言功能分为陈述、阐述、建议、同意、不同意和引出6种类型，以及发起和响应两种方式；修改功能分为添加、删除、改写、重新排序和更正5种类型，以及自发修改和他人修改两种方式；支架策略分为情感涉入、应急响应、指导、主体间性和启发兴趣5种类型。

本研究提出的同伴互动行为分类方法具有以下特点：首先，基于以往学者们对语言功能的分类，整合、修改和删除一些类别，使方案更精简、操作性更强。其次，基于以往作文修改的分类，精确化"改写"和"更正"两个类别，将词汇选择归为改写，将语法的修改归为更正，增加了"重新排序"的内容。最后，基于语料特点，本研究的支架策略删除了个别类别，使编码方案更有针对性。

基于上述同伴互评类型和同伴互动行为，本研究从平等性和相互性两个维度识别同伴互动模式。小组中写作者和同伴贡献的语言数量平衡则表示高平等，不平衡则表示低平等。高频率地使用响应和他人修改属于高相互性，反之则属于低相互性。

在跨洋互动写作的网络互评过程中,二语学习者和母语者对同伴写作文本进行反馈,本研究关注的焦点是中美同伴互评类型、互动行为和互动模式。

本章为中美同伴互评研究提供了理论框架。下面三章将逐一研究中美同伴互评类型、互动行为和互动模式。

第四章 中美跨洋互动写作中同伴互评的特征

本章分析跨洋写作互动中同伴反馈的使用特点，共包括 5 个小节。第一节介绍语料与统计结果；第二节从反馈者视角对收集到的数据进行分析，包括从反馈者视角描述同伴反馈的总体特征及其子类的特征，并进行推断性分析；第三节从写作者视角描述回评的总体特征及其子类的特征，再进行推断性分析；第四节详细讨论中美同伴反馈类型的异同并具体分析其原因；最后是本章小结。

4.1 语料与研究问题

4.1.1 语料

本章语料选自"英语写作跨洋互动"项目，该项目旨在通过中美大学生的网上写作活动促进不同文化之间的交流。本研究选取第 17 轮和第 19 轮互动写作语料作为研究对象，结合作文修改报告和后续访谈，描述网络环境下混合同伴小组的中美同伴反馈的使用特征。

第 17 轮跨洋互动写作始于 2015—2016 年第一学期期中，历时共 5 周。写作活动的实施步骤如下：第一步，中美大学生观看《秋菊打官司》和《永不妥协》（*Erin Brockovich*）两部电影。两部电影主题相似，都是女主角用法律武器争取正义的故事。观赏影片之后，中美大学生撰写一篇不少于 500 字的文章（以一两个中美文化或非言语交际策略为视角），比较和讨论这两部电影。第二步，中美大学生将文章上传至在线写作平台。第三步，中美大学生进行为期两周的多轮网上互评。每篇文章都由两个美国同伴和两个中国同伴依据反馈清单实施在线反馈，反馈清单内容包括对作文进行总体评价，概括文章的主题，指出文章在组织、设计、语言等方面存在的问题，归纳需要修改的重点等。第四步，中美大学生根据反馈修改文章，并上传修改稿。学生可以根据自己的需要和判断决定是否采用同伴反馈，以及是否修改他们的文章。第五步，学生附上反思日志，反思的内容包括是否在修改稿中采纳了同伴反馈及原因、对跨洋互动写作活动的感想和对同伴反馈或者讨论话题的感想等。学习者们对此次跨洋互动写作进行反思，可能会谈论他们从这轮交流中学到了什么、他们修改后的文章与初稿相比的变化，以及他们采纳反馈的原因、他们对这轮交流的态度等。第六步，项目主持人和一名硕士生用汉语分别对 5 名中国学生进行半结构式访谈。后续访谈的内容包括参与者对跨洋互动写作的态度、二语学习者对母语者同伴反馈的期望、双方反馈焦点的异同、参与者最有信心提出哪些方面的反馈等。第 19 轮跨洋互动写作始于 2015—2016 年第二学期期末，历时共 5 周。中美学习者观看《盲山》和《噩梦》（*Nightmare in Badham County*）两部电影，两部电影都讲述了女大学生遭遇噩运，最终被解救的故事。任务与第 17 轮相同。

中美跨洋互动写作中同伴互评特征的研究选取第 17 轮中的中美写作者各 16 名和第 19 轮里的中美写作者各 23 名（其中有 4 名美国学习者的写作文本未搜集到，只选取剩余 19 名学习者的语料），语料包括 35 名中美大学生针对 70 篇写作文本的在线反馈文本、写作者附在修改稿之后的反思日志和后续访谈。因此，研究数据包括中国学生反馈文本（对美国学生 35 篇写作文本的反馈，共计 84 人次）、美国学生反馈文本（对中国学生 35 篇写作文本的反馈，共计 81 人次）、中国写作者回评文本（对美国反馈者的反馈的反馈，共计 66 份）、美国写作者回评文本（对中国反馈者的反馈的反馈，共计 60 份）、中美写作者的反思日志（中美各 30 份，中美学习者各有 5 人没有附上反思日志），以及 5 名中国学习者的后续访谈。

4.1.2　研究问题

对于中美同伴反馈的使用特点，主要设计了 3 个研究问题：

① 在网络自然互动环境下（而非教学环境下）的混合小组中，中美大学生为同一体裁作文提供了哪些同伴反馈类型？

② 中美同伴反馈类型存在哪些异同？它们具体体现在哪些方面？

③ 中美同伴反馈类型出现的频次是否存在差异？

在同伴反馈分类的基础上，首先，我们分别从写作者视角和反馈者视角制订适合本研究的同伴反馈和回评编码方案，计算同伴反馈和反馈之反馈的出现频次，了解中美同伴反馈类型的分布，对比中美同伴反馈类型的异同；其次，根据作文修改报告和后续访谈，从写作者视角和反馈者视角了解同伴反馈的类型，三方检测中美同伴反馈类型的异同；最后，探究产生异同的深层原因，以期拓宽二语写作反馈研究的视角。为使研究更具可操作性，我们将研究问题细化为以下具体内容：

① 同伴反馈的编码。对同伴反馈和回评的类型进行分类，选择分析单元（意义单元/句法单元），设计具体的编码方案并阐释识别分析单元的方法，保证编码过程中评价者间的信度。

② 中美同伴反馈类型的分布。根据上述编码方案，计算每种反馈类型的出现频次，进行卡方（χ^2）检验，确定中美同伴反馈类型是否一致；根据反馈类型的出现频次，统计分析中美同伴反馈类型的分布情况；详细描述各种反馈类型的特征。

③ 反思日志和后续访谈的文本分析。对中美大学生的反思日志进行文本分析，从中美写作者的视角总结同伴反馈类型，计算提及上述反馈类型的人数，并根据后续访谈的内容三方验证中美同伴反馈类型的异同。

④ 中美同伴反馈类型的异同及产生原因。根据数据分析，归纳、总结中美同伴反馈类型之间的共性和差异性，并探究其产生的深层原因。

4.2 中美反馈者的反馈特征

4.2.1 中美同伴反馈的总体特征

表 4.1 所示是中美大学生同伴反馈的两个大类的总体分布情况。表中的数据是经过一定程度的标准化处理后的数据。由于中美学生反馈者人数不同（分别为 84 人和 81 人），本研究对反馈类型的出现频次进行了标准化处理。处理方式为"原始反馈频次/反馈人数×100"，得出的结果就是表 4.1 中的数据。从表 4.1 可以看出，中美大学生对不同反馈类型的使用频次具有相同的顺序，都是评价类反馈最多，占所有反馈类型的绝大多数（超过 90%），中美大学生的评价类反馈分别占各自反馈总数的 92.4% 和 95.7%。中美大学生的情感反馈类型的占比较小，不到总数的 10%，分别占各自反馈总数的 7.6% 和 4.3%。

表 4.1 中美大学生同伴反馈大类的总体分布

频次		学生		
		中国学生	美国学生	总计
类型	评价类反馈	2 160 (92.4%)	2 093 (95.7%)	4 253 (94%)
	情感反馈	178 (7.6%)	93 (4.3%)	271 (6%)
	总计	2 338 (100%)	2 186 (100%)	4 524 (100%)

卡方检验结果显示，中国大学生在两大反馈类型的使用频次上存在显著性差异（表 4.2），美国大学生的两大反馈类型的使用频次也存在显著性差异（表 4.3）。中美大学生的两大反馈类型的使用频次总体上存在显著性差异（$\chi^2=22.64, df=1, p=0.000$），如表 4.4 所示。具体来说，中美大学生在评价类反馈的使用上存在显著性差异（$\chi^2=10.38, df=1, p=0.001$），美国学生使用评价类反馈的比例（95.7%）高于中国学生比例（92.4%）。在情感反馈的使用上，中美大学生之间也存在显著性差异（$\chi^2=32.64, df=1, p=0.000$），中国学生使用情感反馈的比例（8%）高于美国学生（4%）。

表 4.2 中国大学生同伴反馈大类的卡方检验

	类型	评价类反馈	情感反馈	总计
频数	实际频数	2 160	178	2 338
	理论频数	1 169	1 169	2 338
	卡方检验	$\chi^2=1 680.21, df=1, p=0.000$		

表 4.3 美国大学生同伴反馈大类的卡方检验

	类型	评价类反馈	情感反馈	总计
频数	实际频数	2 093	93	2 186
	理论频数	1 093	1 093	2 186
	卡方检验	$\chi^2=1 829.83, df=1, p=0.000$		

表 4.4　中美大学生同伴反馈大类的卡方检验

	频次	中国学生	美国学生	总计	卡方检验
类型	评价类反馈 （理论频数）	2 160 (2 198)	2 093 (2 055)	4 253	$\chi^2=10.38$, $df=1$, $p=0.001$
	情感反馈 （理论频数）	178 (140)	93 (131)	271	$\chi^2=32.64$, $df=1$, $p=0.000$
	总计	2 338	2 186	4 524	$\chi^2=22.64$, $df=1$, $p=0.000$

从反馈类型的角度来说，中美大学生提供反馈通常遵循如下规律：从评价类反馈的验证性反馈开始，尤其是从整体的或具体的肯定性评论开始，然后进行具体的指正性评论，最后再转向情感性评论或者回到整体的肯定性评论。一些研究者指出，从整体的或具体的肯定性评论，到具体的指正性评论，再转向情感反馈或者一般性的肯定性评论的同伴反馈模式，以及详细的局部肯定性反馈、以修改为导向的具体性建议和有说服力的意见解释，再加上反馈者分享自己对话题的理解，都表明网上同伴反馈本身就是一种好的写作实践（Jordan-Henley & Maid，1995；Mabrito，1991；Strenski 等，2005）。

以下示例具体呈现这种反馈模式（节选自第 17 轮跨洋互动写作中中国学生第 1 篇的评论）。

> I really like this response. It was very descriptive and elaborate, and it is made quite clear what you think about the subject. However, I saw a few syntax errors that might stand some improvement. I will elaborate upon them in the following excerpts. I hope this helps you out.
>
> My first comment is concerning "justified right" in the first sentence. This isn't exactly a grammar error, just an issue of lexical semantics …
>
> In the second paragraph, the first sentence needs "die" to be an infinitive (in other words, "to die") …
>
> In the last sentence of the third paragraph, the word "goes" should probably have a "which" or "that" before it …
>
> At this point, I will comment on the style, meaning, and content

of the essay.

　　Even though I do not see Qiuju's concern as merely a selfish whim, I found it interesting how you compared these women's goals as divergent in this way …

　　However, if I were to make one suggestion for your writing, it would be to choose one main focus (or thesis) and subordinate the others to it. In other words, concentrate on "persistence" or "no pain, no gain" while making all points apply directly to this topic. Otherwise, great writing! Thanks for sharing.

　　上述反馈先以一种一般性的、积极的语气提出了评论"I really like this response.",属于验证性反馈;紧接着具体指出写作的优点"It was very descriptive and elaborate, and it is made quite clear what you think about the subject.",属于肯定性反馈。接着,反馈者用一个转折连词 however 开始所有具体的指正性反馈,表示反馈者从积极反馈向消极评论转变;反馈者委婉地提出建议"I saw a few syntax errors that might stand some improvement.",批评的意图显而易见,属于否定性反馈。然后,反馈者非常具体地指出文章中有待改进的地方,包括语法问题("My first comment is concerning 'justified right' in the first sentence. This isn't exactly a grammar error, just an issue of lexical semantics.")、观点("Even though I do not see Qiuju's concern as merely a selfish whim, I found it interesting how you compared these women's goals as divergent in this way.")和结构〔"However, if I were to make one suggestion for your writing, it would be to choose one main focus (or thesis) and subordinate the others to it. In other words, concentrate on 'persistence' or 'no pain, no gain' while making all points apply directly to this topic."〕,并给出具体建议。最后,以一般性的肯定评论("Otherwise, great writing!")和情感评论("Thanks for sharing.")结束反馈。

4.2.2　中美同伴反馈的子类特征

　　表 4.5 所示是中美大学生同伴反馈 21 个子类的分布情况。表中的数据是经过一定程度的标准化处理后的数据。从表 4.5 可以看出,两种反馈

类型中子类的比例不平衡。总体而言,指正性反馈的数量明显多于验证性反馈(2 561 vs 1 692),其中内容解释(1 389)和局部肯定(990)两个子类数量最多、使用频率最高;理解核实(14)、谦辞(15)等子类数量最少。具体而言,第一,在验证性反馈中,肯定性反馈的数量明显多于否定性反馈(1 306 vs 386),其中局部肯定性反馈的数量明显多于整体肯定性反馈(990 vs 316)。也就是说,反馈者倾向于对写作文本的具体内容或具体方面做出肯定性评价并给出支持的理由和原因,而不仅仅是对写作文本的总体质量进行概括性的评论。局部肯定性反馈使得评论更具体也更有针对性,让写作者明白自己的写作优点并清楚知道原因;而整体肯定性反馈是对同伴的写作文本给予笼统的、抽象的肯定,通过积极的、正面的话语发挥激励的作用。以下示例(第 17 轮跨洋互动写作中中国学生第 5 篇的评论)具体说明这两种反馈类型:

表 4.5　中美大学生同伴反馈子类的总体分布

(单位:次)

大类	子类		组别		总计
			中国	美国	
评价类反馈	验证性反馈	肯定性反馈	整体肯定	121	195	316
			局部肯定	501	489	990
		否定性反馈	批评	124	85	209
			质疑	88	89	177
	指正性反馈	重述类反馈	定位	85	62	147
			直接纠错	23	44	67
			错误分析	27	83	110
		提出问题	理解核实	7	7	14
			解释需求	48	19	67
		信息性反馈	内容解释	795	594	1 389
			回应	11	56	67
			信息补充	145	101	246
			总述	67	47	114
		建设性反馈	意见解释	37	75	112
			建议	81	147	228

续表

大类	子类	组别 中国	组别 美国	总计
情感反馈	讨论邀请	99	41	140
	谦辞	15	0	15
	移情	7	10	17
	问候	33	11	44
	祝愿	18	6	24
	感谢	6	25	31
总计		2 338	2 186	4 524

I really enjoyed reading your essay! In my essay, I mainly focused on the differences between the movies, so it was interesting to read your comparisons. Overall, this is a great essay!

Your argument is very well-developed. Every point is supported by scenes from the movies. Your direct quotes really enhance your argument, too!

I found the organization of your essay to be very easy to follow, with one paragraph transitioning into the next. This organizational layout provides a great design, too!

在上述同伴反馈中，反馈者首先用"I really enjoyed reading your essay！""Overall，this is a great essay！"对写作文本做出整体的积极性评价，属于整体肯定性反馈。接着，反馈者具体阐释了写作文本论证充分（Your argument is very well-developed. Every point is supported by scenes from the movies. Your direct quotes really enhance your argument, too!）和组织有条理（I found the organization of your essay to be very easy to follow, with one paragraph transitioning into the next. This organizational layout provides a great design, too!）等优点，这些就是局部肯定性反馈。

在指正性反馈类型中，信息性反馈的数量最多（1 816），提出问题类反馈最少（81）。信息性反馈中的内容解释（1 389）是指正性反馈中数量最多的评论形式。这就意味着，反馈者侧重于向同伴解释自己对话题的理解及重新陈述（总结或复述）写作文本的内容，以表达自己对论文部分的理解或重读。另外，信息性反馈中的信息补充类反馈的数量也不少（236），说明反馈者善于提供一些与当前讨论主题相关的额外信息。以下两个示例（第17轮跨洋互动写作中美国学生第3篇的评论）具体呈现这两种反馈类型：

例1

　　When one sits down to read the essay, one is confronted with three paragraphs: an introduction, a paragraph of similarities, and a paragraph of differences. It seems that your main focus at first is to show the similarities rather than the differences of the two movies. First you explain how both women honor the justice code of their own culture in spite of the liberties they take and their audacious attitudes. You also mention some differences as well. Part of this dissimilarity is the effect class has on each woman. For Erin, she is capable of benefiting for her modest class origins, whereas Qiuju suffers from her quaintness and lack of wherewithal.

例2

　　Each is dictated by situational and cultural factors. For example, I can see why it would seem strange that Erin is so concerned with getting money from Pacific Gas and Electric, rather than an apology like Qiuju. But, as soon as a case like this is made public in America, there is no way the company won't publicly apologize. For this reason, an apology is not really a concern. In America, government officials and companies need to maintain a good opinion with the public (because they need votes to get reelected, and they need people to buy their goods). It is obvious then that if it is made public that someone in the government or a company does something, they will apologize to gain favor again with the public. In other words, in America we think of course they'll apologize, and that's not enough. That's not justice. They have to pay for what they did and help the people they wronged. I think that in China, however, it is different. I think that Qiuju's sense of justice is also accurate.

在例 1 中，反馈者首先概要地总结写作文本的组织结构：引言、阐述对比和比较的段落（When one sits down to read the essay, one is confronted with three paragraphs: an introduction, a paragraph of similarities, and a paragraph of differences.），然后找出文章的关注焦点是展示两部电影的相似之处而不是它们的不同之处（It seems that your main focus at first is to show the similarities rather than the differences of the two movies.），并且复述写作者的主要观点（First you explain how both women honor the justice code of their own culture … For Erin, she is capable of benefiting for her modest class origins, whereas Qiuju suffers from her quaintness and lack of wherewithal.），这个复述就是信息性反馈中的内容解释。

在例 2 中，反馈者分享自己的观点（Each is dictated by situational and cultural factors.）。联系影片内容，反馈者认为 Erin 更关心是否可以从太平洋煤气电力公司得到钱，而不是像秋菊那样道歉；向写作者陈述自己对上述细节的理解，如 "But, as soon as a case like this is made public in America, there is no way the company won't publicly apologize. For this reason, an apology is not really a concern."；然后提供额外信息，即在美国，政府官员和公司需要在公众中保持良好的口碑（因为他们需要选票来获得连任，他们需要人们购买他们的产品），如果有人在政府或公司做了什么事情被公开，他们会道歉，以再次赢得公众的青睐。换句话说，在美国，只道歉是不够的，他们必须为自己的所作所为付出代价。这个反馈属于信息性反馈中的信息补充。

指正性反馈中存在一定数量的建设性反馈（340）和重述类反馈（324）。这说明反馈者会给出建议（228），同时会具体解释建议（112），有时甚至还会精确地指出问题所在位置（147），也会直接给出正确形式即直接纠错（67）或者进行详细的错误分析（110）。这些评论类型表示反馈者发表的意见是一种以修改为导向的评论，具有针对性且可操作性强。下面的例子（第 17 轮跨洋互动写作中中国学生第 8 篇的评论）展现反馈者如何通过提出这一系列评论达到以修订为导向的目的。

In the first sentence of the last paragraph, "costumes" should be plural, since we are talking about both women's attire (comparatively). Other than a few issues in grammar and semantics, I would focus on making the thesis statement (or focus) be a little more central to the piece. I would take filming methodology, character focus, and wardrobe and make them specifically return to the topic of documentary versus biography genres. It might be better if the later two paragraphs specifically mentioned these two words (documentary, biography) in your focus statement.

在上述反馈中，反馈者直接定位即指出问题所在位置（In the first sentence of the last paragraph），然后给出正确形式即直接纠错（costumes should be plural），并且给出解释［since we are talking about both women's attire (comparatively)］。反馈者表达了对同伴语法的否定性评价即批评（Other than a few issues in grammar and semantic）之后；概括性地提出自己会将反馈重点放在写作的内容上［I would focus on making the thesis statement (or focus) be a little more central to the piece.］，即"概括句"反馈，为写作者的修改指明方向；接着从反馈者的视角具体解释建议［I would take filming methodology, character focus, and wardrobe and make them specifically return to the topic of documentary versus biography genres. It might be better if the later two paragraphs specifically mentioned these two words (documentary, biography) in your focus statement.］，增强了建议的可操作性，反映了反馈者对读者需求的关注。

卡方检验结果显示，中国大学生的评价类反馈（表4.6）和情感反馈（表4.7）的使用频次存在显著性差异。在中国大学生的子类使用频次方面，评价类反馈中的验证性反馈（表4.8）和指正性反馈（表4.9）的使用频次存在显著性差异；各种反馈子类的出现频次都存在显著性差异（表4.10）。用同样的方法检测美国大学生的反馈类型，发现评价类反馈（表4.11）、情感反馈（表4.12）、验证性反馈（表4.13）和指正性反馈（表4.14）的使用频次存在显著性差异。但是美国大学生对各子类反馈的使用频次不是都存在显著性差异，除了否定性反馈（$\chi^2=0.09$, $df=1$,

$p=0.762$）的使用不存在显著性差异外，其他子类的使用频次都存在显著性差异（表 4.15）。

表 4.6　中国大学生评价类反馈的卡方检验

类型		验证性反馈	指正性反馈	总计
频数	实际频数	834	1 326	2 160
	理论频数	1 080	1 080	2 160
卡方检验		$\chi^2=112.07$，$df=1$，$p=0.000$		

表 4.7　中国大学生情感反馈的卡方检验

类型		讨论邀请	谦辞	移情	问候	祝愿	感谢	总计
频数	实际频数	99	15	7	33	18	6	178
	理论频数	29.67	29.67	29.66	29.67	29.67	29.66	178
卡方检验		$\chi^2=210.45$，$df=5$，$p=0.000$						

表 4.8　中国大学生验证性反馈的卡方检验

类型		肯定性反馈	否定性反馈	总计
频数	实际频数	622	212	834
	理论频数	417	417	834
卡方检验		$\chi^2=201.56$，$df=1$，$p=0.000$		

表 4.9　中国大学生指正性反馈的卡方检验

类型		重述	提出问题	信息性反馈	建设性反馈	总计
频数	实际频数	135	55	1 019	118	1 327
	理论频数	331.75	331.75	331.75	331.75	1 327
卡方检验		$\chi^2=1\,908.98$，$df=3$，$p=0.000$				

表 4.10　中国大学生同伴反馈子类的卡方检验

大类		子类		频数	卡方检验
评价类反馈	验证性反馈	肯定性反馈	整体肯定	121	$\chi^2=232.15$，$df=1$，$p=0.000$
			局部肯定	501	
		否定性反馈	批评	124	$\chi^2=6.11$，$df=1$，$p=0.013$
			质疑	88	

续表

大类			子类	频数	卡方检验
评价类反馈	指正性反馈	重述	定位	85	$\chi^2=53.51, df=2, p=0.000$
			直接纠错	23	
			错误分析	27	
		提出问题	理解核实	7	$\chi^2=30.56, df=1, p=0.000$
			解释需求	48	
		信息性反馈	内容解释	795	$\chi^2=1468.93, df=3, p=0.000$
			回应	11	
			信息补充	145	
			总述	67	
		建设性反馈	意见解释	37	$\chi^2=16.41, df=1, p=0.000$
			建议	81	
情感反馈			讨论邀请	99	$\chi^2=210.45, df=5, p=0.000$
			谦辞	15	
			移情	7	
			问候	33	
			祝愿	18	
			感谢	6	
总计				2 338	$\chi^2=6 017.95, df=19, p=0.000$

表 4.11 美国大学生评价类反馈的卡方检验

	类型	验证性反馈	指正性反馈	总计
频数	实际频数	858	1 235	2 093
	理论频数	1 046.5	1 046.5	2 093
卡方检验		$\chi^2=67.91, df=1, p=0.000$		

表 4.12 美国大学生情感反馈的卡方检验

	类型	讨论邀请	移情	问候	祝愿	感谢	总计
频数	实际频数	41	10	11	6	25	93
	理论频数	18.6	18.6	18.6	18.6	18.6	93
卡方检验		\multicolumn{6}{c}{$\chi^2=44.80$, $df=4$, $p=0.000$}

表 4.13 美国大学生验证性反馈的卡方检验

	类型	肯定性反馈	否定性反馈	总计
频数	实际频数	684	174	858
	理论频数	429	429	858
卡方检验		$\chi^2=303.15$, $df=1$, $p=0.000$		

表 4.14 美国大学生指正性反馈的卡方检验

	类型	重述	提出问题	信息性反馈	建设性反馈	总计
频数	实际频数	189	26	798	222	1 235
	理论频数	308.75	308.75	308.75	308.75	1 235
卡方检验		$\chi^2=1\,105.03$, $df=3$, $p=0.000$				

表 4.15 美国大学生同伴反馈子类的卡方检验

大类		子类		频数	卡方检验
评价类反馈	验证性反馈	肯定性反馈	整体肯定	195	$\chi^2=126.37$, $df=1$, $p=0.000$
			局部肯定	489	
		否定性反馈	批评	85	$\chi^2=0.09$, $df=1$, $p=0.762$
			质疑	89	
	指正性反馈	重述	定位	62	$\chi^2=12.09$, $df=2$, $p=0.002$
			直接纠错	44	
			错误分析	83	
		提出问题	理解核实	7	$\chi^2=5.54$, $df=1$, $p=0.019$
			解释需求	19	

续表

大类	子类		频数	卡方检验
评价类反馈	指正性反馈	信息性反馈		
		内容解释	594	$\chi^2=1\,048.53,df=3,p=0.000$
		回应	56	
		信息补充	101	
		总述	47	
		建设性反馈		
		意见解释	75	$\chi^2=23.35,df=1,p=0.000$
		建议	147	
情感反馈	讨论邀请		41	$\chi^2=44.80,df=4,p=0.000$
	移情		10	
	问候		11	
	祝愿		6	
	感谢		25	
总计			2 186	$\chi^2=4\,250.87,df=19,p=0.000$

接下来，我们对比中美大学生的各反馈子类的使用频次。首先，中美大学生评价性反馈的各子类的使用频次不是都存在显著性差异。在双方的验证性反馈的两大子类中，肯定性反馈的使用频次存在显著性差异（$\chi^2=14.56,df=1,p=0.000$），否定性反馈的使用频次不存在显著性差异（$\chi^2=3.58,df=1,p=0.059$）。在中美大学生指正性反馈的四大子类中，重述反馈（$\chi^2=30.54,df=2,p=0.000$）和信息性反馈（$\chi^2=44.69,df=3,p=0.000$）的使用频次存在显著性差异，提出问题反馈（$\chi^2=2.49,df=1,p=0.115$）和建设性反馈（$\chi^2=0.21,df=1,p=0.650$）的使用频次不存在显著性差异，如表 4.16 所示。其次，为了检验中美同伴反馈的差异体现在哪些子类上，对上述中美同伴反馈子类中存在显著性差异的类型做进一步的统计。检验结果显示，在肯定性反馈中，中美大学生的整体肯定的使用频次存在显著性差异（$\chi^2=10.67,df=1,p=0.001$），而局部肯定的使用频次不存在显著性差异（表 4.17）。在重述反馈中，中美大学生的定位（$\chi^2=16.14,df=1,p=0.000$）和错误分析（$\chi^2=15.27,df=1,p=0.000$）的使用频次都存在显著性差异，

而直接纠错的使用频次不存在显著性差异（表 4.18）。在信息性反馈中，中美大学生的内容解释（$\chi^2=44.33, df=1, p=0.000$）和回应（$\chi^2=40.80, df=1, p=0.000$）的使用频次都存在显著性差异，而信息补充和总述的使用频次不存在显著性差异（表 4.19）。最后，中美大学生情感反馈的 5 个子类的使用频次不是都存在显著性差异。双方的移情（$\chi^2=4.12, df=1, p=0.042$）和感谢（$\chi^2=27.62, df=1, p=0.000$）的使用频次存在显著性差异，但是讨论邀请、问候和祝愿的使用频次不存在显著性差异，如表 4.20 所示。

表 4.16　中美大学生同伴反馈子类的卡方检验

大类	子类		组别		卡方检验
			中国	美国	
评价类反馈	验证性反馈	肯定性反馈			
		整体肯定	121	195	$\chi^2=14.56, df=1, p=0.000$
		局部肯定	501	489	
		否定性反馈			
		批评	124	85	$\chi^2=3.58, df=1, p=0.059$
		质疑	88	89	
	指正性反馈	重述			
		定位	85	62	$\chi^2=30.54, df=2, p=0.000$
		直接纠错	23	44	
		错误分析	27	83	
		提出问题			
		理解核实	7	7	$\chi^2=2.49, df=1, p=0.115$
		解释需求	48	19	
		信息性反馈			
		内容解释	795	594	$\chi^2=44.69, df=3, p=0.000$
		回应	11	56	
		信息补充	145	101	
		总述	67	47	
		建设性反馈			
		意见解释	37	75	$\chi^2=0.21, df=1, p=0.650$
		建议	81	147	

续表

大类	子类	组别 中国	组别 美国	卡方检验
情感反馈	讨论邀请	99	41	$\chi^2=46.08$, $df=5$, $p=0.000$
	谦辞	15	0	
	移情	7	10	
	问候	33	11	
	祝愿	18	6	
	感谢	6	25	
总计		2 338	2 186	$\chi^2=242.06$, $df=20$, $p=0.000$

表 4.17 中美大学生肯定性反馈的卡方检验

大类	子类	实际频数（理论频数） 中国	实际频数（理论频数） 美国	卡方检验
肯定性反馈	整体肯定	121 (150)	195 (166)	$\chi^2=10.67$, $df=1$, $p=0.001$
	局部肯定	501 (472)	489 (518)	$\chi^2=3.41$, $df=1$, $p=0.065$

表 4.18 中美大学生重述的卡方检验

大类		子类	实际频数（理论频数） 中国	实际频数（理论频数） 美国	卡方检验
指正性反馈	重述	定位	85 (61)	62 (86)	$\chi^2=16.14$, $df=1$, $p=0.000$
		直接纠错	23 (28)	44 (39)	$\chi^2=1.53$, $df=1$, $p=0.216$
		错误分析	27 (46)	83 (61)	$\chi^2=15.27$, $df=1$, $p=0.000$

表 4.19 中美大学生信息性反馈的卡方检验

大类		子类	实际频数（理论频数） 中国	实际频数（理论频数） 美国	卡方检验
指正性反馈	信息性反馈	内容解释	795 (718)	594 (671)	$\chi^2=44.33$, $df=1$, $p=0.000$
		回应	11 (37)	56 (30)	$\chi^2=40.80$, $df=1$, $p=0.000$
		信息补充	145 (134)	101 (112)	$\chi^2=1.98$, $df=1$, $p=0.159$
		总述	67 (62)	47 (52)	$\chi^2=0.88$, $df=1$, $p=0.347$

表 4.20　中美大学生情感反馈的卡方检验

大类	子类	实际频数（理论频数）		卡方检验
		中国	美国	
情感反馈	讨论邀请	99（92）	41（48）	$\chi^2=1.55, df=1, p=0.213$
	移情	7（11）	10（6）	$\chi^2=4.12, df=1, p=0.042$
	问候	33（29）	11（15）	$\chi^2=1.62, df=1, p=0.203$
	祝愿	18（16）	6（8）	$\chi^2=0.75, df=1, p=0.386$
	感谢	6（20）	25（11）	$\chi^2=27.62, df=1, p=0.000$

4.3　中美写作者的回评特征

4.3.1　中美写作者回评的总体特征

中美大学生的回评数量分别为 66 份和 60 份，相较于首轮同伴反馈的 84 人和 81 人，中美大学生对同伴反馈的回复率分别为 78.5% 和 74%，中国大学生对同伴反馈的回复率要高于美国大学生。由于中美大学生的回评数量不同，因此对回评类型的出现频次进行标准化处理。处理方式为"原始反馈之反馈频次/反馈之反馈人数×100"，得出的结果就是表 4.21 中的数据。表 4.21 所示是中美写作者对反馈之反馈（同伴反馈者的反馈）类型的总体分布情况。从中可以看出，中美大学生的不同回评类型的使用频次具有相同的顺序，从高至低依次是模糊性反馈、接受性反馈、不接受性反馈。

表 4.21　中美大学生回评类型的总体分布

类型	学生		
	中国	美国	总计
接受性反馈	230（16.8%）	273（20.7%）	503（19%）
模糊性反馈	1 119（82%）	1 036（78.4%）	2 155（80%）
不接受性反馈	17（1.2%）	13（0.9%）	30（1%）
总计	1 366（100%）	1 322（100%）	2 688（100%）

卡方检验结果显示，中国大学生在 3 种回评类型的使用频次上存在显著性差异（表 4.22），美国大学生在 3 类反馈的使用频次上也存在显著性

差异（表 4.23）。总体来说，中国大学生回评的总数要略高于美国大学生（1 366 vs 1 322）。其中，中美大学生使用的模糊性反馈数量最多，比重最大，接近反馈总数的五分之四，占各自反馈总频数的 82% 和 78%；美国大学生的接受性反馈的数量和比例（273，20.7%）高于中国大学生（230，16.8%）；中美大学生不接受性反馈的数量和比例相当。

表 4.22　中国大学生回评类型的卡方检验

	类型	接受性反馈	模糊性反馈	不接受性反馈	总计
频数	实际频数	230	1 119	17	1 366
	理论频数	455.3	455.4	455.3	1 366
卡方检验		$\chi^2=1\,500.80$, $df=2$, $p=0.000$			

表 4.23　美国大学生回评类型的卡方检验

	类型	接受性反馈	模糊性反馈	不接受性反馈	总计
频数	实际频数	273	1 036	13	1 322
	理论频数	440.67	440.67	440.66	1 322
卡方检验		$\chi^2=1\,283.13$, $df=2$, $p=0.000$			

卡方检验结果显示（表 4.24），中美大学生回评的使用频次总体上存在显著性差异（$\chi^2=6.69$, $df=2$, $p=0.035$）。具体来说，中美大学生在接受性反馈的使用上存在显著性差异（$\chi^2=5.21$, $df=1$, $p=0.022$），美国大学生使用接受性反馈的数量明显高于中国大学生。中美大学生在模糊性反馈的使用上也存在显著性差异（$\chi^2=6.50$, $df=1$, $p=0.011$），中国大学生使用模糊性反馈的数量明显多于美国学生。但是双方的不接受性反馈的使用频次不存在显著性差异。

表 4.24　中美大学生回评类型的卡方检验

	频次	中国学生	美国学生	总计	卡方检验
类型	接受性反馈（理论频数）	230 (255.6)	273 (247.4)	503	$\chi^2=5.21$, $df=1$, $p=0.022$
	模糊性反馈（理论频数）	1 119 (1 110.4)	1 036 (1 074.6)	2155	$\chi^2=6.50$, $df=1$, $p=0.011$
	不接受性反馈（理论频数）	17 (15.2)	13 (14.8)	30	$\chi^2=0.65$, $df=1$, $p=0.422$
	总计	1 366	1 322	2 688	$\chi^2=6.69$, $df=2$, $p=0.035$

中美大学生回评一般遵循以下模式：从接受性反馈开始，写作者表达对反馈者的观点或建议的接受或赞同，然后进行模糊性反馈，澄清自己的观点、为自己的观点或行为做辩护抑或是回答反馈者的问题，或者启发反馈者就某一话题继续讨论。以下示例具体呈现了这种回评模式（选自第19轮跨洋互动写作中国学生第6篇写作者的回评）：

> Your enlightening comments make me rethink my thesis statement. Then I agree with your opinion that anyone should be able to see that abuse is wrong and they do not need a law to tell them that. But they put their own selfish desires first rather than the law or morality. Bai was trapped by the males who cast their covetous eyes on her body, while Cathy and Diane were locked in the farm labor prison where their labor and lives were squeezed by people who abused their power for selfish desires. Since everyone there do the same thing, breaking the law without getting punishment, they don't feel it is abnormal.
>
> "To be honest, I haven't considered the effects that the society's dynamic has had in the town's people." Actually, I can't understand this sentence thoroughly. Could you please give a further explanation?

在上述回评中，首先，写作者肯定反馈者的启发性评论让他重新思考自己的主题句（Your enlightening comments make me rethink my thesis statement.），再表达对反馈者观点的赞同（Then I agree with your opinion that anyone should be able to see that abuse is wrong and they do not need a law to tell them that. But they put their own selfish desires first rather than law or morality.）。其次，写作者澄清自己对他们讨论的话题的看法（Bai was trapped by the males who cast their covetous eyes on her body, while Cathy and Diane were locked in the farm labor prison ... they don't feel it is abnormal.）。最后，针对反馈者提出的另一个观点（社会动态对乡民的影响），写作者表达了自己的兴趣和不解，在结束回评的同时表达了自己想针对该话题与反馈者继续交流的愿望（"To be honest, I haven't considered the effects that the society's dynamic has had in the town's people."... Could you please give a further explanation?）。

4.3.2 中美写作者回评的子类特征

表 4.25 所示是中美大学生回评子类的总体分布情况,是经过一定程度的标准化处理后的数据。

表 4.25 中美大学生回评子类的总体分布

大类	子类	频数 中国	频数 美国	总计
接受性反馈	局部接受	215	263	478
	整体接受	15	10	25
模糊性反馈	澄清	412	610	1 022
	辩护	191	150	341
	反思	33	0	33
	答疑	280	177	457
	解决方案	18	18	36
	回应	0	3	3
	经验求教	185	78	263
不接受性反馈		17	13	30
总计		1 366	1 322	2 688

第一,回评子类的出现频次比例不平衡。澄清的数量最多、使用频率最高;局部接受和答疑也较多;回应和整体接受两个子类的数量最少。

首先,在接受性反馈中,局部接受的数量明显多于整体接受(478 vs 25);也就是说,写作者倾向于对反馈者的评价给予具体的、有针对性的积极回应,具体阐述赞同反馈者哪些方面的评论,只有极少数的回评笼统地表达对反馈者观点的赞同或者是全部赞同。以下(第 17 轮跨洋互动写作中国学生第 8 篇写作者的回评和第 17 轮跨洋互动写作中国学生第 7 篇写作者的回评)是接受性反馈中局部接受和整体接受两种回评类型的典型范例:

例 1

  I love your idea of specifically returning to my topic after comparing the filming methodology, character focus and wardrobe.

Because when I read my passage again and again, I found that the other paragraphs are not as concentrate to my thesis statement as I think. And your suggestion is good, I will use it in my review.

例2

It's a long and detailed comment. I really appreciate it.

在例1中,写作者首先赞成反馈者关于写作文本需要明确的主题句的建议(I love your idea of specifically returning to my topic after comparing the filming methodology, character focus and wardrobe.),接着阐释自己赞同反馈者意见的原因,即在多次阅读自己文章后发现其他段落的确如反馈者指出的那样未能围绕主题句展开(Because when I read my passage again and again, I found that the other paragraphs are not as concentrate to my thesis statement as I think.),之后表示将接受并采纳反馈者的意见(And your suggestion is good, I will use it in my review.)。由此可见,例1是局部接受性反馈。相较于局部接受性反馈,整体接受性反馈比较模糊、笼统,如例2中写作者直接表达"反馈者的评论很长很详细,非常感谢"。

其次,在模糊性反馈中,澄清的数量最多(1 022),答疑次之(457),辩护(341)和经验求教(263)的数量也较多。这意味着写作者侧重于向反馈者解释意图或提供额外的信息,以帮助反馈者了解所写的内容,或举例解释自己的观点;同时,写作者的回评中也有大量内容用于回答反馈者提出的问题或者是为自己的观点或行为进行辩护。小部分写作者会对反馈者提出的问题进行反思(33),并提出相应的解决方案(36)。

以下示例(第17轮跨洋互动写作美国学生第7篇写作者的回评)具体呈现上述提及的回评类型:

The dictionary definition of rhetoric is, "language designed to have a persuasive or impressive effect on its audience". That being said, I believe that rhetoric goes beyond written and spoken language and branches out into almost every aspect of our lives. In a traditional sense, rhetoric involves the use of language (either written or spoken) as a means of persuading. However, my use of the term "rhetoric" goes beyond that, because I believe that things outside of language (for example, physical appearance) play a huge role in a rhetorical situation. That is to say that when an individual tries to persuade someone to take a certain position or act in a certain way, language is not the only factor that plays a role. My professor pointed out in class one day that even hats can be rhetorical. For example, if a man on the street is trying to get you to buy his product, it is not only his language, but his appearance, the way he carries himself, etc. that plays a role in your decision. Perhaps the man has an old worn-down hat, and you purchase his product because you feel that he needs the money.

在上述反馈中，写作者向反馈者解释 rhetoric 的含义，他首先指出字典中 rhetoric 是指对听众具有说服力或能给听众留下深刻印象的语言，但是他认为 rhetoric 不仅仅指书面和口头语言，还涉及生活中的其他方面（The dictionary definition of rhetoric is, "language designed to have a persuasive or impressive effect on its audience". That being said, I believe that rhetoric goes beyond written and spoken language and branches out into almost every aspect of our lives.）。该回评是在回答反馈者对 rhetoric 的疑问，属于答疑类反馈。接着写作者提供了与该词相关的额外信息，包括它的传统意义［In a traditional sense, rhetoric involves the use of language (either written or spoken) as a means of persuading.］，阐释自己对 rhetoric 的理解并举例说明（However, my use of the term rhetoric goes beyond that ... language is not the only factor that plays a role.）；之后用学习中的实例解释 rhetoric 的所指和用法（My professor pointed out in class one day that even hats can be rhetorical ... My definition of rhetoric includes all of the factors that play a role in the making of a rhetorical decision.），以帮助反馈者了解写作文本的内容。这些反馈都属于澄清。

又如（第 17 轮跨洋互动写作中国学生第 1 篇写作者的回评）：

I must admit that I haven't focused too much on the grammar during my writing. Some stereotypes of erroneous usages still remain in my mind (such as "there is an old saying goes ..."). Maybe I should pay more attention to enhancing my accuracy and referring to my grammar book frequently from now on.

上述回评的写作者针对反馈者指出的语法问题进行反思，分析出现问题的原因，并且提出将多参考语法书以解决存在的问题。

最后，不接受性反馈的总体数量较少，表明大多数写作者不会直接拒绝或者否定反馈者的评论。

第二，中美大学生回评子类的使用频次也有很大差异。具体而言，在接受性反馈中，美国大学生的局部接受的数量明显多于中国大学生（263 vs 215），整体接受的数量略少于中国大学生（10 vs 15）。其次，在模糊性反馈中，中国大学生的辩护（191 vs 150）、答疑（280 vs 177）、经验求教（185 vs 78）和反思（33 vs 0）的数量明显多于美国大学生，但是澄清的数量明显少于美国大学生（412 vs 610）。中国大学生的不接受性反馈的数量高于美国大学生（17 vs 13）。值得注意的是，在回评中，反思类回评只出现在中国大学生的反馈中，回应类反馈只出现在美国大学生的回评中。

卡方检验结果显示（表 4.26），中国大学生回评的 10 个子类的使用频次存在显著性差异（$\chi^2=1\,052.02$，$df=8$，$p=0.000$），中国大学生的接受性反馈中的整体接受和局部接受的使用频次存在显著性差异（$\chi^2=173.91$，$df=1$，$p=0.000$）；模糊性反馈的 7 个子类的出现频次都存在显著性差异（$\chi^2=598.23$，$df=5$，$p=0.000$）。表 4.27 显示，美国大学生的回评子类的使用频次也存在显著性差异（$\chi^2=2\,094.08$，$df=8$，$p=0.000$），美国大学生的接受性反馈中的整体接受和局部接受的使用频次存在显著性差异（$\chi^2=234.47$，$df=1$，$p=0.000$），模糊性反馈的 7 个子类的出现频次也存在显著性差异（$\chi^2=1\,467.93$，$df=5$，$p=0.000$）。

表 4.26 中国大学生回评子类的卡方检验

大类	子类	频数		卡方检验
		实际频数	理论频数	
接受性反馈	局部接受	215	115	$\chi^2=173.91$，$df=1$，$p=0.000$
	整体接受	15	115	

续表

大类	子类	频数		卡方检验
		实际频数	理论频数	
模糊性反馈	澄清	412	159.86	$\chi^2=598.23$, $df=5$, $p=0.000$
	辩护	191	159.86	
	反思	33	159.86	
	答疑	280	159.86	
	解决方案	18	159.85	
	回应	0	159.85	
	经验求教	185	159.86	
不接受性反馈		17	17	
总计		1 366	1 366	$\chi^2=1\,052.02$, $df=8$, $p=0.000$

表 4.27 美国大学生回评子类的卡方检验

大类	子类	频数		卡方检验
		实际频数	理论频数	
接受性反馈	局部接受	263	136.5	$\chi^2=234.47$, $df=1$, $p=0.000$
	整体接受	10	136.5	
模糊性反馈	澄清	610	148	$\chi^2=1\,467.93$, $df=5$, $p=0.000$
	辩护	150	148	
	反思	0	148	
	答疑	177	148	
	解决方案	18	148	
	回应	3	148	
	经验求教	78	148	
不接受性反馈		13	13	
总计		1 322	1 322	$\chi^2=2\,094.08$, $df=8$, $p=0.000$

表 4.28 显示，中美大学生回评子类的使用频次总体上存在显著性差异（$\chi^2=151.71$, $df=9$, $p=0.000$），但是具体子类的使用频次不是都

存在显著性差异。在 10 个回评子类中，中美大学生使用的澄清数量最多、比重最大，中国大学生的澄清超过了反馈总频数的约六分之一（30%），美国大学生的澄清数量接近反馈总频数的一半（46%）。具体来说，只有模糊性反馈（$\chi^2=143.05$，$df=6$，$p=0.000$）的使用频次存在显著性差异，中美大学生的接受性反馈和不接受性反馈的使用频次都不存在显著性差异。为了检验中美回评的模糊性反馈差异体现在哪些类型上，我们对模糊性反馈做了进一步统计。检验结果显示（表 4.29），在中美回评的模糊性反馈中，澄清（$\chi^2=11.50$，$df=11$，$p=0.001$）、辩护（$\chi^2=15.33$，$df=1$，$p=0.000$）、答疑（$\chi^2=31.55$，$df=1$，$p=0.000$）和经验求教（$\chi^2=53.04$，$df=1$，$p=0.000$）的使用频次存在显著性差异。其中，美国大学生的澄清（610 vs 412）的出现频次要明显多于中国学生，而中国大学生的辩护（191 vs 150）、答疑（280 vs 177）和经验求教的（185 vs 78）使用频次明显多于美国学生。

表 4.28　中美大学生回评子类的卡方检验

大类	子类	频数		卡方检验
		中国	美国	
接受性反馈	局部接受	215	263	$\chi^2=2.16$，$df=1$，$p=0.142$
	整体接受	15	10	
模糊性反馈	澄清	412	610	$\chi^2=143.05$，$df=6$，$p=0.000$
	辩护	191	150	
	反思	33	0	
	答疑	280	177	
	解决方案	18	18	
	回应	0	3	
	经验求教	185	78	
不接受性反馈		17	13	$\chi^2=0.65$，$df=1$，$p=0.422$
总计		1 366	1 322	$\chi^2=151.71$，$df=9$，$p=0.000$

表 4.29　中美大学生模糊性反馈的卡方检验

大类	子类	实际频数（理论频数）		卡方检验
		中国	美国	
模糊性反馈	澄清	412（531）	610（491）	$\chi^2=11.50$，$df=1$，$p=0.001$
	辩护	191（177）	150（164）	$\chi^2=15.33$，$df=1$，$p=0.000$
	反思	33	0	无
	答疑	280（237）	177（220）	$\chi^2=31.55$，$df=1$，$p=0.000$
	解决方案	18	18	无
	回应	0	3	无
	经验求教	185（137）	78（126）	$\chi^2=53.04$，$df=1$，$p=0.000$

第三，反思日志显示（表4.30），中美写作者对于反馈类型的关注主要集中于写作主题、文化、语言和写作技巧4个方面。为了监督和调节自己或他人的学习，写作者被要求写一篇反思性的文章（反思日志），我们对中美大学生的反思日志进行了文本分析，从写作者的视角归纳、总结同伴反馈和回评的特征，以期达到双重验证中美大学生同伴反馈和回评类型的异同的目的。

表 4.30　中美写作者视角的同伴反馈类型统计

写作者的反馈内容	反馈类型的频数	
	中国大学生	美国大学生
写作主题	15	22
文化	14	17
语言	15	8
写作技巧	16	6
读者意识	1	4
批判性思维	3	1
解决方案	2	0
反馈时间	0	4
反馈形式	0	3

首先，美国写作者指出，中国反馈者对美国学生关于写作主题和文化

的反馈要明显多于美国同伴对中国学生的反馈（分别为 22 vs 15 和 17 vs 14），即 30 位美国写作者中分别有 22 位认为中国反馈者的评论涉及写作主题，17 位美国写作者认为中国反馈者的评论讨论了中西文化。下面的举例节选自美国学生的反思日志（第 17 轮跨洋互动写作中美国学生第 7 篇）：

> The comments surrounding my essay were more a conversation centering primarily on cultural differences and interpretations of the film rather than a critique of my essay or suggestions of revision. The only things that I could change with the input I was given were minor clarifications and expansions on certain ideas, in particular those about Qiuju. I did end up taking all suggestions and making the necessary changes within my essay, as well as rereading it myself and finding things that I wanted to change about it. I did not necessarily disagree with any interpretation of my essay because I believe that any opinions provided that differed from my own had more to do with varying interpretations of the films.

该例中美国写作者首先概括性地总结了中国反馈者对其写作文本的评论是围绕文化差异和电影解读进行的，即文化和主题两个方面，而不是对写作文本进行批评或给予相关的修改建议（The comments surrounding my essay were more a conversation centering primarily on cultural differences and interpretations of the film rather than a critique of my essay or suggestions of revision.）。接着，写作者指出反馈信息主要是关于文化和主题的，其他方面的修改意见较少，因此自己只对内容进行了少量修改（The only things that I could change with the input I was given were minor clarifications and expansions on certain ideas, in particular those about Qiuju.）。然后，写作者表达了对反馈者意见的态度，即采纳了所有建议，除此之外因为进行了再次的自我检查，还做出部分的自发修改（I did end up taking all suggestions and making the necessary changes within my essay, as well as rereading it myself and finding things that I wanted to change about it.）。最后，写作者表达了自己对待不同观点的态

度，即不会反对反馈者对自己的文章做出的任何解释，因为他相信任何不同的意见都是关于影片的不同阐释（I did not necessarily disagree with any interpretation of my essay because I believe that any opinions provided that differed from my own had more to do with varying interpretations of the films.）。美国写作者对待不同意见的态度与美国反馈者对待中方写作文本的反应一致，既不表示支持也不会直接反对；即使意见不一致，他们也会尊重对方意见，认为观点的不一致只是源于双方看待问题的视角不同。

中国写作者则认为，美国反馈者对中国写作者的关于语言和写作技巧的反馈要明显多于中国同伴对美国学生的反馈（分别为 15 vs 8 和 16 vs 6）。也就是说，30 位中国写作者中分别有 15 位认为美国反馈者的评论涉及语言问题，16 位认为美国反馈者的评论提到了写作技巧。下面的两个实例节选自中国写作者的反思日志（第 19 轮跨洋互动写作中国学生第 8 篇和第 17 轮跨洋互动写作中国学生第 7 篇），具体呈现美国反馈者对语言问题和写作技巧的关注。

例 1

  Shannon mentioned the language usage，which I think is interested to both of us. It is a cultural thing or linguistic thing to be exact. For example，Shannon said，"I think I can safely say that most Americans don't use that word（chagrined）. We would probably use the word，annoyed or irritated." I am glad to know about this because it seems that there is little chance to figure out the common language usage in English-speaking countries. All I can do is to bear in mind.

例 2

  Shannon would give wonderful suggestions，such as rephrasing a sentence into a slightly different one which I think was better organized，too. Moreover，she reminded me of the problem that can be the most likely to be ignored：run on sentence. In fact，I had never been aware of this problem. And I will work on it.

在例 1 中，中国写作者提到美国反馈者指出其写作文本里出现的词汇选择问题，反馈者认为大多数母语者不会使用 chagrined 这个词，并建议选择 annoyed 或 irritated，以帮助写作者规范使用语言（Shannon mentioned the language usage, which I think is interested to both of us ... We would probably use the word, annoyed or irritated."），中国写作者对反馈者关于语言的建议表达了高度赞赏之意和感激之情（I am glad to know about this because it seems that there is little chance to figure out the common language usage in English-speaking countries. All I can do is to bear in mind.）。

在例 2 中，美国反馈者也关注到了句子层面的问题，包括提到改写句子结构（Shannon would give wonderful suggestions, such as rephrasing a sentence into a slightly different one which I think was better organized, too.）和指出存在流水句问题（Moreover, she reminded me of the problem that can be the most likely to be ignored: run on sentence.）。中国写作者乐于接受和采纳针对句子层面问题的建议。

除此之外，美国反馈者善于给予写作技巧方面的建议和意见，例如：

  Thanks to Stephen. He pointed out a clearer structure for my essay. So, in my revision, I mainly changed the design of my essay. I made the opening shorter and briefer, and then I wrote about Erin from two aspects and then I also commented on Qiuju from two aspects.

  In fact, for me, structure is a problem because sometimes when I write, some other ideas pop up in my head, and I also want to put them in my essay. But sometimes those ideas seem to be irrelevant, so I don't know how to conclude them in the first and then the last paragraph or connect them naturally between paragraphs.

  About this problem, Kaitlan also gave me some suggestions, such as picking top five or so key ideas to work with and trying the best to forget the rest. Additionally, her essay with a clear structure inspired me. I will pay more attention on the structure later in my writing.

在这则反思日志中，中国写作者感谢两位美国反馈者在写作技巧方面给予的帮助。首先，感谢 Stephen 指出论文组织结构的问题并给出一个有关更清晰的结构的建议(He pointed out a clearer structure for my essay. So, in my revision, I mainly changed the design of my essay. I made the opening shorter and briefer, and then I wrote about Erin from two aspects and then I commented on Qiuju also from two aspects.);然后,写作者反思写作存在的组织结构问题,如在写作过程中会突然冒出其他一些想法,想把这些想法放进论文里,但有时候这些想法与主题并不相关,导致不知如何在文章的开头和结尾处进行总结,也无法在段落之间自然地加入这些想法(In fact, for me, structure is a problem because sometimes when I write, some others ideas pop up in my head, and I also want to put them in my essay. But sometimes those ideas seem to be irrelevant, so I don't know how to conclude them in the first and then the last paragraph or connect them naturally between paragraphs.)。针对写作者提出的组织结构问题,另一位美国同伴 Kaitlan 通过自己的写作实践经历给出了解决方案,即选择 5 个最重要的想法,并尽力忘记其余的(About this problem, Kaitlan also gave me some suggestions, such as picking top five or so key ideas to work with and trying the best to forget the rest.)。

最后,美国学习者的修改报告提及同伴互评可以增强写作者的读者意识。例如:

> I really like the fact that both parties posted and commented on each other's essays. It was very helpful to me as a writer to read the comments the Chinese students had on the structure of my essay or point out parts in my writing that wasn't clear. I guess I never really thought about how my writing may be confusing or unclear to someone whose first language is not English. In composition classes, we always talk a lot about trying to get rid of ambiguity in your writing.

在该修改报告中,美国学习者指出,阅读中国学生对自己文章结构的评论或者指出写作文本中不清晰的部分的评论,是非常有帮助的,因为他从未想过自己的文章会让非母语者感到困惑或不理解。中美互评的方式让写作者增强了读者意识,开始思考如何消除写作中的歧义,如何让说不同语言和来自不同文化的人理解自己的观点。

而中国学习者则强调反馈可以培养写作者的批判性思维。例如：

> Though there are something I can do better, such as not just sticking on whether the disasters happened in the movies are true or not, increasing the frequency of exchanging comments, it is a very valuable experience for me to improve my English writing and critical thinking ability.

这份中国学习者的修改报告指出，在中美同伴互评过程中，双方在学习和写作思考方面相互交流，提高自身的英语写作能力，增强批判性思维。

此外，中国学习者发现美国学习者善于思考文章中提出的（社会）问题，并实施解决方案，如"What Alexandra reminds me of is to think of how to conduct a solution but not just a solution and then stop ever."；美国学习者提出将反馈的时间提至学期初的效果会好于在学期末，并且认为一对一的同伴反馈形式要优于小组反馈，如"I did not like that this project was assigned to us so late into the semester. We did this project at the same time as the final project, and it was too overwhelming … I would have preferred if this project was assigned and implemented at the beginning of the semester … In addition, I would have preferred to have only had one pen-pal … I think the program would have worked better if we just had one, maybe two at the most, pen-pals to communicate with. This would allow us to have much more in deep conversations and more personalized feedback."。

然而，有些修改报告只是解释了学习者对文章做出修改的原因及反馈的重点，还不足以检查学习者对母语者同伴反馈的态度。后续访谈可以深入地了解中国参与者对母语者同伴反馈的期望和双方同伴反馈关注点的异同。访谈结果显示，几乎所有中国学生都对跨洋互动写作持肯定态度，他们认为同伴反馈不仅有助于他们更好地理解影片的文化背景，使修改稿的内容更深入、客观；还可以帮助他们修改文章，提高他们的英语写作技巧。但是，母语者反馈的关注点是写作内容，中国学习者更期望对方关注自己语言方面的问题。整体而言，二语学习者在反馈时会先关注内容再考虑语言，以学习的态度对待美国同伴的文章；二语学习者不会为了维持和谐关系而放弃提出批评，会以礼貌的形式指出对方的问题；二语学习者在提出反馈的过程中，最有信心提出与写作内容（尤其涉及中国文化方面的内容）相关的反馈，对写作技巧的评价也比较有信心，对语言方面的评价最没有自信。

4.4 中美同伴互评类型的比较

4.4.1 中美同伴互评类型的共性分析

同伴互评过程涉及不同形式的同伴评论。不论是反馈者的同伴反馈还是写作者的回评，中美大学生同伴互评的类型都具有一致性。双方的同伴反馈都包括评价类反馈和情感反馈两种类型，且以评价类反馈为主；回评都包括接受性反馈、模糊性反馈和不接受性反馈3种类型，且以模糊性反馈为主。这表明中美大学生对同伴互评类型重要性次序的认识是一致的。

第一，在中美大学生同伴反馈的评价类反馈中，指正性反馈数量最多。换言之，中美反馈者为同伴提供了大量的关于当前表现与期望表现之间差距的信息。此类反馈数量多，分析其原因有二：一方面，在参与跨洋互动写作项目之前，双方学习者都已接受过议论文的写作训练，在提供反馈方面具有相当丰富的经验，这可以部分地解释指正性反馈类型数量之多。此外，本研究选取的语料是跨洋互动写作活动的第17轮和第19轮，受前面多轮同伴互评训练和实践的启发，中美大学生已经学习和熟悉了反馈视角，在给对方的写作文本进行反馈时，学习使用对方的反馈方式。另一方面，双方教师为学生提供了写作反馈的指导提纲，列出鉴析同伴写作的视角，避免学生读后感式的反馈（郑超等，2013）。后续访谈和修改报告显示，大多数评论者会根据反馈清单，提供关于同伴写作文本和写作主题的个人观点的叙述性片段。综合上述两个原因，中美大学生的指正性反馈数量最多且反馈的类型相似。

第二，指正性反馈类型中的信息性反馈是最常见的评论形式。这意味着同伴反馈主要围绕着与写作内容相关的话题展开。中美大学生在同伴互评过程中既是写作者也是反馈者，他们熟悉同一主题的写作内容，在评阅同伴写作的过程中，既提供与主题相关的附加信息、重读或者阐释自己对写作文本的理解，又积极为同伴提供与讨论主题相关的信息或者解释自己对话题的理解。同时，双方可能对涉及对方文化的部分不熟悉或者理解有误，所以与文化相关的信息补充类反馈的数量也不少。因此，在网络环境中，学生最优先关注的是意义的创造，当他们被要求凸显内容和更正语言时，提供的反馈主要与内容有关，这表明相对于语言特征，学生更倾向于传达内容意义（Kessler，2009）；关于内容的协商所指比例最高（Edasawa & Kabata，2007）。信息性反馈数量多是因为英语跨洋互动写作项目的活动初衷是通过网上互评，使二语学习者了解自己的二语水平与母语者之间的差距，并根据母语者提出的建议反思自己的二语学习，以期在后续学习中做出必要的调整，跨越互动中所发现的差距（郑超等，2013）。大量的信息性反馈说明跨洋互动写作活动为中美大学生提供了文化交流的机会，让双方反思文化差异，促进双方对彼此文化和自己文化的了解（Liaw，2006）。

第三，中美反馈者的验证性反馈中的肯定性反馈，尤其是局部肯定性反馈所占比例很大，说明中美反馈者倾向于对同伴写作文本的具体内容或具体方面给予肯定性评论，并说明支持的理由和原因。本研究中的局部肯定性反馈主要是针对文章的语篇组织、结构、连贯和逻辑等写作方面做出的评价。二语学习者尤其是高水平的二语学习者已经具备一些写作方面的专业知识（Cumming，1989），这是与二语语言能力无关的基础写作能力。通过母语写作的实践，二语学习者可能已经能够运用这种专业知识来评价同伴的总体写作水平，而非语言特定问题。另外，本研究中的中国参与者是广东外语外贸大学英语专业的大二学生，由于他们自身的二语语言能力的发展，他们有能力对写作文本做局部评价而不仅仅是整体评论。后续访谈也证实了二语学习者会更关注对方的写作思路。因此，二语学习者的肯定性反馈尤其是局部肯定，与母语者的一样，成为主要反馈类型之一。

第四，中美写作者的模糊性反馈以澄清为主；接受性反馈以局部接受为主，以整体接受为辅。中美写作者接受的同伴反馈以指正性反馈为主，尤其是信息性反馈中的内容解释数量最多，针对同伴对主题的不同理解和重读，中美写作者需要阐释意图或者举例帮助同伴理解自己的观点，因此澄清的数量最多。另外，在同伴互评过程中，无论是母语者还是二语学习者，都不会全盘地否定或者完全接受同伴反馈，双方会进行意义协商，及时调整语言。修改报告显示，母语者不认为自己的语言就是规范表达或标准英语，而是认为自己也需要及时更新语言储备。后续访谈显示，在双方互评过程中，二语学习者也不会一味地将母语者的语言视为标准英语。在面对母语者对写作内容的观点（尤其是关于中国文化的观点）时，中国大学生会坚持自己的观点。因此，在同伴互动过程中，中美大学生都在调整语言资源，部分接受同伴的观点，产生共适应（co-adaption）行为。（伍志伟，2018）

第五，中美大学生的同伴反馈和回评有相似的反馈模式。同伴反馈一般遵循以下模式：先给予写作文本评价（验证性反馈），然后详细阐释问题，提出修改建议（指正性反馈），最后给予情感反馈。验证性反馈指对论文进行总体评价（赞成或否定）；问题的详细阐释解决文本中不清楚或模棱两可的部分；修改建议可以向写作者说明如何改善写作文本；情感反馈多指邀请同伴继续讨论。回评一般遵循的模式如下：从接受性反馈开始，陈述对反馈者的观点或建议的态度（赞同或反对），然后澄清自己的观点，为自己的观点或行为做辩护或是回答反馈者的问题。

在跨洋互动写作活动中，母语者和二语学习者轮流给对方提供书面的同伴反馈和回评，双方的地位是平等的，不存在口语反馈过程中二语学习者处于不利地位，须确保混合小组中母语者与二语学习者平等的问题，也进一步证实了混合同伴小组中书面反馈的价值，即书面反馈使二语学习者有更多机会传达反馈意见，这表明同伴反馈的书面模式可能是混合同伴小组特别有价值的工具。（Zhu，2001）此外，异步同伴反馈让反馈者在提出反馈之前有足够的时间思考反馈的内容，以便提供详细的、全面的反馈（Bradley，2014）。本研究的语料是在线异步反馈，我们发现评价类反馈多，这区别于"在线同步反馈中情感反馈占大多数"（Luo，2016：156）的研究结论。

综上所述，同伴反馈的培训、二语学习者较高的写作能力、与写作文本内容相关的反馈内容和延时书面反馈的形式是中美同伴反馈类型之间存在共性的影响因素。高水平二语学习者的同伴反馈类型和与学习资历相当的母语者的同伴反馈类型具有一致性，这也证明了反馈策略使用的普遍性和有效性。

4.4.2　中美同伴互评类型的差异性分析

无论是作为反馈者还是写作者，中美大学生的同伴反馈和回评类型及其子类的出现频次都存在显著性差异,双方的差异主要体现在批判意识与读者意识、权威对话与平等对话、静态文本与动态话语3个方面。

4.4.2.1 批判意识与读者意识

首先,中美大学生同伴反馈中的重述和回评中辩护的使用频次存在显著性差异。中国大学生的定位、批评和辩护的数量明显多于美国大学生。中国大学生善于提出批评,如"However, the paper does not clearly state the similarities and differences; rather, it just summarizes the films, which is not the objective of the assignment."。此例中中国大学生认为美国大学生的写作文本未明确陈述两部影片的共同点和不同点,只是总结了影片的内容,未达到本次写作任务的目标,因此对美国大学生的写作给予了直接的、否定性的评价。中国大学生倾向于用语言实现和缓和批评方式。当他们重述、批评同伴时,他们倾向于郑重指出问题而不仅仅是描述问题,如"Maybe more variation of transitional words would be better. I notice there are repetitions, like 'despite' and 'similarly'. And maybe you can add more personal opinions and other supporting evidence.";他们的建议有时更加强烈,如"The descriptions are not enough to make your opinions deeper and clearer." "So it is wrong to say that Bai was forced to work on their farm, which is only one of the functions of this 'wife'.";他们对分歧的表达过分自信,如"I disagree that Erin Brockovich is not at all concerned with saving face."。这些可能使他们的批评看起来不够得体。

中国大学生在回评中经常使用辩护型反馈,例如:

> At the very beginning I was fully convinced by your logical analysis, but later on, I found that there might be some slightly difference between "group polarization" and "bystander effect", so I don't think the bystander effect can totally incorporate "group polarization" … I reserve my opinion on the idea that "the bystander effect incorporates both of these concepts".

在上例中,中国写作者不赞同美国反馈者提出的"群体极化"和"旁观者效应"相同的观点,他认为两者存在一些细微差别,因此保留自己的观点,即"旁观者效应"包含了"群体极化"和其他概念。中国写作者对美国反馈者给予的反馈持否定态度。

又如，反馈者提出"Those anti-feminists argue that some of the activities generated from the women's right movement are themselves paradoxes.", 中国学生辩护称"As far as I am concerned, I don't think it is a paradox. To me, Girl's Day is not a holiday for people to scorn at girls but to show respects and care to girls. Here is the definition I've found on the Internet about feminism, 'A feminist advocates or supports the rights and equality of women.' We celebrate Girls' Day doesn't mean that we view girls less privileged or disadvantaged than boys. It's the same with Mother's Day, Children's Day or even just like any other holidays. On Girls' Day, what we get is happiness, joy and fun, but not discrimination. In my opinion, the establishment of Girls' Day is to appreciate the cuteness, the youthfulness, and the other merits or virtues a girl has in her entire life. Therefore, the activities that generate from the women's rights movement are not paradoxes at all, and it's just a matter of different people's perspectives."中国大学生针对美国反馈者的"那些反女权主义者认为，妇女权利运动产生的一些活动本身就是悖论"的评论进行反驳。中国大学生使用大量的批评和辩护反馈，这说明他们倾向于对同伴的写作文本或同伴的评论观点给予直接的、否定的和消极的反馈，具有很强的批判意识；使用这两种反馈可能会给人留下这样的印象，即他们会支配同伴的行为（Murphy & Neu, 1996）。在后续访谈中，中国大学生也证实不会为了维持和谐关系而放弃提出批评。

在回评中，中国大学生使用反思类反馈，美国大学生没有使用此类反馈。例如，"After reading your article, I feel that I still have a long way to go to improve my English comparing with the native speaker.", 中国大学生认为与母语者的英语相比，自己提高英语水平的路还很长；"I think the ideas of my article only depend on these two movies, which are absolutely not enough to elaborate more social issues.", 中国写作者的回评提到自己重新审视自己的文章后发现，只依赖两部电影不足以解释更多的社会问题。中国大学生的反思类反馈数量说明他们常常将自身的写作文本与同伴的写作内容、观点、组织和语言等方面相比，认识到自己的二语水平与母语者之间的差距，讨论语言的选择，协商语言的使用，进一步反思自己的二语学习目的。这也表明同伴反馈的数量也受批判性阅读技能影响，而不仅仅是语言能力。另外，中国大学生能够为美国大学生的写作提供许多有效的建议，对于美国同伴的反馈做出批判性回应，并思考是否在修改稿中采纳同伴的建议；这样的批判性思维过程不但可以提高学生写作的质量，而且可以促使他们获取自主写作技巧进而发展成为独立写作者。

其次，中美写作者回评中的接受性反馈和不接受性反馈类型的出现频次不存在显著性差异。在同伴互评过程中，二语学习者和母语者一样，不会全盘地否定或者完全接受同伴反馈，双方会进行意义协商，及时调整语言。后续访谈显示，面对母语者对写作内容的观点（尤其关于中国文化的观点）时，中国大学生会坚持自己的观点。这说明二语学习者已经具备了一定的批判意识，已经可以根据对方的语言水平来决定是否采纳对方的建议，不会因为对方的母语者身份就不假思索地采纳其意见，因此，中国大学生的局部接受性反馈的数量和美国大学生相差不大。

再次，中美大学生同伴反馈在错误分析的使用频次上存在显著性差异（$\chi^2=15.27$，$df=1$，$p=0.000$），美国大学生的错误分析的数量明显多于中方（83 vs 27）；双方的回评在澄清的使用频次上也存在显著性差异（$\chi^2=11.50$，$df=1$，$p=0.001$），美国大学生的澄清数量明显多于中国大学生（610 vs 412）。错误分析主要是学习者针对同伴的语法、词汇和句型等语言使用问题给予的反馈信息。母语者的反馈焦点集中于词汇、词法和句法（薛红果，2011），美国大学生因对自身母语的熟练程度，会更关注二语学习者的语言问题，讨论词汇的选择，这说明"语言熟练程度越高的学习者，提供反馈数量越多，也更专注与语言相关的反馈"（Allen & Katayama，2016：104）。美国大学生的澄清数量说明他们重视解决问题，作为反馈者，不仅以修改为目的给予意见，还会考虑到意见的可理解性，解释给予意见的原因，以帮助同伴理解；作为写作者，针对同伴提出的问题或是解释需求等反馈，通过澄清的方式具体阐释或者举例解释自己的意图，以达到让同伴理解的目的。这与美国教师的教学理念有关，他们认为教学的主要任务是将理论知识运用于实践，解决实际生活中的问题（孙亚玲等，2015）。这反映出母语反馈者具有很强的读者意识，主动为二语学习者考虑；表明高水平的反馈者有写作者需求意识，会为写作者考虑。因此,在互动过程中,母语反馈者"将读者的需求放在首位,以达到清晰的共生关系"(Merkel,2018:22)。

以下两个实例节选自第17轮跨洋互动写作中国学生第1篇的美国大学生的反馈和第19轮美国学生第15篇美国大学生对中国反馈者的回评:

例1

However, if I were to make one suggestion for your writing, it would be to choose one main focus (or thesis) and subordinate the others to it. In other words, concentrate on "persistence" or "no pain, no gain" while making all points apply directly to this topic.

例2

I truly believe the prison population faces some of the most and worst oppression and discrimination in present-day America than any other population. It is horrific how inhumanely prisoners are treated regardless of their crimes. In fact, it is due to America having one of the worst social justice systems that we have the most inmates and highest recidivism rate than majority of countries all over the world. One day, I hope out society realizes the importance and benefits of a rehabilitative system rather than a punitive one.

在例1中,美国反馈者首先提出建议,要求写作者关注一个写作主题,围绕这个主题展开写作[However, if I were to make one suggestion for your writing, it would be to choose one main focus (or thesis) and subordinate the others to it.];接着具体说明这个反馈建议,即专注于"坚持"或"一分耕耘,一分收获"的观点,而且让所有的内容都集中于这个话题(In other words, concentrate on "persistence" or "no pain, no gain" while making all points apply directly to this topic.)。例2中的美国写作者回评,介绍了美国司法制度存在的一些问题,如犯人面临着一些最严重的压迫和歧视,受到非人道的对待,美国囚犯人数最多,其累犯率也高于全球大多数国家(I truly believe the prison population faces some of the most and worst oppression and discrimination ... It is horrific how inhumanely prisoners are treated regardless of their crimes ...)。这些解释

和澄清是为了协助同伴了解影片涉及的美国司法背景知识并提出自己的想法，希望社会认识到康复体系的重要性和好处。

大量的辩护和局部接受性反馈说明中国大学生具有很强的批判性思维，批判意识是学习并掌握其他文化表达的一个重要方面（Helm & Guth，2010），反馈策略的培训可以增强批判思维能力。这个观点与"中方学习者受中国传统文化（如面子问题、和谐）影响，倾向于提供积极和模糊的评论，有时以牺牲提供修改所需的反馈意见为代价维持和谐"（Carson & Nelson，1996：1）的结论不同。这可能与以下几点有关：第一，他们的二语语言能力不足。第二，他们缺乏必要的二语语用知识，无法进行更复杂和更巧妙的否定。使用诸如"I don't agree"或者"I disagree"这样直接的、纯粹的不同意表达，是因为他们缺乏表达不赞同的其他语言形式。第三，在选择一定的策略和语义公式表达否定时，借鉴了母语社交语用知识。例如，访谈数据倾向于证实，二语学习者认为提供建议是一种礼貌的、间接的批评方式，二语学习者会以礼貌的方式提出不同意见。

美国大学生的错误分析和澄清反馈类型数量之多说明母语者更关注语言问题，倾向于解决问题，具有很强的读者意识。在同伴互评过程中，美国大学生思考如何让说不同语言和来自不同文化的人理解自己的观点，关注二语学习者的语言问题，倾向于解决问题。中国大学生倾向于指出问题出现的具体位置，然后纠正并提供正确的形式；而美国大学生提供元语言解释，以帮助同伴理解复杂的词汇项目和语法结构。跨洋互动写作过程让中美大学生充当写作者和反馈者的双重角色，作为反馈者，学生要弄清楚想要反馈的内容，并安排好要表达的信息，确保这些反馈内容能清晰地被传达给写作者和其他读者；同时应具有读者思维，要弄清楚写作者或者其他读者需要什么样的信息。双方在互评的实践过程中积极提供关于如何修改论文的具体建议，说明同伴互评增强了他们对读者需求的关注。因此，中美同伴互评增强了反馈者在跨文化方面的敏感度和批判性的文化意识（Helm & Guth，2010）。

最后，在线同伴反馈活动创造的氛围保留了传统书面反馈的优点，即写作者对读者需求敏感。不管反馈意见如何传递，反馈任务本身鼓励写作者对读者需求有高度感知能力。在线平台的同伴反馈同时兼具了在线反馈

和传统书面反馈的优点,是有益的教学实践。第 17 轮跨洋互动写作中第 12 篇中国大学生的反思日志也证实了以上观点:

> Another thing I want to talk about is our e-mails. From an e-mail, we can also tell a distinct difference between Chinese style and English style. When I was writing an e-mail to my American partner, I found it seemed that I was writing a note in TEM-4. I strictly obey the rules, from salution to signature, in a formal way. After receiving a reply from them, I made a comparison between two e-mails. I found that the e-mail from my American partner was written in a more casual and friendly way. They would use some expressions like, "please feel free to look at it", "but if is okay" or "but if it is convenient to you". It gives us a feeling that they are considerate of us. And my e-mail was written in a more direct way and completely took my own wishes into consideration, such as "expecting your early reply".

中国大学生观察双方反馈邮件的写作格式,发现中美学习者的反馈文本的语言特征有明显区别,指出中国学生的反馈非常正式,严格遵守从打招呼到签名的写作格式;而美国同伴的邮件更加随意,如美国学生会说"请随意查看""如果可以的话""如果方便的话",给人一种体贴的感觉;而中国学生会以直接的方式,如"期待您的早日答复",表达自己的意愿。另一篇修改报告也提及相似的发现,第 19 轮跨洋互动写作中第 9 篇中国大学生的修改报告写到"And they don't mind stating distinctively like oral speech, which my Chinese peers found too stiff in structure.",美国大学生不介意口语化,而中国学生的写作结构僵化,遵循一定的形式。这与美国大学生的写作呈现口语化特征、个性化特征,而中国大学生的写作较正式,遵守特定的格式(马广惠,2002)的观点相符。这说明中美同伴互评的过程增强了双方批判性的跨文化意识和读者意识。

4.4.2.2 权威对话与平等对话

首先,中国大学生同伴反馈中的内容解释多于美国大学生(795 vs 594),但是美国大学生回评中的内容解释明显多于中国大学生(610 vs 412)。作为反馈者,中国大学生倾向于表达与主题相关的话题,阐释与文化相关的内容，这反映了中国大学生关注文化交流和思想碰撞，也反映出美国大学生对中国文化的了解还不够充分，中国大学生需要详细解释中国文化。中国反馈者注重自身对于写作文本意义的理解和建构，重视文化思想的输出和不同观点的交流，这源于汉语写作的传统目的——"文以载道"，强调文章的内容应关乎宇宙和人类社会的真理（刘立新、游晓晔，2018），认为写作的意义在于启发和教育读者。这体现了中国大学生将自己置于权威者地位，将同伴放在对话互动的依赖位置，这源于中国的教材将读者（本研究中的被反馈者）放在被教育者的地位，要求读者接受写作者（本研究中的反馈者）的观点。在后续访谈中，中国大学生提及国内英语写作教师强调写作主题须与社会问题相联系，以提升写作内容和水平。此外，中国反馈者的解释需求多于美方（48 vs 19），他们对美国学生写作文本中的不清楚部分提出了质疑，所以美国学生在回评中需要澄清自己的意图或举例解释自己的观点，他们的内容解释比作为反馈者时更多。例如，第19轮跨洋互动写作中第13篇美国大学生的回评：

> However, the concept you brought up confused me, "use of convicts for labor fuel the economy development since minimal expenses for food, clothing and shelter were necessary. There is always a ready supply of replacement labor, so incentives against the mistreatment of convict workers were non-existent".

中国反馈者对美国学生的观点感到困惑，要求写作者做进一步的解释，即解释需求。为了回复反馈者的质疑，美国写作者澄清如下：

> I can offer an explanation for "use of convicts for labor fuel the economy development since minimal expenses for food, clothing and shelter were necessary. There is always a ready supply of replacement labor, so incentives against the mistreatment of convict workers were non-existent". The American movie was made in 1976 in the South. Even though Civil War has already ended in America, Southern still had a hard time dealing with slavery and racial issues. I thought the farm owners used convicts since they don't have to legally provide anything more than they need (they just need basic food, clothing, and

shelter). Most people wouldn't dig deep into convicts, doing farming labors. It was easier for the owner to get away with mistreating people, and they don't have to pay them.

美国写作者解释了美国影片制作的时间和地点（1976年拍摄于南部），介绍了当时的社会状况（即使美国内战已经结束，南部在处理奴隶制和种族问题上仍然很艰难），从而达到澄清、解释自己观点的目的（农场主们使用因犯，因为他们除此之外，不必提供任何其他的东西，只需要为因犯提供基本的食物、衣服和住所；大多数人不会深入了解从事劳动的因犯，这让农场主们更容易摆脱虐待人口的嫌疑，而且不需要付工资给他们）。

中美大学生在同伴反馈和回评中的内容阐释或澄清反馈数量之多，体现了中国学生善于提出问题和美国学生注重解决问题的不同反馈方式。这从另一个侧面说明中国反馈者似乎承担了导师或教师的作用，将美国写作者看作学生；而美国写作者却注重回应同伴的问题，体现了他们协商互动的立场；同时，中国大学生的读者意识比较薄弱，没有考虑到不同的文化可能会影响反馈的接受度。

其次，中美大学生使用回应的频次存在显著性差异（$\chi^2=40.80$，$df=1$，$p=0.000$），美国大学生的回应类反馈居多（56 vs 11）。美国反馈者在对写作者观点做出反应时，有时既不表示支持也不直接反对，常用 interesting 一词表达对同伴观点的回应。例如，第19轮跨洋互动写作中第7篇美国大学生对中方写作文本的反馈如下：

I think your choice of words are so interesting because if I were trying to convey the same message you were saying, I would probably use different words. This is not to say that my words are any better. I just find this interesting enough to bring attention to.

美国大学生对中国学生选词的回应使用了 interesting 一词，未直接指出用词的问题，但是委婉地提出母语者不会选择这个单词，以引起写作者的注意。母语者经常"缓冲"（mitigate）所提出的不同意见（Nguyen, 2008），较多采用间接、隐晦的反馈（Sotillo, 2005）。这不仅体现出美国反馈者的读者意识强，还表明他们平等合作的态度。此外，即使美国大学生有不同的意见，他们也会尊重对方意见，正如他们在反思日志中提到"Even though I disagree with some people's point of views, I learned to respect their opinion."。回应类反馈可以使反馈者避免观点的绝对性，给写作者留有思考和判断的余地，有效维系反馈者和写作者之间的平等合作关系，体现出美国大学生对角色平衡的注重。这也反映了美国教育重视培养学生的分析能力，鼓励学生提出不同的观点，调动学生的积极性和主观能动性。在修改报告和后续访谈中，中国大学生都提到美国大学生属于读者友好型，会关注双方地位的平等。

再次，中美大学生在使用重述的频次方面存在显著性差异（$\chi^2 = 30.54$, $df=2$, $p=0.000$），美国大学生使用重述较多（189 vs 135）。由于中国大学生的词汇知识掌握得不太精确，美国大学生倾向于指出同伴对词汇的不准确或不恰当使用，包括惯用语。重述是识别引起学习者注意的错误形式精确位置的快速方法，借此注意母语和二语形式之间的差距。例如，第17轮跨洋互动写作第1篇美国大学生对中方写作文本的反馈如下：

> In the second paragraph, the first sentence needs "die" to be an infinitive (in other words, "to die"). Usually, in the language, when a verb phrase acts as a clause, and another verb precedes it, the non-auxiliary verb becomes an infinitive. In other words, when both "seem" and "die" act as verbs, the one that comes after the preliminary verb must become an infinitive. This is a tough rule to get right because you also have those auxiliary verbs (such as "can" or "will") than never precede an infinitive. Present participles are also confusing to compare in these instances since they can also act as clauses (just like infinitives). It's is probably best to memorize these forms rather than learn any of the weird conditions involving their transitive verb and intransitive verb forms.

在该例中，美国大学生不仅定位错误形式的精确位置，还具体分析错误，指出同伴的不定式使用不当，解释不定式的正确用法，分析不定式与现在分词的区别，并给出学习语法的建议。这说明美国大学生倾向于提供元语言解释，帮助同伴理解复杂的词汇和语法结构。

中美大学生的经验求教的使用频次存在显著性差异（$\chi^2=53.04$，$df=1$，$p=0.000$），中国大学生的经验求教的数量明显多于美国学生（185 vs 78）。二语学习者将母语者的语言视为权威，对于他们来说，通过提高自己对地道目标语单词或短语的认识来增强语言技能是至关重要的，他们通过比较和对比自己的母语和目标语言，可以更深入地理解词汇单元或表达如何被实际使用，并进一步发展他们的语言学知识和观点。例如，在回评"I wonder whether or not it'll seem odd to English natives when using 'first, second, etc.' in writing. Then which words or phrases English-speaking people prefer to use as transitional signals?"中，中国大学生想知道英语中是否经常使用"first, second, et."，以及英语常用哪些单词或短语作为过渡词。

最后，作为反馈者，中国大学生的情感反馈要多于美国大学生，用于评论其同伴的语言技能的高低。在反馈过程中，perfect、excellent、impressive、brilliant等评价词语反复出现。以下摘录来自第17轮跨洋互动写作第3篇中国大学生对美方写作文本的反馈，表现出中国大学生对同伴反馈的印象深刻：

> It was a pleasure reading your essay. I like your unique and insightful perspectives, some of which really open my mind, and other of which I surprisingly find we have seen eye to eye on. Also, you elaborated your arguments with precise and powerful evidence. Good work!

尽管美国大学生提供的情感反馈少于中国学生，但他们利用类似的赞誉作为开场白来评论他们同伴的写作，即肯定性反馈数量较多，美国大学生的整体肯定明显多于中国学生（195 vs 121）。例如，"I really liked this response. It was very descriptive and elaborate, and it is made quite clear what you think about the subject."。美国大学生通常在开头部分对同伴的写作进行总体评价，一般是积极、正面的评价，然后指出问题，给出建议，最后在结尾处再给出总体评价，这体现了美国典型的批评行为准则，即"即使是在不可接受的情况下，也要首先表扬，再提出温和的改进建议"（Belz，2003：78）。但是，作为写作者，美国大学生的回评的局部肯定性反馈略多于中方（501 vs 489）。作为母语者，美国写作者会选择性地接受对方意见，体现为对反馈意见的局部肯定。同时，美国学生通过写作文本感知和识别中国学生的情绪与心理状况，设身处地为中国学生着想，表达自己对同伴观点和语言表达等方面的理解，因此，美国学生的反馈中有一定数量的移情。美国学生的感谢也多于中方，这与美国教材要求读者站在和写作者相等或平行的位置看待写作文本有关。这些体现了美国学生具有合作意识，倾向于肯定同伴的优点和感谢同伴的意见，是鼓励式教育的结果。

对中美大学生的内容解释、澄清、回应、重述、经验求教、移情、整体肯定性评价和感谢等反馈类型出现频次差异的分析发现，中国大学生在陈述与写作内容（尤其是文化）相关的观点时，倾向于将自己置于权威地位，注重表达自身观点，美国大学生更关注意义协商；在协商与语言使用相关的反馈内容时，中国大学生将美国大学生视为权威，美国大学生具有读者意识，重述反馈类型较多，以提高二语学习者使用目标语言的准确性。中美大学生的权威立场和合作立场呈现出动态特征。这也说明具有权威性和解释性立场的读者发挥更多的"给予意见"功能（如写作评价），具有探究性和合作立场的读者执行更多的"给予信息"功能（如见解和示例）（Lockhart & Ng，1995）。例如，中国大学生对涉及本国文化的讨论具有话语权，而美国大学生在语言方面具有权威性；双方在交流写作主题、文章组织结构等方面时，却体现了合作立场。中国大学生的反思日志也印证了该观点：

> Interestingly, when I was communicating with American partners, we reached an agreement very smoothly, and we both thought the comments from each side were reasonable. However, my essay was greeted with more questions and disagreements when we were doing peer assessment with my classmates. Even though we tried to convince each other, we ended up with reservations. Anyway, I enjoyed the discussion with both sides of my partners, which allowed me to make improvement in different perspectives.

中国大学生指出与美国同伴进行反馈互动时，注重双方的意义协商，认为双方的意见都是合理的，容易达成一致意见（Interestingly, when I was communicating with American partners, we reached an agreement very smoothly and we both thought the comments from each side were reasonable.）；但是与中国同伴交流时，会收到更多的质疑和不同意见，双方都注重自身观点的表达，反而不容易形成一致意见（However, my essay was greeted with more questions and disagreements when we were doing peer assessment with my classmates. Even though we tried to convince each other, we ended up with reservations.）。最后，中国大学生表达了对同伴反馈的积极态度，即认为不管是二语同伴还是目标语同伴的反馈，都只是看待同一个问题的不同视角而已（Anyway, I enjoyed the discussion with both sides of my partners, which allowed me to make improvement in different perspectives.）。由此可见，同伴互评时写作者和反馈者之间的关系是动态的，会在权威立场和合作立场之间切换。

4.4.2.3 静态文本与动态话语

Bakhtin（1981）的对话主义观点认为，一个词在被个人或其他个体注入意义之前是没有意义的，"每一个话语都是说话者与产生话语的（置于整个复杂的社会场景中的）更广泛语境的产物之间相互作用的产物"（Bakhtin，1994：41）。他认为，语言不是独立于说话者或言语的一系列理想化形式，而是说话者在与他人斗争过程中创造的有意义的情景话语。对于巴赫金而言，个体话语的概念是虚构的，因为话语是共同构建的，个体话语不是孤立的，要以与他人对话为前提。言者需要努力去适应他人的声音，并使之服从自己的目的。因此，我们需要分析同一写作文本的不同话语之间的对话（Bakhtin，1981、1986）。

写作文本不是单向的、静态的描述性文本，它既包括写作者表达的意义，也包括读者（反馈者）建构的意义。学习者需要知道他们的写作不是静态的，意义不仅在于词汇，还在于读者（反馈者）对这些词汇的理解。只有学习者得到读者的反馈意见时，学习者才能知道自己的意图是否达到。反馈也是一种写作，是反馈者与写作者之间的对话和交流。同伴反馈不是静态文本，而是动态话语，是围绕语言使用、主题和文化等相关话题的协商交流，这些互动会促进更丰富的语言学习、思想和文化交流，体现了"共享解释，协商意义和澄清期望的互动"（Carless 等，2011：396）。

在互动过程中，同伴通过提供交流信息并借助传达信息的手段，促进多个反馈者参与文本的社会构建（Perpignan，2003）。在中美大学生的互动过程中，既有反馈者和写作者之间一对一的双向互动，也有多个反馈者之间的多向互动。这具体体现在以下几个方面：

第一，反馈者在与写作者的互动过程中会引用其他反馈者的观点，如第 19 轮跨洋互动写作中国大学生第 16 篇中美国反馈者赞同另一个反馈者的意见：

> I agree with all of the feedback Taylor already presented to you. I was going to also suggest that *Nightmare in Badham County* illustrated discrimination against women using the same evidence Taylor previously offered.

又如第 19 轮跨洋互动写作中美国学生第 8 篇中国反馈者对其他反馈者评论的反馈：

> I want to share my opinion after reading comments from both Shirley and Shannon. Shirley mentioned that brutality of the authority figures wasn't demonstrated in *Blind Mountain*. From my point of view, I think the movie may not expose the brutality but the indifference. As for Shannon's comments, I think it is concise, to the point and it work for me, such as "expanding on the common themes more and highlight the scenes of the movie …"

中国反馈者不赞成 Shirley 的观点，但是认同 Shannon 的评论。这种双向互动表明两个或两个以上的同伴会对同伴文本的相同方面分别进行评论，如 "I agree with all of the feedback Taylor already presented to you." "As for Shannon's comments, I think it is concise …"。当学习者收到多个同伴反馈时，可能会收到至少两个相似的同伴反馈。当多个同伴就一些具体问题达成一致意见时，这种反馈对于写作者修改论文尤为可靠，因其有效性高。换言之，多个同伴反馈更具说服力，比单个反馈更有效。

第二，中美大学生之间的另一种互动方式是多个反馈者之间的互动，如第 17 轮跨洋互动写作中学生第 5 篇美国反馈者的反馈：

Great work, Max! I believe your essay highlights some of the issues I discussed in my work and adds depth to the discussion by focusing specifically on dialectic and demotic speech patterns and how they impact the movie. Although I am unable to comment upon the dialectical disconnect between different regions of China, I think your observations on Erin's informal style of speaking provide us with much fodder for discussion.

As you mention briefly in the opening to your essay, both women protagonists come from a lower-class background; this is advantageous for Erin, and the source of great misfortune for Qiuju is evident. I wonder if one could make an argument as to how these different endings reflect cultural or literary developments in China and the U.S. The triumph of the little guy over the corporate behemoth is a well-established trope in the American and Western tradition, traceable even to stories like that of David and Goliath. Does such a plot appear often in Chinese literature?

As a final note, you mention the clash between mandarin and local Chinese dialects. As a student of the Spanish language, I know that a similar suppression of dialects is occurring in Spain itself, as less common dialects such as Basque and Catalan are being subsumed by Castellan or traditional Spanish. Is it a similar thing happening in China now?

Thanks.

Nick

随后，另一位中国反馈者参与互动，进行反馈：

To Nick,

As a Chinese student, I think such plots about David and Goliath indeed existed in Chinese literature, especially in Ancient war stories, which presented the wisdom of ancient people. And those are true stories. But with time going, maybe Chinese become more practical.

They are focusing more on collective capacity instead of individualistic heroism, which we can often see in Hollywood movies such as *Spider-Man* or *Mission Impossible*.

About the Chinese dialect, well, most of them are similar with mandarin, especially the dialect coming from the north part of China. So people can communicate with each other in their own languages. But some dialects, for example, Shanghainese and Cantonese, are hard to be understood. Although every dialect has its own features and we will not combine them, yet for the convenience of communication, we have mandarin as the national language.

Yolanda

在互动中,美国反馈者(Nick)首先对中国写作者(Max)的写作进行评价,提出两个问题:一是两个故事的结局是否反映了中国和美国的文化与文学的发展?这种小人物胜过企业巨头的故事是否也经常出现在中国文学中?二是在普通话和地方方言之间的冲突方面,西班牙语也会出现类似的方言压制现象,汉语中是否有类似现象?针对这两个问题,另一位中方反馈者(Yolanda)做出回复。由此可见,中美大学生之间的同伴反馈是多向的、多轮的和动态的。互动协商意味着利用对话来建立或维持同伴之间的一定程度的平等或平衡,从这个层面上说,中美大学生的交流和对话都具有动态的特征。

此外,在反思日志和后续访谈中,中美大学生从写作者的视角,说明自己接收到的反馈类型。中国学生认为,美国学生对中国学生的关于语言和写作技巧的反馈要明显多于中方对美国学生的反馈,这进一步证实了美国学生的直接纠错和错误分析两种反馈类型数量多于中国学生。美国写作者指出,中国反馈者对美国写作者所做的关于写作主题和文化的反馈多于美国反馈者对中国写作者的反馈,这也验证了中国学生的内容解释和信息补充两种反馈类型数量多于美国学生。更重要的是,美国学生的报告提及同伴互评可以增强写作者的读者意识,而中国学生则强调反馈可以培养写作者的批判性思维。中美大学生的同伴反馈文本、反思日志和后续访谈验证了中美同伴反馈的使用特点和出现频率之间存在的差异。

概括而言,中国大学生同伴反馈的使用特点说明中国大学生具有很强的批判性思维，倾向于表达自身观点，这可能是与汉语写作的传统目的——"文以载道"有关，受"读者是被教育者"的教育理念的影响。美国同伴反馈中高频率的反馈类型表明美国大学生关注意义协商，他们的读者意识和平等对话意识强，体现了美国学生写作的批评行为准则，这源于"写作为交际服务"的教育理念。在同伴互评过程中，写作者和反馈者之间的关系是动态的，反馈者的态度会在权威立场和合作立场之间切换。

4.5 结语

我们通过描述同伴互评的类型和学生对写作的反思，并结合后续访谈，追踪中美大学生的反馈实践发现，中美大学生的同伴反馈类型都包括评价类反馈和情感反馈，双方的同伴反馈的使用频次顺序相同，评价性反馈占大多数，其中指正性反馈数量最多。中美大学生的回评类型都包括接受性反馈、模糊性反馈和不接受性反馈3种。双方的回评的使用频次顺序相同，模糊性反馈占大多数，接受性反馈次之，不接受性反馈最少，其中澄清类反馈数量最多。这说明二语学习者和母语者在对同伴反馈重要性次序的认识上是一致的，有丰富的同伴互评经验的二语学习者和母语者的书面同伴反馈类型之间具有一致性。

总的来说，中美大学生的同伴反馈大类的使用频次存在显著性差异。指正性反馈的数量明显多于验证性反馈；验证性反馈中肯定性反馈的数量明显多于否定性反馈，其中局部肯定性反馈的数量明显多于整体肯定性反馈；指正性反馈类型中信息性反馈的数量最多，建设性反馈和重述类反馈较多，指出问题类反馈最少。具体而言，中美大学生的评价性反馈各子类的使用频次不是都存在显著性差异。在双方的验证性反馈中，肯定性反馈的使用频次存在显著性差异，否定性反馈的使用频次不存在显著性差异；在指正性反馈中，重述反馈和信息类反馈的使用频次存在显著性差异，提出问题反馈和建设性反馈的使用频次不存在显著性差异。在肯定性反馈中，中美大学生整体肯定的使用频次存在显著性差异。在重述反馈中，双方的定位和错误分析的使用频次存在显著性差异。在信息性反馈中，中美大学生的内容解释和回应的使用频次存在显著性差异。在情感反馈中，移情和感谢的使用频次存在显著性差异。

中美大学生的回评大类的使用频次存在显著性差异。在接受性反馈中，局部接受的数量明显多于整体接受；在模糊性反馈中，澄清的数量最多，答疑次之，辩护和经验求教的数量也较多。具体而言，在中美大学生的模糊性反馈中，澄清、辩护、答疑和经验求教的使用频次存在显著性差异，其中美国大学生的澄清的使用频次要明显多于中国学生，而中国大学生的辩护、答疑和经验求教的使用频次明显多于美国学生。

中美大学生提供同伴反馈通常从评价类反馈的验证性反馈开始，尤其是从一般的或具体的肯定性评论开始，然后进行具体的指正性评论，最后再转向情感性评论或者回到整体的肯定性评论，即"评价类反馈（肯定性反馈→指正性反馈）→情感反馈/肯定性反馈"模式。而提供回评时一般从接受性反馈开始，写作者表达对反馈者的观点或建议的接受或赞同，然后进行模糊性反馈，澄清自己的观点、为自己的观点或行为做辩护抑或是回答反馈者的问题，或者启发反馈者就某一话题继续讨论，即"接受性反馈→模糊性反馈"的模式。

双方反馈的使用频次说明中国大学生的权威意识强，在跨文化交流中已经具备批判性思维；美国大学生的读者意识和平等对话意识强。中美大学生的反馈文本都体现出动态特征，双方利用对话建立和维持互动交流；同伴之间的关系是动态的，反馈者的态度在权威立场和合作立场之间切换。

在考察中美大学生同伴互评类型的异同和反馈模式的过程中，我们发现同伴反馈的过程是动态的、多向的。然而，同伴在互动交流后是否会进行相应的修改，哪些反馈类型更容易被采纳、接受和理解，双方在互动过程中如何互为支架，形成了什么样的互动模式，这些都值得进一步的探讨，下一章将对此进行详细论证。

中美跨洋互动写作中的同伴互动行为

本章分析中美同伴反馈的互动行为,共包括5个小节。第一节介绍本章的研究语料和研究问题;第二节分析中美同伴的互动行为,包括中美同伴在修改稿中实施的基于反馈的修改、对同伴反馈的采纳和互动过程中的支架策略,具体统计和详细地描述中美写作组的互动行为;第三节对比中美大学生上述3种互动行为的异同;第四节讨论由上述3种互动行为生成的4种互动模式;最后进行本章小结。

5.1 语料与研究问题

本章语料选自第17轮跨洋互动写作中的13个小组,分别是对中国大学生写作文本进行反馈的7个小组(称为中方写作组),其中包括美方14人和中方7人;对美国大学生写作文本进行反馈的6个小组(称为美方写作组),其中包括中方15人和美方8人。选择这两组进行案例研究的原因是这两组的反馈者中既有中方学习者也有美方学习者,可以借此考察同一小组中母语反馈者和二语反馈者与写作者的互动模式是否存在差异。另外,这两组里中国和美国反馈者人数相同(各22人),排除人数不同引起的反馈数量差异。

对中美同伴反馈互动行为进行研究,主要思考以下4个问题:

① 根据同伴反馈,混合小组成员在修改稿上做出了哪些修改?

② 在基于在线平台的混合小组写作过程中,学习者易于接受、理解和采纳哪些反馈?

③ 在混合小组写作过程中,学习者使用了哪些反馈策略?

④ 在相同的在线反馈任务中,中方写作组和美方写作组形成了怎样的互动模式?

具体来说，本研究将通过以下途径回答上述研究问题：第一，通过分析在线平台历史记录揭示小组成员会根据同伴反馈做出哪些修改，考察同伴在线交流共同构建书面文本的过程。第二，通过分析在线交流中体现的反馈类型，以及学习者的反思日志和后续访谈，考察哪些反馈易于被接受、理解和采纳。第三，通过分析在线评论语言中反映的反馈策略及学习者的反思日志，考察中美同伴互动的反馈策略。第四，根据对上述3种互动行为的统计和分析，得出中方写作组和美方写作组相互作用的总体模式，接着以迭代和整体的方式分析数据，对两组的数据进行比较，通过对两组互动模式的进一步比较，探索相同写作任务的同伴互动的动态性质。

5.2 中美同伴的互动行为

5.2.1 中美同伴的修改行为

5.2.1.1 中国同伴的修改行为

中方写作组里小组成员共同讨论写作文本的优缺点，帮助写作者完善写作文本，参与文本构建。同伴讨论了对方写作文本的各个方面，然而因成员参与程度不同，不同小组采纳反馈的数量和类型不同，修改稿中作文修改数量相差较大，展现了不同的支架策略和互动模式。本研究首先分析写作者的修改稿，查看对写作文本的哪些部分进行了修改。下面具体分析中方写作组在完善写作文本时执行的更改功能。

如表5.1所示，在中国大学生（7人）修改文章的过程中，写作组成员总共实施了168个写作修改，最多的修改类型是更正（64个，9.1个/人），其次是改写（52个，7.43个/人），接着是26个删除、21个添加和5个重新排序。在168次修改中，99个（约59%）是自发修改，69个（约41%）是他人修改。平均每人实施24个作文修改；其中第3篇、第7篇和第1篇的写作者实施的修改数量高于均值（分别是52个、34个和28个），而第2篇、第5篇、第4篇和第6篇低于均值（分别是10个、14个、15个和15个）。值得关注的是，在变化最多的第3篇写作中，52个修改中的49个是自发修改；而在变化最少的第2篇写作中，10个修改中的7个是他人修改；特别是第5篇写作，所有修改都是他人修改。

表 5.1　中国大学生作文修改的描述性统计

(单位：个)

中方写作	添加		删除		改写		重新排序		更正		总计
	自修	他修	自修	他修	自修	他修	自修	他修	自修	他修	
第1篇	2	1	5	2	5	0	0	0	4	9	28
第2篇	1	0	2	2	0	3	0	0	0	2	10
第3篇	5	0	10	0	17	0	0	2	17	1	52
第4篇	2	1	0	0	2	8	0	0	2	0	15
第5篇	0	1	0	0	0	2	0	0	0	11	14
第6篇	0	2	0	0	4	2	0	1	5	1	15
第7篇	0	6	5	0	8	1	0	2	3	9	34
小计	10	11	22	4	36	16	0	5	31	33	168
总计	21		26		52		5		64		
均值	3		3.71		7.43		0.72		9.14		24

我们查看了小组成员的在线讨论和写作者的反思日志后发现，在第3篇写作的在线讨论中，反馈者提出的修改意见以语法和论文结构的修改为主，导致修改稿中有大量的作文修改。但是关于语法的修改意见是笼统的（如"Apart from some minor mistakes, your language and grammar are very good!"），写作者自行查找、修改语法，因此出现了大量的更正和改写类的自发修改；而关于论文结构的两个意见是具体的，因此有两个他人修改。在同伴互动过程中，写作者积极参与活动，但是小组成员没有展示共同所有权，小组成员之间协作互动较少。在第5篇写作的在线讨论中，反馈者提出的关于语法和结构的修改意见都是具体的、详细的（写作者的反思日志也提到"a lot of useful suggestions with detailed illustrations"），表现出更高程度的互动，写作者的所有修改都属于他人修改；在线讨论中也有一些笼统的建议，如"some ideas are a little abstract""the author can further explain the point from the perspective of the readers"，写作者没有对此做出相应的互动交流和修改。因此，修改稿的修改总数不多，作文修改程度不大。

5.2.1.2 美国同伴的修改行为

美方写作组成员以不同的方式完成了写作任务，与中方写作组展示的作文修改、采纳类型和支架策略存在相似性和差异性。在线评论记录显示，美方写作组成员在在线评价互动过程中采用了多种类型的写作修改，如表5.2所示。

表5.2 美国大学生作文修改的描述性统计

（单位：个）

美方写作	添加		删除		改写		重新排序		更正		总计
	自修	他修	自修	他修	自修	他修	自修	他修	自修	他修	
第1篇	0	3	0	1	1	1	1	1	3	0	11
第2篇	0	1	0	0	0	0	0	1	0	1	3
第3篇	2	2	0	0	1	1	0	0	2	0	8
第4篇	0	4	0	0	2	1	1	0	0	0	8
第5篇	0	5	1	1	2	0	1	0	0	0	10
第6篇	0	1	2	1	1	1	0	0	0	1	7
小计	2	16	3	3	7	4	3	2	5	2	47
总计	18		6		11		5		7		
均值	3		1		1.83		0.83		1.17		7.83

美方写作组成员总共执行了47次作文修改行为，平均每人实施7.83个作文修改，数量上明显少于中方写作组（7.83 vs 23.86）。在美国大学生（6人）修改文章的过程中，执行最多的修改行为是添加（18个，3个/人），其次是改写（11个，1.83个/人），其余的依次是更正（7）、删除（6）和重新排序（5）。在47次修改中，20个（约43%）是自发修改，27个（约57%）是他人修改；不同于中方写作组以自发修改为主，美方写作组的修改中他人修改更多。第1篇和第5篇的修改数量（分别是11个和10个）明显高于均值，而第2篇的修改数量（3个）远远低于均值。与中方写作组不同，在美方写作组修改最多的第1篇写作中，11个修改中有7个是他人修改；写作变化最少的第2篇作文中所有的修改都是他人修改。

我们查看了在线讨论和反思日志后发现，中国同伴对美国大学生的母语写作提出的修改意见主要集中于文章结构，如增加主题句、结尾句或者调整排序，因此添加类修改数量最多。关于语法的修改意见很少，即使有这方面的意见，有的也未被采纳（如时态问题），因此更正类修改数量较少。例如，在第 4 篇写作中，反馈者提出 "However if there was one thing I would fix, it would be to have a clear thesis statement. The thesis was implied, but having a clear statement …" 后，写作者积极回应 "In my revised essay, I added a thesis for the first sentence stating strongly that both stories are tied by a theme of justice.", 并在修改稿中添加了主题句。但是在第 5 篇写作中，反馈者提出修改意见 "I think maybe the past tense should be used when retelling the story." 后，写作者未采纳这个建议并给出理由 "Concerning writing about the films in the past tense, I do not believe that that is the correct approach. It is true that they are based in true events, but as stories they can be experienced in the past, in the future, and even in the present. The tense should reflect all of these possibilities."。尽管美方写作组的总体修改数量较少，但是小组成员展示了共同所有权，表现出积极的协作互动倾向。

5.2.2 中美同伴的采纳行为

5.2.2.1 中国同伴的采纳行为

基于在线反馈、修改稿中的他人修改及中美大学生的反思日志，本研究归纳、总结了小组成员易于接受、理解和采纳的反馈类型，以探究中美大学生对反馈类型的偏好。下面讨论中方写作组在完成和完善初稿任务的过程中采纳的反馈类型。

如表 5.3 所示，7 名中国大学生的修改稿共采纳了 69 个同伴反馈意见，采纳的同伴反馈中数量最多的是关于词汇的意见（21 个，3 个/人），其次是关于时态的反馈（16 个，2.29 个/人），再次是关于句法、组织、标点和内容的反馈。在采纳的 69 个同伴修改意见中，57 个（约 83%）是关于写作文本形式的建议，12 个（约 17%）是关于写作文本语篇层面的修改意见。平均每人采纳 9.86 个修改意见，第 7 篇、第 5 篇和第 1 篇的写作者采纳的修改意见高于均值（分别是 18 个、14 个和 12 个），而第 3 篇、第 6 篇、第 2 篇和第 4 篇的作者采纳的修改意见低于均值（分别是

3个、6个、7个和9个)。

表5.3 中国大学生采纳反馈的描述性统计

(单位:个)

中方写作	形式层面			语篇层面			总计
	句法	词汇	时态	标点	组织	内容	
第1篇	2	3	0	7	0	0	12
第2篇	3	4	0	0	0	0	7
第3篇	0	0	1	0	2	0	3
第4篇	1	8	0	0	0	0	9
第5篇	1	3	8	0	2	0	14
第6篇	0	1	0	0	4	1	6
第7篇	6	2	7	0	2	1	18
小计	13	21	16	7	10	2	69
总计	57 (≈83%)			12 (≈17%)			
均值	1.86	3	2.29	1	1.43	0.29	9.86

需要特别注意的是,在采纳修改意见最多的第7篇写作中,写作者采纳的修改意见主要集中于时态和句法层面(分别为7个和6个);而在采纳修改意见最少的第3篇写作中,时态和句法层面(分别为1个和0个)的意见很少。除了第6篇外,中国大学生采纳的同伴反馈主要集中于形式层面的修改意见。这说明中国大学生采纳的反馈数量的多少与反馈内容有关,若反馈集中于写作形式层面,则采纳的数量就多。

另外,我们在详细审查了写作者和反馈者之间的在线讨论和写作者的反思日志后发现,中国大学生未采纳笼统的、不具体的或者抽象的反馈意见。例如,在第5篇的在线讨论中,反馈者提出"I still find this passage not that easy to follow because some ideas are a little abstract, and there are some grammatical mistakes. All in all, it's a well-written passage but it would be much better if the author can further explain the point from the perspective of the readers."。针对这个反馈意见里的"有些观点抽象""有些语法错误""从读者视角解释观点",写作者做出回应"I also think there are some grammatical mistakes in my passage, with some sentences are difficult to follow, but it is not that easy for me to find and correct them. So would you please point it for me? And I would revise it according to your suggestions.",阐明了未采纳的原因：写作者知道文章有问题，但是不知道具体有哪些问题，需要反馈者指出具体问题，但是反馈者并未指出。在随后的反思日志中，写作者明确提出自己更倾向于具体的、详细的建议（I am so grateful for the suggestions from one friend who has given me quite a lot of useful suggestions with detailed illustrations.）。

中国大学生未采纳自己不赞成的反馈意见。例如，在第 6 篇的在线讨论中，反馈者提出"I would also add more references to the stories in order to solidify the argument being made."的建议。针对反馈者"增加电影内容的引用"的建议，写作者提到由于在写作之前被告知不要写太多电影内容，因此对反馈者的这个建议感到困惑，所以未采纳反馈者的建议（As to the lack of examples from the film, I myself is very confused because I was told not to mention too much about the film but I have found in your essays much about it.）。

5.2.2.2 美国同伴的采纳行为

美方写作组的采纳类型也分为形式层面和语篇层面，但是呈现的采纳类型不同于中方写作组。美方写作组采纳的关于形式层面的同伴反馈中没有关于时态的修改意见，但是在关于语篇层面的同伴反馈中，采纳的类型增加了关于观点的修改意见。

表 5.4 显示，美方写作组中 6 名美国大学生的修改稿共采纳了 27 个同伴反馈意见，人均采纳意见的数量明显少于中方写作组（4.5 vs 9.86）。采纳的意见中最多的是关于组织的反馈（15 个，2.5 个/人），其次是关于句法的反馈（4 个），接着是观点（3 个）、词汇（2 个）、内容（2 个）和标点（1 个）。采纳的 27 个修改意见中 20 个（约 74%）是对写作文本语篇层面的修改，7 个（约 26%）是对写作文本形式层面的修改，平均每人采纳 4.5 个修改意见。第 1 篇、第 5 篇和第 4 篇的写作者采纳修改意见的数量高于均值（分别是 6 个、6 个和 5 个），而第 6 篇、第 2 篇和第 3 篇的写作者采纳修改意见的数量低于均值（分别是 4 个、3 个和 3 个）。值得关注的是，在采纳修改意见较多的第 1 篇和第 5 篇写作中，写作者采纳的修改意见都集中于文本组织方面（分别为 5 个和 4 个）。除了第 6 篇外，美国大学生采纳的同伴反馈主要集中于语篇层面的修改意见。

表 5.4　美国大学生采纳反馈的描述性统计

（单位：个）

美方写作	形式层面			语篇层面			总计
	句法	词汇	标点	组织	内容	观点	
第 1 篇	1	0	0	5	0	0	6
第 2 篇	0	1	0	2	0	0	3
第 3 篇	0	0	0	0	0	3	3
第 4 篇	0	1	0	4	0	0	5
第 5 篇	0	0	0	4	2	0	6
第 6 篇	3	0	1	0	0	0	4
小计	4	2	1	15	2	3	27
总计	7（≈26%）			20（≈74%）			
均值	0.67	0.33	0.17	2.5	0.33	0.5	4.5

同样，我们也详细审查了在线讨论和写作者的反思日志，发现以下 4 点：

第一，美方写作者未采纳关于时态和词汇的建议。例如，在第 5 篇的在线讨论中，中方反馈者提出"For these two movies are all adapted by a true story, I think maybe the past tense should be used when retelling the story."，但是写作者认为"Concerning writing about the films in the past tense, I do not believe that that is the correct approach. It is true that they are based in true events, but as stories they can be experienced in the past, in the future, and even in the present. The tense should reflect all of these possibilities."。美国学生不赞成用过去式描述电影，因为虽然电影是基于真实的事件，但是观影者在过去、未来甚至现在都能看到这些故事，而时态应该反映所有这些可能性。

第二，美方写作者未采纳关于影片观点的反馈意见。例如，在第 6 篇的在线讨论中，中方反馈者都提出"I think it's hard to say that Qiuju was aimed at saving face."的反馈，写作者回应"Many people from China believed that Qiuju was not trying to save face, only the chief of the village was. Even though I respect their comments, I feel that Qiuju was not just wanting an apology. She wanted to protect her family honor. I believe that honor and saving face coincide. This is why I felt that I should not change this part of my essay.",中方反馈者认为秋菊不是为了挽回面子,只有村主任是要面子的。尽管尊重反馈者的意见,但写作者仍然认为秋菊不仅仅想要道歉,她还想要维护她的家庭荣誉。因此,写作者坚持自己的观点,没有在修改稿中修改这部分内容。

第三,美方写作者未采纳与写作技巧相关的部分建议。例如,在第 5 篇的在线讨论中,中方反馈者提出 "And if there is any possible, you can add some examples to show that what kind of advantage or trouble will be brought under the influence of the way of expression and what we should do. Anyhow, contacting with the real life is the ultimate purpose for us to write an argument.",但是写作者认为 "Concerning your point that arguments should always connect to real life, I don't entirely agree. Many critics contend that it is enough to discuss art for art's own sake. Furthermore, there is a growing trend among many writers to allow the reader to be the final interpreter of art. When writing in that way, it is better to have a more general conclusion, rather than dictating to the reader what the moral should be. Still, I admit I had not considered what the function of my paper should be before I started writing and will try to do that more in the future."。写作者不赞成总是将论点与现实生活联系起来,因此没有采纳相关意见。

第四,美方写作者未采纳增加大量内容的建议。例如,在第 6 篇的在线讨论中,反馈者提出 "It's unclear what you mean when you say Erin is fighting for a cause—couldn't one say that Qiuju is fighting for the cause of honor? I think that you have highlighted an interesting difference between the two movies, but you'd have to specify what cause Erin is fighting for. Is it the rights and dignity of the underrepresented country folk against corporate overreach? There is much promise here, but the arguments you make need to be fleshed out a bit more.",建议写作者详细地阐释某个观点,使论点更加充分,但是写作者并未增加相关信息。这可能与大量增加内容的可操作性不强有关。

5.2.3 中美写作组的支架策略

5.2.3.1 中方写作组的支架策略

支架策略具有人际性质，在互动中才能体现，因此我们对支架策略的讨论以小组的互动（至少一对一的互动）为单位，而不是计算每个成员采用的支架策略。中方写作组中共有 7 个互动小组，我们依次查看了每个小组在线讨论过程中实施的支架策略及其体现的在线互动的特点，发现中方写作者和美方反馈者通过指出对方的问题和给出建议提供指导（Donato，1994），及时响应小组同伴的问题并做出适当的回应，向小组成员表达感谢，通过提出新的问题引起小组成员对话题的兴趣等支架策略参与共同任务。特别是在协商写作文本的语言和文本结构时，使用支架策略明显，美方反馈者指出问题，中方写作者赞同反馈者的意见，双方对该情形有共同的理解，并且保持一致，主体间性的支架策略（Rommetveit，1985）应用很广泛。例如，第 2 组（节选自第 17 轮第 5 篇）中方写作者（W—writer）和美方反馈者（R—responsor）之间的在线讨论：

> R：Overall, your language and grammar are very good! My only suggestion would be to review some of your idiomatic expressions; some of your wording is only slightly incorrect, and I can still understand what you are trying to say. For example, "What she is in face of" in the sixth paragraph might also be worded as "What she faces is …"
>
> W：Aha, I think you do a better job in summarizing my own essay, and I do try to convey that idea. By "some of your idiomatic expressions", do you mean those idioms like "as poor as a church mouse"? Since that is my first trying, I'm not quite sure whether I have made it right.
>
> R：Idioms are a type of figurative language. They are phrases that have a different meaning than what is literally said. They aren't quite comparisons like "as poor as a church mouse". An example that I can think of that we use are "It's raining cats and dogs". We say it to mean that it is raining a lot; it isn't literally raining cats and dogs. I know this

expression is pretty weird. Have you ever heard this saying, or do you have something similar to it in Chinese? I'm afraid this isn't going to help much if this is strictly part of Western culture!

W: I guess the expression "as poor as a church mouse" is more a metaphor than an idiomatic expression, is it correct? I think we also have this kind of idiomatic expressions in Chinese. We use "an iron clock" to address someone who is very mean.

R: Yes, I think saying someone is "an iron clock" would be an idiom. "As poor as a church mouse" would actually be classified as a simile. Similes and metaphors are very similar in that they both compare two unsimilar things. The difference between the two is that similes make the comparison using the words "like", "as", or "than", and metaphors make the comparison without those key words. Since "as poor as a church mouse" uses the word "as", it is considered a simile. Similarly, "she is like a church mouse" and "she is poorer than a church mouse" would also be similes. A metaphor might be something like "she is a church mouse". When learning metaphors, the first saying I learned was "he is a fish out of water". Have you ever heard this saying or do you have something similar to it?

Figurative language can be pretty tricky to understand. As a native speaker, it took me years to grasp the concepts. Even now, I can still have trouble figuring out what kind of figurative language a phrase is …

W: Thank you so much for your detailed explanation, which helps me know more about figurative language.

Aha, I come to realize I must have confused the equivalent expressions of simile and metaphor in English. Thanks to your elaboration, I'm clear about their difference now …

如节选所示，反馈者先对写作者的词汇和习惯用语进行诊断，接着对习惯用语存在的问题进行确认，然后对习惯用语进行具体指导并举例说明，之后给出自己对习惯用语的理解，认为习惯用语是一种暗喻，并用汉语中的习语举例；反馈者赞同汉语举例，但是纠正写作者使用的习语"as poor as a church mouse"是明喻并解释原因,属于指导支架策略。同时反馈者为写作者提供了学习修辞语的资源,是一种应急响应支架策略。最后,写作者感谢反馈者的详细解释和帮助,这是情感涉入支架策略。这样,反馈者和写作者实现了对习语的共同理解,观点达成一致,体现主体间性的支架策略。

又比如,第2组中中方写作者和美方反馈者之间的在线讨论:

R: To me, this passage reads nicely, although it could flow a little nicer, perhaps if there weren't so many small paragraphs, but it is certainly easy to follow along and understand the main point. Although I would request that the author explain what the Chinese translation of *Erin Brockovich*, because without it the entire opening line is lost. I like the sum up in the end with the disclaimer about taking advice...

W: As to the translation of the film *Erin Brockovich*, it's actually the title of my passage: "never compromise". I didn't find it difficult to understand until you and Mark, the other member of our group both raise the same question in the feedback. And you also think that too many small paragraphs in the beginning of the passage make it difficult to follow. Would it be much better if I combine the first and fourth paragraphs by adding some conjunction words?

R: I think that yes, combining paragraphs into one would make it read easier. Also, hearing that your focus is "never compromise", that adds much clarification. I think your paper is very good and it sends this message, I think a few minor changes could really add clarification and keep your message consistent throughout.

W: It is really a good opportunity for me to talk with you native speakers. In addition, I am curious about what you think of Qiuju. I once thought that she should give up when all the people around her consider it unnecessary. I think most Chinese will agree with me. But finally Qiuju's perseverance touched the bottom of my heart, and I realized that we all should struggle for what we deserve. What's your opinion? Or what will most American people think about it?

在上述互动中,反馈者针对写作文本的组织和结构进行诊断,属于指导支架策略;接着两位反馈者都指出英文影片的中文译名问题,写作者承认自己没有意识到这个问题,并针对段落结构存在的问题进行确认;然后反馈者肯定写作者对反馈意见的理解,写作者感谢反馈者的建议和帮助,这些属于情感涉入支架策略;同时写作者提出新的问题,这是为了引起反馈者对讨论主题的兴趣,属于激发兴趣支架策略。这样,反馈者和写作者实现了对组织和结构的共同理解,观点达成一致,体现主体间性的支架策略。

在大多数中方写作者和美方反馈者的小组里,双方的互动涉及积极的指导、应急响应、热情的情感涉入和主动的兴趣激发,主体间性的支架策略明显。但是,在中方写作组的7个小组中,中方写作者和中方反馈者互动时,支架策略出现显著变化,相互作用表现为缺乏主体间性,指导未得到回应,支架策略并不明显。在少数美方反馈者提出在线讨论时,中方写作者没有做出回应或者未在规定时间内做出回应;或者中方写作者提出新的讨论话题时,美方反馈者未及时回复。这些都会导致双方的参与度降低,书面贡献的参与度下降,缺少主体间性。例如,第2组中中方写作者和中方反馈者之间的在线讨论:

R: Here are some suggestions:

(1) When you describe the movie plots, I think it will be better if the past tense is used.

(2) In your last paragraph, you said that "From beginning to end, they won't give up until they are offered the final judgment they expect". But the truth is that, Qiuju had already "given up" before the final judgment was offered because the village chief lent a hand when she was about to give birth regardless of the past embarrassment. I think some correction is needed to make your expression more accurate.

中国大学生给出修改意见后,写作者没有做出回应,虽然在写作者的反思日志中,写作者提到中方反馈者的意见,但是没有明确表示赞同还是反对,在修改稿中也没有做出相应的修改。在阅读了写作者的修改稿之后,反馈者继续做出如下反馈:

> In your essay, it seems that the simple present tense is still used. I searched on the Internet and found most people believe that the simple present tense should be used to make people feel immersive. I have never thought about that before.

反馈者查找自己的修改意见未被采纳的原因,发现反馈意见不合理,即叙述影片不一定必须用一般过去时。反馈者在互动中习得了新的知识。但是在这个过程中,反馈者和写作者并无互动,缺少主体间性,没有使用支架策略。

中方写作者与中方反馈者的互动较少,可能的原因是双方在进行在线讨论之前已经在课堂上进行了大量的互动反馈,所以后期的在线互动较少。反馈者的回复可以证实这一点,他提到同班同学在进行在线写作之前已经在课堂上就两部影片进行了大量的讨论,所以很难再对本班同学的写作给予修改意见(It's harder to reply to one's written by fellow students because they are more influenced by discussions that we all had in class.)。

5.2.3.2　美方写作组的支架策略

美方写作组的支架策略有显著变化。本研究依次查看美方写作组中的6个互动小组的在线讨论过程,考察每个小组的支架策略后发现,在美方写作小组中,中方反馈者给对方提供指导,写作者响应小组同伴提出问题并做出赞同或反对的回应,写作者向小组成员表达感谢,同一小组中不同的反馈者共同参与任务,小组成员经过协商达成共同的理解,观点保持一致。与中方写作组不同,在多数情况下美方写作组中,中方反馈者和美方写作者协商写作文本的语言和文本结构时,中方反馈者指出问题,美方写作者不赞同反馈者的意见,观点无法达成一致,缺少主体间性。例如,第5篇美方写作者和中方反馈者之间的在线讨论:

> R: As an argumentative composition, maybe the conclusion or the ending should be added to perfect the structure of the whole article. And if there is any possible, you can add some examples to show that what kind of advantage or trouble will be brought under the influence of the way of expression and what we should do. Anyhow, contacting with the real life is the ultimate purpose for us to write an argument.

For these two movies are all adapted by a true story, I think maybe the past tense should be used when retelling the story. What do you think?

W: Thank you for all the comments! They were very insightful. Concerning your point that arguments should always connect to real life, I don't entirely agree. Many critics contend that it is enough to discuss art for art's own sake. Furthermore, there is a growing trend among many writers to allow the reader to be the final interpreter of art. When writing in that way, it is better to have a more general conclusion rather than dictating to the reader what the moral should be. Still, I admit I had not considered what the function of my paper should be before I started writing and will try to do that more in the future.

Concerning writing about the films in the past tense, I do not believe that it is the correct approach. It is true that they are based in true events, but as stories they can be experienced in the past, in the future, and even in the present. The tense should reflect all of these possibilities.

R: I do appreciate for your comments. I believe different opinions are based on different educational and cultural background and they are meaningful, aren't they?

如节选所示，反馈者对写作文本的结尾和时态进行诊断，认为议论文的结尾应该将论点和现实生活联系起来，并且认为写作者复述影片中的故事时应该用过去时，这属于指导支架策略；但是写作者对于这两个建议持反对意见，并详细解释不接受反馈意见的原因。中方反馈者对于美方写作者的解释持保留意见。由此可见，反馈者与写作者对结尾和时态的理解不同，他们进行了一些发散性思维，但没有形成共同的理解，所以观点未达成一致，未呈现主体间性。

另外，在协商写作文本的内容时，若中方反馈者提出不同观点，同一小组中其他的中方反馈者会共同参与任务，反馈者之间不仅体现主体间性的支架策略，他们还共同努力提出不同观点，并通过具体解释观点提供指导。主体间性的支架策略在协商写作内容时很明显，属于集体支架。例如，第6组的互动：

R1: In Paragraph Two, there is a sentence saying "This is because in China honor/saving face is everything". Well, in fact, not all Chinese people do things just for their face. Besides, Qiuju suing the head of village was neither for her husband's nor her own face. She wanted an apology, just for a respect from others instead of dirty languages and humiliation.

By the way, there are many slashes appeared in this article. What do they mean? Some words were used too many times, such as "tainted". Maybe you can try to change your expressions to let the article be more vivid. As these two movies are both adapted from two true stories, maybe the past tense should be used when retelling the story.

在这组的互动中，第一个中方反馈者对美方写作者的绝对性表述"对中国人来说，荣誉/面子就是一切"提出质疑；对标点符号、用词和时态提出了建议。尽管中方反馈者希望能与写作者在观点、符号和时态几个方面达成共识，自己给出的建议能够为写作者的修改提供帮助，但是美方写作者未做出回应，双方无互动，缺少主体间性，没有使用支架策略。但是这并未打消反馈者的积极性，在写作者修改后，该反馈者继续给出反馈意见：

R1: You believe that "honor and saving face coincide". So I think maybe you aren't intended to say something bad, just confused by the concept. Saving family honor is very distinguished from saving face. Saving family honor is positive and commendatory. It is for a group of people, family members. But saving face is absolutely for the individual herself. It has a negative and derogatory. Qiuju was not just fighting for herself. She asked for an apology from the head of village, for the respect from ours. It's quite different.

The other thing I want to mention is the word "taint". The charming of language is that we have different ways to express ourselves. If we keep using one certain word when talking with others for so many times, people may get bored. And so does writing articles. You may use "pollute", "contaminate" or "pollution", "contamination" to paraphrase "taint". That is just what I suggest.

反馈者对于写作者的"荣誉和面子是一致的"的观点提出不同意见，并且详细阐释两者的不同；因为写作者在修改稿中仍然用词不当，所以反馈者具体解释 taint 的用法，并给出修改建议。另一个中方反馈者（R2）读完第一个反馈者的意见后，表达了对其反馈意见的认同：

R2：I want to share with you my ideas.

First, I also feel the same that saving family honor and saving face is different, but I think the meaning of saving face could be neutral. But indeed, I'm not sure if native speakers have similar thoughts on this.

The difference between saving face and honor as you mentioned reminds me of an interesting turning point of Qiuju's story. At first, Qiuju may want to save face, but later she insists on appealing, which makes her lose face because she exposes something shameful to the public (her husband was kicked on the crotch by the village chief). Meanwhile it's an act of saving family honor.

Second, you mentioned for the second time on the word "tainted". As a language learner, variety of word choices bothers me a lot, while what bothers me this time is necessity on changing the word "tainted". Would it be less common and meaningful to paraphrasing such a term? It seems to me that it's a proper name that is not necessary to paraphrase. In addition, I would be more interested to know the difference among the synonyms "taint", "pollute" and "contamination", and consider proper use afterwards.

第二个反馈者对第一个反馈者的"荣誉和面子不同"的观点表示赞同，并且举例对 taint 用词不当的观点表示支持。这种反馈者之间的在线互动具有面对面反馈的优势，呈现多向性特征。

值得一提的是，虽然认知冲突（Tocalli & Swain, 2005）可能发生在协作活动中，但对不同观点的协商可以让小组成员建立新的理解并达成新的共识。例如，第 4 组写作者和反馈者的在线互动：

> R：However, there are also some points I cannot agree on. The first one is about the word at the back of the first paragraph——retribution, which means severe punishment for something seriously wrong that somebody has done; I do think Qiuju is not seeking for severe punishment but a sincere apology.

反馈者指出写作者的 retribution 用词不当，解释 retribution（报复）意味着惩罚某人所犯的严重错误，但是秋菊寻求的不是严厉的惩罚，而是真诚的道歉。写作者和反馈者双方都不是试图对文本进行绝对控制：中方反馈者没有提供直接的解决方案要求写作者修改，而是指出了自己对这个单词的理解并阐释原因；写作者虽然未在回复反馈者时提及该点，但是在反思日志中做出了回应，即 "One commenter brought up that I had used the word 'retribution' and believed that the definition of the word did not match the context. After rechecking the definition myself, I found the definition to be vague, while I was correct in my understanding; the commenters' understanding of it was not incorrect. Therefore in my revisions I chose a better way of phrasing my point that would be more clear and avoid this vagueness."，写作者在收到反馈者关于 retribution 的反馈后，查阅相关资料时发现该词的定义模糊，为了避免模糊性，需要使用更加精确的词。反馈者在修改稿中提供了一个替代方案，这与原始文本不同，反馈者没有直接给予"解决方案"。这说明了双方为提供互惠援助做出努力，最后达成了双方都同意的理解（Tudge，1992）。

5.3 中美同伴互动行为的异同

5.3.1 中美同伴互动行为的共性

中美写作者修改稿中修改数量的多少与反馈内容有关。若反馈内容以语法、结构、词汇和用法规范的修改意见为主，则修改稿中写作变化就多，作文修改程度大；若修改意见以观点和写作内容为主，则修改稿中的修改就少。对于笼统的修改意见，写作者以自发修改为主或者不进行修改；对于具体的、详细的修改意见，写作者以他人修改为主，表现出更高程度的写作者与反馈者的互动。中美学习者不会采纳笼统的、不具体的、抽象的及自己不赞成的反馈意见。

中美大学生关于写作内容和主题的讨论较多，双方对不同的观点进行协商交流，但是大多数学生都会对同伴的观点持保留意见。中美大学生会采纳关于文本结构的修改意见，可能的原因有两个：一是对新文体的关注度高于语言；二是中美大学生都具备一些写作方面的专业知识，这是与语言能力无关的基础写作能力，无论是母语者还是二语学习者，都能够应用这种专业知识评价同伴的总体写作水平。

中美大学生不易采纳要求增加举例、具体阐释及大量内容的建议，因为这些建议要求写作者对论文的某些具体部分进行重写，这在同伴反馈过程中操作性不强。中美大学生易于采纳多个同伴提出的相同的反馈意见，这与"如果两位及以上的反馈者给出相似的评论意见，那么写作者在后续修改稿中进行修订的可能性比单一同伴的评论意见要高出 3.5 倍"（Leijen，2017）的结论一致，也证实了多种同伴反馈比单一同伴反馈更有利（Cho & Schunn，2007）。

中美大学生对于同伴反馈的接受和采纳建立在理解并赞同的基础上。例如，中国大学生倾向于接受和采纳关于时态的建议，而美国大学生则不接受。这是因为美国大学生具有母语优势，不赞同二语反馈者对于时态的建议；在词汇、语法等语言问题方面，二语学习者将母语者视为权威。

中美大学生和本国反馈者的互动较少，没有对指导和激发兴趣等支架策略做出回应，缺乏主体间性，支架策略并不明显。这是因为双方在进行在线讨论之前已经进行了大量的课堂互动反馈，后期的在线互动较少。

5.3.2　中美同伴互动行为的差异性

中国大学生平均每人实施 24 个作文修改，美国大学生实施的作文修改的数量明显少于中方写作组（7.83 vs 23.86）。中美大学生采纳的修改类型的数量完全不同，按照数量多少，中国大学生的修改类型依次是更正、改写、删除、添加和重新排序；美国大学生是添加、改写、更正、删除和重新排序。反馈者对中国大学生写作文本提出的关于语法和结构的修改意见多，对美国大学生写作文本的修改意见主要集中于文章结构。

中美大学生的修改方式也不同，中国大学生以自发修改为主（约59%是自发修改，约41%是他人修改），修改总数多的文本以自发修改为主；美国大学生的他人修改更多（约57%是他人修改，约43%是自发修改），修改总数多的文本以他人修改为主。

中美大学生在主题内容、语篇结构和语言形式等方面进行互动协商，中国大学生采纳的反馈集中为对写作文本的语言形式和语篇结构方面的建议；而美国大学生更倾向于接受对文本语篇层面的意见。中国大学生尤其重视关于时态、用词和句子表达的建议；美国大学生更注重对文本结构和组织的反馈。美国大学生接收到的同伴反馈较多，但是被采纳的反馈意见不多；关于时态、词汇和写作技巧的建议不易被美国大学生采纳。

在中方写作组中，美方反馈者和中方写作者的互动涉及积极的指导、应急响应、热情的情感涉入和主动的兴趣激发，主体间性的支架策略明显。但是在美方写作组中，当中方反馈者指出写作文本的语言和文本结构问题时，美方写作者会反对反馈者的意见，观点无法达成一致，缺少主体间性。虽然双方在互动中出现了认知冲突，但对不同观点的协商可以让小组成员形成新的理解并达成新的共识。另外，在协商写作文本的内容时，中方反馈者与其他反馈者之间偶尔出现互动，共同参与反馈任务，体现集体支架策略。

5.4 同伴互动模式的生成

在检查和重新审视数据之后，本研究形成的主要观点是，中美同伴使用各种互动行为的组合创造了不同的互动模式。将这个观点概念化，可以将同伴互动分为4种关系类型：集体互动关系、合作关系、从属关系和常规关系。这里的同伴互动行为指同伴互动时实施的反馈行为、做出的写作修改行为、采纳的不同反馈行为及执行反馈策略的行为。形成的互动模式如图5.1、图5.2所示：

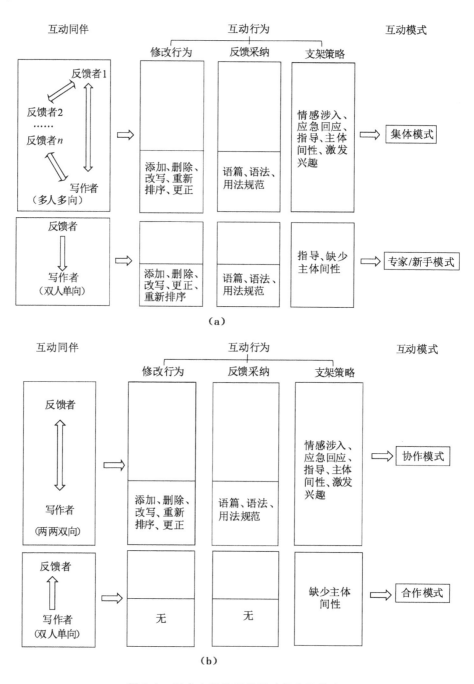

图 5.1 混合小组的同伴互动行为及模式

图 5.1 从左至右的方向反映了本研究论点,即某些行为组合会导致某

些关系模式。本研究认为,互动行为和互动关系模式是以持续的方式通过语篇实现的,并且互动关系的性质会发生改变。面对面反馈有,书面反馈较少。在线延时反馈的经历也会对中美大学生在反馈中的自我定位产生影响,因此,即使是某种特定关系类型的暂时和偶然存在也会影响中美同伴在随后的互动中选择采取的行动。换句话说,中美学习者的行为都来自并导致某种关系模式的存在。

5.4.1 集体互动模式

具体而言,图5.1显示了中美大学生互动的行为及其形成的互动模式。第一种是集体互动模式。这种互动模式涉及建构性的互动和集体支架,小组成员在完成任务和相互参与文本构建方面显示出高度的个人责任感,反映在小组成员会积极参与反馈、在写作变化行为中出现他人修改类型、采纳对方的反馈意见及互为支架策略等方面。所有参与者之间的支架策略是该互动模式的一个显著特征。小组中没有一个成员是专家,每个小组成员共同担任专家角色,写作者在修改稿中采纳了小组成员的反馈,并且在写作任务中共同努力,互为支架。例如,中方写作组第5组的互动:

> R1: As you mention briefly in the opening to your essay, both women protagonists come from a lower-class background; this is advantageous for Erin, and the source of great misfortune for Qiuju is evident. The triumph of the little guy over the corporate behemoth is a well-established trope in the American and Western tradition, traceable even to stories like that of David and Goliath. Does such a plot appear often in Chinese literature?
>
> As a final note, you mention the clash between mandarin and local Chinese dialects. As a student of the Spanish, I know that a similar suppression of dialects is occurring in Spain itself, as less common dialects such as Basque and Catalan are being subsumed by Castellan or traditional Spanish. Is a similar thing happening in China now?
>
> R2: As a Chinese student, I think such plots as David and Goliath indeed existed in Chinese literature, especially in ancient war stories, which presented the wisdom of ancient people. And those are true

stories. But with time going, maybe Chinese become more practical. They are focusing more on collective capacity instead of individualistic heroism, which we can often see in Hollywood movies such as *Spider-Man* or *Mission Impossible*.

About the Chinese dialect, well, most of them are similar with mandarin, especially the dialect coming from the north part of China. So people can communicate with each other in their own languages. But some dialects, for example, Shanghainese and Cantonese, are hard to be understood. Although every dialect has its own features and we will not combine them, yet for the convenience of communication, we have mandarin as the national language.

W: The depth of conversation that we have had about the nature of arguments is something that I did not think I would have with speaking in a secondary language. Commenter 2 and Commenter 3, you have both been very engaging conversationists and written in a way that was easy to read, but also gave me much to think about.

第一位反馈者（美国学生）对写作文本的内容进行评论后，指出小人物战胜大公司的情节是美国和西方传统的一个完美组合，甚至可以追溯到David和Goliath的故事。他想知道这样的情节在中国文学中是否经常出现。另外，关于写作者提及的汉语中普通话和方言之间的冲突，反馈者作为学习西班牙语的学生，知道西班牙语会出现类似的方言言语压制，他想知道现在中国是否也有类似的事情发生。这位反馈者提出的两个问题明显不是针对美方写作者，而是向其他中方反馈者提出的问题。这体现了该小组成员之间的互动不仅仅局限于反馈者与写作者之间的交流。第二位反馈者（中国学生）回答了这两个问题。之后，写作者感叹小组成员之间的话题讨论具有一定的深度，并且称赞两位中方反馈者是非常有吸引力的对话者。在这上述互动中，小组成员并不是简单地并行工作，各自完成分配给他们每个人的任务，而是集体努力，反馈者和写作者及反馈者之间交流相关话题，每位成员都为修改做出贡献，成员之间的互动是多人多向的、积极且富有成效的。

5.4.2 协作互动模式

第二种是协作互动模式。当反馈互动的参与者试图一起处理书面文本时就形成了协作互动模式。这种关系的关键性特征是反馈者和写作者双方不会对书面文本拥有绝对的控制权。相反,他们试图一起探讨什么样的作品对目标读者来说是成功的作品。下面举例展示的互动包含了表示协作关系的行为,双方针对写作结构和观点进行协商,反馈者评论写作者的写作(美方写作组第 4 篇):

> The passage above mainly talks about the average civilian ... It's easy to follow the author's idea which is supported by some vivid scenes from the two movies. What's more, the author is so considerate that the passage is easy for us non-native speakers to understand ...
>
> However, it would be much better if there is a topic sentence for the third paragraph and a conclusion at the end.

中方反馈者首先对写作文本进行评估,对文本的中心论点、论据和文章的组织结构与语言给予正面的、积极的评价;接着反馈者发现问题并予以纠正,使用了重述反馈策略。

美方写作者对中方反馈者评论的回复如下:

> I have received comments and totally agree that some topic sentences would help organize and add flow to my essay. If I reworked this, I would definitely incorporate that. I would love to receive any other criticism that anyone may have.

美方写作者收到了相关的评论后表示,完全赞同主题句可以增强文章的流畅性,并表示会采纳建议,在修改稿中加入主题句。接着,反馈者回复写作者:

> As your topic is how the lowest of society fight for justice, I want to know whether this kind of case occurs frequently in your country. You see, in China, there is an idiom "xi shi ning ren", which means that we had better not conflict with others if it is not that much important.

中方反馈者欲激发写作者对相关话题的讨论兴趣,又提出新的话题:

社会最低层为正义而战,美国是否有这种情况?反馈者提到中国的一个习惯用语"息事宁人",并解释了成语的意义:如果事情不那么重要,最好不要与别人发生冲突。写作者继续回复反馈者:

> Thank you for your insight. That's a really great question. I'm very interested in hearing about the Chinese perspective and your idiom. That's really interesting to me that people are told not to make trouble. I'd say in the U.S. people aren't afraid to stand up and challenge people… I would like to ask, how do you feel people in China use the media (TV, Internet, radio, etc.) to voice their opinions?

美方写作者对反馈者提出的问题很感兴趣,他不能接受被人告知不要惹事。他好奇中国人如何使用媒体发表意见,中方反馈者回答了写作者的问题:

> Like Americans, nowadays people in China also like to give voice to their feelings and opinions on the Internet, such as the Microblog, that is Weibo in Chinese. As long as what is said doesn't break the law and it's factual, people are free to say whatever they want. Also, there are many Weibo accounts registered by the government for civilians to give their opinions about the policies or the civil servants. Some people can also get the answer to their question from the authorities.

中方反馈者回答,现在中国人也喜欢在互联网上发表自己的感受和看法。写作者又提出新的问题:

> Would you mind giving me the "汉字"? I'd be excited to learn a new idiom! So I would like to know how you think Chinese people see Qiuju and Erin in terms of "面子" (I think that's the characters) or saving face. We seem to have some mixed ideas here about what that means and whether or not Qiuju is saving face. Do you have any comments?
>
> I'm glad you are interested in Chinese. The Chinese characters are

"息事宁人". In my opinion, this idiom doesn't relate to "面子", but I agree with you that Qiuju is saving face in doing so, to some extent. And I have to admit that most of our Chinese people care much about "面子".

美方写作者表达了对汉字的兴趣。另外，因为美国大学生之间关于"从面子或挽回面子的角度看待 Qiuju 和 Erin，以及 Qiuju 是否在挽回面子"的观点不一致，美方写作者想征询中方反馈者的意见。中方反馈者赞同写作者的观点，认为 Qiuju 是在挽回面子。在写作者上传修改稿后，双方进一步交流，并对此次互动进行总结：

R: I am glad that you find my comment of use. This essay is much easier to follow as you have added a topic sentence for each paragraph and there is also a conclusion at the end which has summed up the essay and helped me better understand it. I agree with you that although Erin and Qiuju are in different sides of the world, they are struggling for the same thing, justice which exists across the world and in every time of our history, both America and China.

W: I'm glad you like my improved essay, and I found your comments very helpful. I agree that all these changes do make my essay easier to read, and I'm glad my argument comes through clearly, and is well-defended. Overall I'm much happier with my second draft, I think all the comments and suggestions really helped.

中方反馈者肯定了修改稿的进步，写作者采纳了反馈者增加主题句和结论的建议，并且双方统一了看法，认为世界各地都存在正义。写作者感谢反馈者的意见使得修改后的论文可读性更强，而且通过双方的交流互动，观点更加清晰明了。

这个实例呈现了反馈者和写作者的多次互动，反馈者首先指出写作者的写作文本的结构问题，即主要为缺少主题句和总结。反馈者没有采取诸如警告或刺激之类的行动来分担双方完善文本的负担，而是实施提供解决方案的反馈策略。写作者接受对方的建议，没有提出任何挑战或异议，而是接受了反馈者的判断。接着，反馈者提出新的问题，激发了对方的讨论兴趣，写作者回答问题并提出新的问题，双方在互动中共同进步。这组成员采取了协作立场，参与的积极性很高。他们相互参与解决对方的问题（反映在积极的指导和激发对方的兴趣方面），反馈者和写作者之间是两两双向互动，主体间性的支架策略明显。

这里需要指出集体互动模式和协作模式之间的不同。集体互动模式展现了集体支架的特征（Donato，1994）：所有小组成员共同协商写作任务，在在线讨论中同时承担共同协商的个人角色。协作模式是指两个成员之间发生互动。如上述举例美方写作组第 4 篇的互动所示，没有证据表明所有成员在一起作为一个集体协商同一写作文本；但是这个小组的两对成员（两两双向互动）积极参与，仍然成功地完成了任务。

5.4.3 合作互动模式

第三种类型是合作互动模式。该模式有明确的分工，小组成员分配写作任务，每个人平行执行各自的子任务，但他们很少接触对方的文本。该模式没有核心人物，组员间没有地位和权威的差别，其缺点是小组成员间缺乏必要的协作，小组决策效率低，成员之间的分歧较大，不能达成共识。最终起决定作用的可能是外部权威。

下面是中国同伴和中国写作者的在线交流：

> I'd like to share about the color, clothing, and accessories in the film with you. The atmosphere of the whole movie is just a section of the special era node after the reform and opening-up. The description of the condensed life state in the movie is the tragedy of the era. At that time, the color of clothes was dim. Especially, the clothes people wore in winter were heavy, which would bring us a very depressing impact on the vision.

中国同伴分享了自己对电影中的颜色、服装和配饰的理解。写作者继续分享影片中色彩的运用：

> You are right. The whole film does use a dark color to reflect the tragedy of the fate of the protagonist …
> When Wang Cailing went home for the Spring Festival after various blows in life, the red touch of her mother setting off

firecrackers rekindled her hope for life. So although no longer clung to her dream of singing at the Paris Opera House, she still did not succumb to the society's view of women at that time and randomly married a man she did not love for the rest of her life.

而中国同伴开始分享其对艺术的理解：

Art has nothing to do with utility. Art is just a way to enjoy life. When Mr. Hu wants to find Wang Cailing to have a fake marriage, just to cover up his lifestyle that has always been rejected by the secular world …

但是，写作者认为王彩玲也是一位艺术家：

But I think Wang Cailing is also an artist. After all, she was duty-bound to pursue her dream. She wants to have a Beijing household, because with this, she may well stay in the Central Art Troupe. With this first step, she can slowly get closer to her ideal …

如摘录所示，尽管互动双方进行对话，但合作不多，即互动性不强，每个人只顾陈述自己的观点，不太在意对方的观点和看法，因此成员之间缺乏协商，未使用支架策略。同时，修改稿中没有他人修改类型。

5.4.4 专家/新手互动模式

第四种是专家/新手互动模式。在这种关系中，交流双方中有一方是更强大的合作伙伴。他们借助自己对写作技巧和规范的知识，以及对相关话题的理解，表达具有权威性的判断；评估和评论写作的整体质量，并且就可接受性发表声明。另一方听从建议并撤回自己原有的表达。下面的摘录给出了专家/新手互动关系的一个实例，选自中方写作组第4篇互动。互动双方讨论词汇的选择：

R: However, I think your and my understandings of the term "human nature" is not the same. You see, what that phrase has come to mean in modern terms is something rather dark. When a writer talks about human nature, they usually do so when they are trying to show the deeper evils of people. For example, a person may say "People are mean to each other. It's just human nature." Now, it is true that the term may be used in a more hopeful context when trying to explain the empathy of a person toward another person's suffering. But for the most part, people try to avoid the darkness associated with "human nature". I might suggest that the term you are looking for is "human decency" or "human kindness". These terms speak toward the brighter aspects of human nature.

W: Thank you for sharing the usage of "human nature", and I am reminded almost simultaneously. I agree with you, and "human decency" serves as a perfect substitute. It's quite important but also challenging to attain the appropriate choice of words, for choosing the improper word may cause a joke especially in front of native speaker. So your suggestion is of great value to me. Thanks a lot!

反馈者质疑写作者用词的准确性（human nature），先详细解释该词的意义，接着举例说明用法，然后给出解决方案，建议使用 human decency 或者 human kindness。写作者感谢反馈者分享 human nature 的用法，赞同反馈者的观点，并且感谢反馈者为其选择恰当的词汇 human decency。接着，反馈者又指出写作文本中存在的其他问题：

R: As I was rereading your essay there was something about its title that caught my attention. It's a small distinction and it's more colloquial than an actual rule:

The question "What composes a good society?" I believe should be rephrased to say "What is a good society composed of?" or "Of what is a good society composed?" The reason for the rephrasing is that society is composed of many things, not by many things. By this I mean that the original question suggests that the elements of society intentionally choose to make the society. Sorry, if that is confusing because it's just a picky thing I noticed. You could also change it to "What constitutes a good society?"

W: Hi, Ava, it's so careful of you to notice the mistake. It's the first time I've known that when its passive form is used, a verb phrase with a "of" does not equal one with a "by". Don't be worried. I've got your point. So "Of what is a good society composed?" can be a better title.

作为英语母语者，反馈者详细阐释了文章标题存在的句法问题，并且给出解决方案。写作者理解了存在的问题并采纳了反馈意见。在反馈者和写作者的多次互动过程中，反馈者首先更正了中方学习者在写作中存在的词汇选择问题，通过举例和提供额外信息等方式完成母语者与二语学习者共同完善文本的任务，并解决了相关问题。母语者是语言的权威裁判，他们发现问题并予以纠正；二语写作者在互动中接受对方的解释和建议，没有提出任何挑战或异议，接受了母语者的判断。

这是专家/新手的互动模式，涉及个人贡献不平衡（主要是美方反馈者给予反馈）和对彼此写作努力的少量互惠反应（中方写作者以接受反馈和感谢对方的反馈为主），这种模式反映在小组成员的不平衡反馈功能实例中，以及写作修改行为中的他人修改上。在这个小组的互动关系中，美方反馈者占优势，他们作为母语者，充当目标文化的代表，他们的判断具有权威性。反馈者评估和评论二语学习者写作的整体质量，并且就可接受性发表声明。写作者听从反馈者的意见，撤回原有的不合理表达。

本研究表明，母语者和二语学习者通过他们的行为共同构建已观察到的4种关系模式，但这并不一定意味着所有参与者都接受这样的关系模式。本研究预测集体互动可以集思广益，反馈者之间的多向多人互动可以促进意义协商和意义构建，但是反思日志的数据也包含了学习者想要获得与我们预想的不同的互动模式。例如，美方写作者提出：

The one thing I would like to be changed would be that we should have been split into partners instead of groups. I feel that I would have had more of a conversation and learned more if I were with a partner instead of a group.

该学习者认为应该组织一对一配对的写作互动活动而不是小组活动，因为两两双向活动可以进行更多的交流，收获更多。"双向同伴修改（不是单向的）提供参与和学习的机会；换言之，同伴双方都可以给予和接受帮助、'教授'和学习如何修改写作文本"（Villamil & de Guerrero, 1996: 69）。

一般观点认为，分担责任的合作风格对学习者有益，但学习者需要一些帮助来实现这一点。本研究对这种观点给予支持，因为它展示了学习者之间大量的合作互动模式。即使学习者最初并没预期到这种关系模式，但本研究表明他们处理得很好，他们的批判意识和读者意识的确有所提高。以下的学习者反思日志说明了这一点：

> Through this, we gradually learn that differences exist because of different traditions, social background, and education systems in line with which comes our different ways of thinking. Finally, communication lets us understand the differences, and we begin to respect others. We had not only to convey our own opinions but also not to offend others. We had to learn to communicate with people we have never seen, try to draw their attention, and make them interested in our topics. This activity has gone far beyond learning writing skills, and we also learn more than that.

由于传统文化、社会背景和教育体系的不同，中西方思维方式之间存在巨大的差异。通过跨洋互动写作活动，中美大学生之间的沟通让双方了解差异，在表达自己意见的同时也尊重他人的不同意见，学会与从未谋面的人进行交流，激发对方的交流兴趣，不让文化差异阻碍反馈的给予和接受。

分析数据发现，中方写作组和美方写作组中体现的写作者和反馈者的互动模式的数量不是均匀分布的。在对中方7个写作组的观察中，一共发现了7个协作互动模式、5个专家/新手互动模式和1个合作互动模式。在对美方6个写作组的观察中，一共发现了7个协作互动模式、4个专家/新手互动模式、2个合作互动模式和2个集体互动模式。中美写作组都以协作互动模式为主，说明中美大学生虽然有认知冲突，但是双方通过互动协商，最终达成共识。由此可见，中美同伴互评是有益的在线协同写作实践，可以被广泛应用于写作教学。中方写作组中协作互动模式最多，说明中国大学生易于接受美国大学生的同伴反馈，尤其是与语言相关的反馈。而美方写作组中出现一定数量的专家/新手互动模式，美国大学生在处理与语言相关的反馈时会坚持自己的观点，无法和中国大学生达成共识并形成合作互动模式，但是会接受与写作文本结构相关的反馈，从而形成专家/新手互动模式。

基于 Unlu 和 Wharton（2015）的一对一师生互动的关系模式，本研究构建了混合小组同伴互评的动态互动模型。图 5.2 展示了通过数据分析得出同伴互评过程中互动行为、互评行为与互动模式的关系。从表面上看，这个论点是线性的：英语母语者和二语学习者在反馈互动中的行为组合有助于形成同伴在线互动中的某些关系模式。实际上，互评行为和互动行为与互动模式之间是相互作用的（本研究用双箭头表示）。本研究具体查看了中美 13 个写作组在在线互动过程中实施的反馈行为，发现双方对写作内容的讨论最多，即信息性反馈最多；双方关于内容的讨论最容易出现认知冲突，但双方会经过协商建立理解并达成新的共识，所以协作互动模式最多。在中方写作小组中，美国大学生会指出中国大学生的语言问题并给出建议，涉及重述、建议、感谢、接受和经验求教等反馈行为较多；中国学生大多会接受母语者的语言建议，做出相应的修改，形成的专家/新手互动模式较多。有时，当美方写作组中的中国大学生指出语言或语法问题时，美方写作者不接受反馈者的意见，不会采纳意见和做出修改，双方无法达成一致，缺少主体间性，不能形成合作互动模式。美方写作小组中不同的反馈者会共同参与任务，形成集体互动。当然，互动模式也会促进写作者的修改和采纳行为，形成多种类型的反馈和支架策略。

本研究支持其他学者的观点，即反馈不应该被看作将自己的写作方式强加给他人，控制学习者写作的简单的、单向的行为，也不单单是写作过程中反馈者和写作者之间的双向行为（Tardy，2006），而是一个多向的过程，反馈者和写作者既要面对其他约束和规范，也要面对其他可感知的权威，如词典、教师反馈等（Unlu & Wharton，2015）。

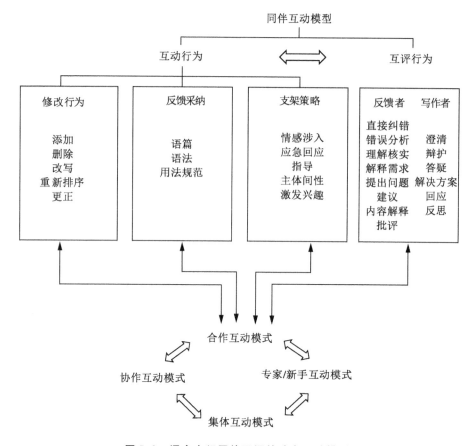

图 5.2 混合小组同伴互评的动态互动模型

5.5 结语

本章描述和分析了网络语境下混合小组中中美大学生的在线反馈互动行为,通过详细对比分析中美大学生的初稿和修改稿,具体地描述中美大学生的在线讨论,并结合小组成员的反思日志,对中美大学生基于反馈的修改、对反馈的采纳和互动中采用的支架策略进行定量与定性分析,有如下发现:

第一,中国大学生在修改稿中实施的作文修改明显多于美国大学生。双方都实施了更正、改写、删除、添加和重新排序 5 种修改行为,但是修改类型的数量排序完全不同。中美大学生的修改方式也不同,中方以自发修改为主,而美方以他人修改为主。第二,中美大学生不会采纳笼统的、不具体的、抽象的及自己不赞成的反馈意见。中国大学生易于采纳关于写作文本的语言形式和语篇结构的建议；而美国大学生更倾向于接受有关文本结构的意见。中美大学生对写作内容和主题进行大量的互动交流，但是不会在修改稿中进行这方面的修改。第三，中美大学生和本国的反馈者之间互动较少，相互作用表现为缺乏主体间性。在中方写作组中，美方反馈者和中方写作者之间使用大量的反馈策略，互动体现主体间性。在美方写作组中，虽然双方互动出现认知冲突，但经过协商建立了理解并达成了新的共识。另外，中方反馈者与其他反馈者之间偶尔出现互动。第四，两个写作组因不同的互动行为和反馈行为形成了不同的互动模式。在中方写作组中，写作者的修改数量多，采纳反馈的数量多，中美大学生之间支架策略明显，形成的互动模式以协助互动模式和专家/新手互动模式为主。在美方写作组中，中美大学生在互动时出现认知冲突，写作者的修改数量和采纳反馈的数量相对少一些，但双方经过协商共建知识并达成了新的共识，形成的互动以协作模式居多。另外，由于中方反馈者与其他反馈者之间偶尔出现互动，因此有少量的集体互动模式。

在混合小组中，中美同伴互评过程中反馈行为、互动行为、互动模式之间是相互作用的，同伴反馈的行为会促成某个互动行为，互动中行为的组合有助于形成在线互动中的某些关系模式；同一个小组的互动模式也呈动态，前几轮互动可能形成从属模式，后几轮互动也可能又转换为合作互动模式。

本章根据编码方案，运用多案例分析方法，定量统计同伴互动行为，构建混合小组同伴互动模型，并在互动理论和最近发展区理论的指导下进行定性分析。下一章将以定量和定性相结合的研究方法，基于社会文化理论，考察二语写作中的中美同伴互动模式，并探讨互动模式生成的影响因素。

第六章 二语写作中的中美同伴互动模式

本章分析二语写作中的中美同伴互动模式，共包括 4 个小节。第一节介绍本章的研究语料和研究问题；第二节分析中美同伴互动模式的生成，通过考察任务协商期间执行的语言功能、协作写作过程中的发起和响应功能，以及文本共建期间执行的修改功能，从平等性和相互性两个维度识别同伴互动模式；第三节结合反思日志和在线讨论，分析中美同伴互动模式生成的影响因素；第四节进行本章小结。

6.1 语料与研究问题

本章语料选自第 18 轮和第 20 轮跨洋互动写作。第 18 轮始于 2017—2018 年第二学期期中，第 20 轮始于 2019—2020 年第二学期期中，这两轮互动的主题相同，项目实施周期相同，都持续两周。在项目实施过程中，中美大学生观看《立春》和《蒙娜丽莎的微笑》(*Mona Lisa Smile*) 两部电影。参与者在规定时间内（两周）完成相同话题和相同体裁的写作任务，上传至在线写作平台。具体步骤如下：首先，中国学生上传初稿；接着，美国同伴和中国同伴对初稿进行反馈，中国学生和同伴的多轮二元互动被自动记录在讨论、评论和历史模块中；然后，中国学生上传修改稿；最后，中国学生写一份反思日志。美国学生也是同样的步骤：上传初稿，进行互动协商，上传修改稿和写反思日志。

数据来自第 18 轮中国写作者 9 人（只选取既有反思日志又有修改稿的 7 人）和第 20 轮中国写作者 26 人（其中 2 人未上传反思日志，1 人无修改稿，符合筛选要求的为 23 人）。根据研究需要只选取中国学生写作互动小组的相关语料（每个小组中有两位美国同伴和一两位中国同伴），收集数据包括中国学生初稿（30 篇）、修改稿（30 篇）、中国学生和同伴的在线讨论（中美 45 对，中中 30 对），以及中国写作者和美国学生的反思日志（各 30 份）。

对二语写作中的中美同伴互动模式的研究，我们主要思考以下两个问题：

① 在跨洋互动写作中，二语写作小组生成了哪些同伴互动模式？

② 互动模式的生成受哪些因素的影响？

本章基于社会文化理论，以定量和定性相结合的方式，从任务协商期间执行的语言功能、协作写作过程中的发起和响应功能、文本共建期间执行的修改功能 3 个方面分析二语写作中的中美同伴互动模式，并结合反思日志和在线讨论，分析同伴互动模式生成的影响因素。

6.2 中美同伴互动模式的生成

6.2.1 中美同伴互动模式的识别

表 6.1 呈现了语言功能的类型、频次和卡方检验结果。总体而言，在二语写作小组互动过程中，写作者与中美同伴在语言功能的使用频次上具有显著性差异（$\chi^2=25.325$，$df=5$，$p=0.000$ vs $\chi^2=35.338$，$df=5$，$p=0.000$），说明写作者与中美同伴的语言贡献不平衡。但是，部分语言功能子类的频次不具有显著性特征。在中中小组中，写作者与同伴的建议和同意两种语言功能的数量具有显著性差异，阐述、陈述、启发和不同意 4 种语言功能不具有显著性差异。在中美小组中，陈述和建议具有显著性差异，阐述、启发、同意和不同意不具有显著性差异。这说明写作者与中美同伴在大部分语言子类上贡献平衡，双方的互动具有一定的平等性。

表 6.1 同伴互动小组语言功能的卡方检验

类型	中中小组（频次）		卡方检验	中美小组（频次）		卡方检验
	写作者	同伴		写作者	同伴	
阐述	62	82	$\chi^2=0.726$，$df=1$，$p=0.394$	87	131	$\chi^2=0.174$，$df=1$，$p=0.676$
陈述	65	78	$\chi^2=2.377$，$df=1$，$p=0.123$	105	116	$\chi^2=7.647$，$df=1$，$p=0.006$

类型	中中小组（频次）		卡方检验	中美小组（频次）		卡方检验
	写作者	同伴		写作者	同伴	
建议	22	86	$\chi^2=15.584$, $df=1$, $p=0.000$	23	102	$\chi^2=21.138$, $df=1$, $p=0.000$
启发	5	6	$\chi^2=0.393$, $df=1$, $p=0.531$	5	16	$\chi^2=1.817$, $df=1$, $p=0.178$
同意	21	15	$\chi^2=5.727$, $df=1$, $p=0.017$	24	22	$\chi^2=3.286$, $df=1$, $p=0.070$
不同意	11	21	$\chi^2=0.518$, $df=1$, $p=0.472$	8	18	$\chi^2=0.650$, $df=1$, $p=0.420$
总计	186	288	$\chi^2=25.325$, $df=5$, $p=0.000$	252	405	$\chi^2=35.338$, $df=5$, $p=0.000$

表 6.2 显示了发起和响应功能的频次和卡方检验结果。在二语写作小组互动过程中，写作者发起与中美同伴响应的频次不具有显著性差异（$\chi^2=1.747$, $df=1$, $p=0.186$ vs $\chi^2=1.056$, $df=1$, $p=0.304$），说明在互动过程中同伴积极地给予回应，双方的互动具有一定的相互性。但是同伴发起和写作者响应的频次具有显著性差异，说明写作者对同伴反馈的响应程度不够，双方相互性不高。无论是中中小组还是中美小组，同伴发起的数量显著高于写作者响应的数量，同伴响应的数量也高于写作者发起的数量。部分原因是同伴数量多（三四人），写作者人数少（一两人）。

表 6.2 同伴互动小组发起和响应功能的卡方检验

组别	写作者发起（频次）	同伴响应（频次）	卡方检验	同伴发起（频次）	写作者响应（频次）	卡方检验
中中小组	14	63	$\chi^2=1.747$, $df=1$, $p=0.186$	225	172	$\chi^2=34.770$, $df=1$, $p=0.000$
中美小组	36	95	$\chi^2=1.056$, $df=1$, $p=0.304$	310	216	$\chi^2=61.812$, $df=1$, $p=0.000$

表 6.3 显示，中国大学生共实施了 904 个修改行为，他人修改的数量

显著高于自发修改的数量（$\chi^2=22.305$，$df=1$，$p=0.000$），高频率地使用他人修改功能表明写作者和同伴之间具有高相互性。

表 6.3 中国大学生修改类型的卡方检验

维度	子类	数量/次	卡方检验
修改类型	他人修改	523	$\chi^2=22.305$，$df=1$，$p=0.000$
	自发修改	381	
总计		904	

6.2.2 中美同伴互动模式的特征

基于上述数据和前人确定的互动模式，互动小组共展示了5种互动模式：集体、协作、合作、专家/新手和主导/主导。表6.4显示，无论是中中小组还是中美小组，都是以协作型互动模式居多（115，57.5%），约占所有互动模式的二分之一。中中小组的互动模式以协作型为主（44%），以合作型（30%）和专家/新手型为辅（23%）；中美小组的互动模式集中于协作型（71%）。中美小组的互动有少量的集体型和主导/主导型，中中小组的互动无主导/主导型。

表 6.4 同伴互动小组互动模式的数据统计

类型	中中小组	中美小组	总计（%）
集体	3	7	10（5%）
协作	44	71	115（57.5%）
合作	30	11	41（20.5%）
专家/新手	23	9	32（16%）
主导/主导	0	2	2（1%）

6.3 中美同伴互动模式的影响因素

分析上述数据发现，中中互动小组和中美互动小组生成的互动模式的数量不是均匀分布的，因此有必要考察影响小组互动模式异同的因素，以及协作型互动模式比其他类型出现更频繁的原因。为此，本研究仔细分析了中美同伴的反思日志和后续访谈，不断"过滤"分析、检查新数据，将新数据的相关部分编码到现有类别中。增加反思日志和后续访谈数据的意义在于提供阐明关系模式的影响因素和关系模式的结果两种视角，这两种视角不能单凭观察获得。对反思日志数据的分析，不仅可以为观测数据得出的概念和类别提供进一步佐证，还可以帮助理解关系模式的可能影响因素及其后果。

本研究在分析所有反思日志和后续访谈数据后，生成了以下几个影响因素的类别：英语母语者对自我英语水平的认知，英语母语者对二语学习者英语水平的认知，二语学习者对自我二语水平的认知，参与活动的动机，写作任务的性质，反馈经验与期望，跨文化交流，以及对写作的批判意识和读者意识。前面几类是同伴互动模式的影响因素；而最后两类不同，它们指的是反馈的潜在后果。上述影响因素分为个体、情境和社会因素，个体因素包括母语者/二语学习者对语言水平的感知、参与动机、反馈经验与期望；情境因素包括写作任务的性质、反馈出现的频次和互动环境等；社会因素包括跨文化交流和思维方式差异等。

6.3.1 个体因素

英语母语者语言水平的自我认知是指母语者如何认识与二语同伴进行网络互动过程中自己的角色。美国同伴的反思日志提到，英语对二语学习者来说很难，对于母语者来说也不容易，每个人都有可能犯错（如"I learned that the English language is hard not only for language learners, but also for the native speakers themselves. Everyone makes mistakes."）。母语反馈者的这种表述可能意味着在提供反馈的同时，他们知道自己的反馈不一定全部正确，双方在互动过程中须互相学习，协作完成任务。或许存在外部权威（譬如老师）对同一篇文章采取不同的处理方式。因此，我们可以假设母语同伴参与反馈互动时受到这种看法的影响。正如某位美国同伴所提及的：

> While I maintain that my analysis was proper, I did take into account a few of the remarks I received and dealt with them to make my analysis more clear. Through the commentaries I received, I was brought to clarify this point, which I believe augments my essay.

虽然母语者认为自己的分析是正确的，但是因为多位中方反馈者质疑母语者写作中的同一个问题，母语者不得不认真思考评论内容，并处理了存在的问题,以便使分析更加清晰。由此可见,英语母语者对自我英语水平的认知影响了他的互动行为。

英语母语者对二语学习者英语水平的认知反映了母语者对二语学习者英语水平的定位。如中美小组互动摘录所示:

> I would like to add one final reflection which is that I have been very impressed by my Chinese pen-pals. The depth of conversation that we have had about the nature of arguments is something that I did not think I would have with speaking in a secondary language. Yolanda and Harv, you have both been very engaging conversationists and written in a way that was easy to read …

美国大学生对中国大学生的印象非常深刻,因为双方关于议论文性质的谈论深度,是美国大学生觉得非母语者无法达到的;他称赞中国大学生非常善于交谈,不仅给出的反馈意见可读性强,同时还给写作者留有思考余地。当然,也有美国大学生认识到二语学习者的困难,如"Reading Chinese students' essays allowed me to contemplate similar difficulties I face when trying to compose an essay or piece of writing in Spanish, my second language.",该母语者阅读了中国学生的论文后,想到自己在尝试用西班牙语(他的第二语言)撰写文章时面临了类似的困难。

二语学习者二语水平的自我认知包括学习者对他们自身缺点的感知。例如"I am not sure whether I have a good command of making English comments on others' articles on paper, but at least I gradually get familiar with and understand it.",中国大学生对自己是否能够很好地对他人的文章发表英文评论表现出不自信,期望同伴尤其是美国同伴给予语言方面的建议。再如,"I understand it would not be that easy to master idiomatic expressions proficiently. I need to immerse myself in more English language context.",中国大学生认为熟练掌握习语有一定的难度。

这些自我认知可能与反馈互动模型中的其他类别相关,如反馈体验。这些体验可能会导致学习者在语言技能方面形成某种自我认知,如"Chinese students tend to care more about the questions that they also held before but lately were solved. For example, they put forward the question about the tense."(摘自中方写作组的"修改报告"),即中国大学生更关心他们之前也遇到过但最近已经解决了的问题,如时态问题;"I don't know it's because we ESL learners are not that sensitive or just because we treat this kind of difference as natural as a part of our life so that we hardly mention about the cultural differences.",即中国大学生很少提及文化差异,可能对这个话题不敏感,或者把这种差异视为生活的一部分。在这种情况下,二语学习者对自身二语水平的自我认知似乎受到反馈体验的影响。反过来,这可能会影响二语学习者反馈的内容和参与反馈互动的方式。

学习者对同伴反馈的感知影响他们的行为和整个群体的互动(Cho, 2017;Sato, 2017)。母语者对二语学习者英语水平的肯定是生成大量协作型互动模式的一个原因。高水平的同伴往往比低水平的同伴提出更多的建议,尤其是当其他同伴的熟练程度较低时。在这种情况下,熟练程度更高的同伴在互动中担当"专家"的角色,而低水平的同伴则担任"新手"的角色(Allen & Mills, 2016)。因此,相对优势的感知差异对互动模式的生成有影响。但是在小组中,专家的角色非常灵活。(Storch, 2002)在专家/新手互动模式中,角色不断切换,写作者在进行中国文化的交流时是专家,在同伴擅长的话题中则变为新手。在执行协作任务期间,即使没有被分配正式角色,小组成员也会根据自身优势或兴趣接任特定角色。(Kost, 2011)

多数参与者的动机是交流文化、学习语言知识和写作技巧,如中国学生的反思日志提及的:

> Of equal importance is that I can acquire more advanced expressions in English when I was reading other people' essays. By reading the passages of native English speakers, I learned quite a lot of idiomatic English. I would note down some expressions to improve my writing skills later.

该日志解释了双方进行多轮主题交流时提供具体反馈的动机,即希望在阅读别人的文章时,可以获得更高级的表达方式。中国学生希望专注于提高他们对目标语中习语的理解水平,如"I can have a better understanding of idiomatic expressions through intensive discussion with native speakers",通过与母语者的密切讨论,他们可以更好地理解习语。除了语言方面外,他们还希望了解不同的写作方式和技巧,如"And through reading the passages of native English speakers, I learned quite a lot of idiomatic English. I would note down some expressions to improve my writing skills later.",即阅读英语母语者的写作段落,可以学到习语和一些表达方式,提高自己的写作水平。

中国学生希望通过互动了解对方的文化或者对方对某一问题的看法,如第20轮跨洋互动写作中第1篇反思日志:

> The comments also led to some very interesting discussion about differences between the American and Chinese culture, and how they affected our views on these two films and the ideals the characters had. I enjoyed my time conversing with the Chinese students very much, and I gained many valuable perspectives from it.

互动评论可以引起一些关于中美文化差异的非常有趣的讨论。中国学生还希望了解来自不同文化的同伴的思维方式,如第3篇反思日志:

> When I read the passages from America, I could feel the different ways of expression between Chinese students and native speakers. Generally speaking, their languages are more concise and accurate. In some cases, although there were no new words involved, some of the sentences in their essays are hard for me to understand. I wonder whether they have the same feeling with us. I think it was the different thinking patterns and language expression customs that affected our understanding. But I regarded it as a great opportunity to narrow the gap in expression.

美国大学生让中国大学生体会到母语者的不同表达方式。美国大学生的语言更简洁准确,不同的思维模式和语言表达习惯影响着双方的理解,但这是缩小表达水平差距的好机会。

学习者不同的参与动机可能会影响他们对待同伴反馈的态度,如反思日志摘录所示,"I did not necessarily disagree with any interpretation of my essay, because I believe that any opinions provided that differed from my own had more to do with varying interpretations of the films.",这位学习者的参与动机是进行观点和文化的交流,因此他不会反对反馈者关于电影的不同意见;"It is beneficial to learn how to operate cohesively in groups with individuals from cultures foreign to your own. Learning ways to offer and receive criticism without allowing cultural differences to block productivity is an important skill set to develop.",学习者的参与动机是学习如何与不同文化的人进行交流,因此学习者认为应该学会给予和接受批评,而不是让文化差异阻碍沟通。中美大学生希望通过互动了解对方的文化或者对方对某一问题的看法,因此他们会对来自不同文化的同伴的不同思维方式和语言表达习惯持积极的态度。

反馈经历与期望是指学习者已有的反馈经历和期待接收的反馈类型。反馈经历可能会导致在语言技能方面形成某种自我认知,如中国大学生更关心自己曾经遇到过但目前已经解决了的问题,如时态问题。

反馈期望类型是指学习者想要接收的反馈类型。有些学生在反思日志中表达了他们的偏好:

> I am so grateful for the suggestions from my group members both from China and America, and especially from one friend called Stephen Messimer, who has given me quite a lot of useful suggestions with detailed illustrations.
>
> This experience of mine is indeed meaningful and inspiring, in that we can not only learn how to write better but also exchange our values with students from two different continents.

在上述两种情况中,写作者表示偏向于具体的建议和与文化差异相关的交流(exchange our values with students from two different continents),这可能与合作关系和常规关系有关。正如上文提到的,这种关系在本书的数据中比较常见,说明学生的期望与他们的反馈体验之间具有一致性。

6.3.2 情境因素

写作任务的性质影响互动模式的性质。该项目的写作任务是借助影片情节，针对中美文化、非语言策略、交际策略等方面表达观点，要求针对写作文本的组织、设计、一致性和语言等方面提供评论。学习者在完成写作任务的过程中，学习如何与来自不同文化或持不同观点的同伴进行积极、有效的沟通，如"It is beneficial to learn how to operate cohesively in groups with individuals from cultures foreign to your own. Learning ways to offer and receive criticism without allowing cultural differences to block productivity is an important skill set to develop."。由此引发大量的协作型和部分专家/新手型互动模式。

然而，部分同伴只发布一次评论，可能觉得仅分享观点就足以完成任务，或者只是为了满足课程要求，抑或观察他人的合作进行间接参与，出现一定数量的一轮互动，这降低了其他互动模式出现的可能性。部分美国同伴小组成员表现出了个体能动性，但未表现出协作能动性（Li & Zhu, 2017b）。也有少量中国大学生和同伴各抒己见，观点未达成一致，生成主导/主导型互动模式的情况。

例如，第 20 轮跨洋互动合作第 6 篇中美同伴评价：

> I thought it was very interesting that you noted how music plays a role in both films. Both films used music to enhance the atmosphere of a scene. Music in *Mona Lisa Smile* is used subtly to convey the feelings of characters to the audience. While never outright stated by the characters themselves, the audience is still able to get a sense of what the characters are thinking and feeling during a scene by what music is playing in a scene. In *And the Spring Comes* music is a very important part of the story. Wang's goal is to become a singer in Beijing. The music also is more focused on Wang herself. The song in the beginning tells the audience all of her hopes and dreams，and the music later on in the film conveys Wang's emotions to the audience when her dreams of being a singer get crushed.

美国同伴对写作者的文章进行了概括性总结和赞赏，未提出意见。写作者感谢同伴的赞赏，希望同伴提出更多的建议（Thanks for your comments. We hope to see more of your suggestions and look forward to your reply.），但是同伴未给予回复，双方只有一轮互动。

反馈出现频次影响互动模式的性质。在二语学习者和中国同伴互动过程中，多个同伴提出相同的反馈意见，增加了反馈被采纳的可能性，多个同伴提出的相同反馈更有利于反馈被采纳。换言之，多个同伴反馈更具说服力，比单个反馈更有效。例如，在第 20 轮跨洋互动写作第 16 篇在线讨论中，中国同伴和美国同伴提出了相似的建议：

R1：But I think you should give a general sentence to tell us about the main meaning of your essay at the beginning，that is，the topic sentence of the whole text. If you can add it and more views about yourself to your essay，I think it will be greater.

R2：From your article，I read a lot of conclusions about two films，but I think you should get more your personal analysis and statement from the two movies. Your theme of the film and culture should be more explicit. Now it is a little vague.

两位都提出增加文章的主题句、更多的个人分析和陈述，以使主题更明确。多个同伴提出相同的反馈意见，同伴之间形成互动，由此生成集体互动模式。

在同伴互动过程中，有互动双方无法解决问题而向其他同伴请教的情况，从而形成集体互动模式。例如，在第 20 轮跨洋互动写作第 2 篇中，中国同伴提出建议"Some paragraph is too long to read, which you can divide into two parts."。写作者赞同同伴的观点，认为有些段落太长，不便于阅读：

Indeed，some paragraphs like the second one are too long to read. We will make appropriate changes without changing the original meaning. But will the separation of paragraphs lead to incomplete content or unclear structure of the article? How do you deal with such a problem? Do you think it will be improved if we replace some of the long sentences in the text with simple sentences，or highlight the central sentence of the paragraph? Do you have any suggestions for our idea?

但是写作者担心分成短一点的段落会导致文章内容不完整或者结构不清晰,并就通过将长句换成简单句或者突出段落的中心句来解决段落太长这个问题是否可行,向中国同伴请教。中国同伴回复:

> We think it may help you to simplify the paragraph by changing a complex sentence into a simple sentence. But will this make you unable to express your thoughts completely? As you said, highlighting the key sentences may have effect.

中国同伴赞同写作者的观点,认为把复杂句改成简单句可以简化段落,但担心简化的段落无法完全表达自己的想法,支持凸显关键句子的方案。写作者也认为将复杂句改为简单句会改变原义,但还未找到解决方案。写作者征询美国同伴关于修改长段落的建议,美国同伴回复:

> I agree that paragraphs can be lengthy, but breaking them up might be confusing. My advice would be to cut back on any non-essential information. I do this in my own writing. I ask myself "Does the reader need this information to understand my point, or would they understand my point if this information wasn't in the essay?" Most of the time, you will find some unnecessary sentences that can be deleted.
>
> Also, headings might be helpful in your essay. It will help the reader stay organized when reading each section and you may feel more comfortable breaking up paragraphs if you decide to include headings.

美国同伴建议删除不必要的信息和使用副标题来划分较长的段落,这不仅可以降低阅读难度,还可以使文章内容一目了然。在这次互动过程中,小组成员共同协商写作任务,承担共同协商的个人角色,形成集体互动模式。

本研究中的跨洋互动写作项目创造了异步在线反馈的互动环境,项目的参与者轮流在讨论区回复,机会均等。写作者先完成文章的写作,接着同伴进行反馈,双方协商,然后写作者再写修改稿。在协作配对的情况下,他们通过轮流回复完成任务。此外,异步协作写作给予参与者充分的回复和反思时间,从而形成较多的协作和专家/新手互动模式。例如,在第20轮跨洋互动写作第3篇在线讨论中,中国同伴提出自己的质疑"But there is only one drawback that is the title is simple and clear, but I don't understand why it is 'like the wind', and its relationship with 'wind' is not very clear.",写作者回应:

> As for your suggestion, the analogy we made in the title, "like the wind" is actually explained at the beginning of the third paragraph of the article … There is also a connection between the style of description and women's view of marriage at the beginning of the fourth paragraph … In the last paragraph, we also made a summary of "brave women, can be the most care-free wind by yourself". So our definition of wind is free and unfettered … We will consider adding more female spirit and the relationship with wind reflected in the two films in the follow-up improvements.

写作者回应在文章第三段、第四段的开头和最后一段中都有 like the wind 的相关解释,考虑在后续的改进中增加更多的对女性精神的描写及两部电影中所体现的与"风"的关系的阐述。同伴感谢写作者对"风"的具体解释(Thank you for your specific interpretation of the image of wind. I understand the meaning of wind. The definition of wind is free and unrestrained, just like the spirit of female courage. This is the use of analogy. I get it. Thank you!)。

6.3.3 社会因素

跨文化因素和思维方式影响互动模式的性质。在跨洋互动写作中,来自不同文化群体的学习者对互动有不同的期望。在线讨论和反思报告都显示,中国学习者希望美国同伴能多关注语言,中国同伴的互动更侧重于修改作文,指出同伴写作中的问题、缺点和错误,提供负面反馈和批评,希望通过批评性和建设性的反馈帮助同伴提高文本质量;而美国同伴对中国的教育和文化差异比对写作本身更感兴趣。相较于中美小组,中中小组中参与者双方对文化差异的观点一致,相关交流较少;而文化差异的交流却是中美小组协商的重点。比如,在第 20 轮跨洋互动写作第 3 篇在线互动中,美国同伴提出问题:

> You also discussed female characters in both films verbally

denouncing marriage. Do you think the timing of both movies (*Mona Lisa Smile* in the 1950s and *And the Spring Comes* in the 1990s) impacts how they viewed marriage? In other words, were Wang Cailing's and Katherine's perspective about marriage the same?

美国同伴就两部不同年代的电影中的主角对婚姻的看法是否一致进行提问，写作者回复：

> Let me talk about my understanding of the background of the times. I am not so familiar with the historical and cultural background of the United States in the 1950s, but I know what China in the 1990s was like. If a woman did not marry, it was a staggering thing, and she would be regarded as a geek or alien. I think Wang Cailing is such a courageous woman that she challenges prejudices and is so brave …
>
> In addition, I think Wang Cailing and Katherine have different understandings of marriage. Katherine encourages students to focus on their own development … The desire to become a housewife has never been completely abandoned … Wang Cailing's view of marriage is even more tragic. If she can't find a suitable lover, she would rather not get married all her life. Her attitude towards the relationship with men actually shows a full affirmation of self-identity—following her heart.

写作者介绍了中国电影的时代背景，但是对美国电影的时代背景不了解，并且陈述了两部电影主角对婚姻的看法。美国同伴就电影背景和主角对婚姻的看法继续与写作者交流：

> I really appreciated your insight about marriage in China in the 1990s. It is quite similar to life for women in the 1950s. To elaborate, there weren't a lot of opportunities for women to be successful in the workforce. Although some women went to college, it was typically reserved for wealthy women. The degree was also looked at as a status symbol, instead of to be utilized for finding a job. To give an example …
>
> I agree with your interpretation of Wang Cailing and Katherine's

views on marriage. It was also really insightful to note that *Mona Lisa Smile* is intended to be a comedy and *And the Spring Comes* is intended to be a tragedy, which definitely plays into how the story ends.

A few scenes that stuck out to me in particular is when Katherine never rejects her boyfriend's proposal. In fact, he is the one … On the other hand, Wang Cailing turns down two proposals …

美国同伴介绍了美国电影的时代背景，赞同写作者对两位主角的婚姻观的解读，列举了对待婚姻态度的令人印象深刻的场景和自己身边的真实案例。接着，写作者又开启新的话题：

In fact, I think our conversation about marriage has benefited both of us. I also noticed that your article mentioned patriarchy. Do you think that only women are oppressed by patriarchy? I find that you have also noticed Hu Jinquan's unfair experience in the movie *And The Spring Comes*. As a man in the movie, he has also been scolded and cursed by other men. If you don't think that only women are victims by patriarchy, then what kind of angle can we use to think about the opposition between men in the men-dominating society?

写作者发现同伴论文中提到的男权制不仅仅是指女性受到父权制的压迫，并就如何思考男人之间的对立向同伴请教。美国同伴交流观点：

The way we discuss patriarchy typically has to do with the oppression of females. But as you pointed out, men can be oppressed by this system. (I will use America as my example because that is the culture I am most familiar with.) Patriarchy is typically seen as forcing both men and women into stereotyped roles … Hu Jinquan is a great example of someone who would be criticized for not being "masculine" enough. Our society has gotten better at …

If you are looking to adding something to your essay, you could mention how Hu Jinquan is excluded from society.

美国同伴表达自己讨论父权制的方式与对女性的压迫有关，建议写作者如果关注男人对男人的压迫，可以提及剧中人物是如何因此被排除在社会之外的。美国同伴关心中国的男女平等程度，写作者回应：

> I read your explanation of patriarchy, that forcing men and women into their own stereotypes, which makes my original vague concept of patriarchy clearer.
>
> I quite agree with you. In fact, in order to meet the expectations of society, many men or women have to play the role they should play, hiding their nature, but the patriarchal oppression of vulnerable groups has never stopped. I used to hear of the "toxic masculinity" in an article about #MeToo movement and it is also the embodiment of the existence of oppression.
>
> To answer your question, maybe because I'm still in school, and I haven't stepped into the society, I don't feel oppressed or excluded by the group. In fact, the equality between men and women in China is relatively high …

写作者感谢同伴对男权主义的解释，详细说明现代中国的男女平等程度已有明显提高。中美同伴关注文化的交流，因此，协作型是中美小组主要的互动模式类型，而以平行的方式表达观点的合作模式在中中小组占有一定比例。

但是，也存在中西思维方式不同导致双方各执己见，观点无法达成一致的情况。例如，在第 20 轮跨洋互动写作第 12 篇在线讨论中，美国同伴提出自己的观点：

> While I feel like your analysis in *And the Spring Comes* is a little far-fetch due to the feminism theme, I can see your point of view. If you want to keep the feminism theme, perhaps you could explain in the beginning that this was a side theme in that particular movie and detail the main overarching theme. This would allow the reader to understand your argument better. I also would try to avoid generalization.

美国同伴认为电影中女权主义的主题有点牵强，如果写作者想保留女权主义的主题，需要解释这是电影的一个次要主题，并详细说明主要主

题。写作者不赞同同伴的观点:

> I am honored that you can understand my point of view, but I think it is not far-fetched to analyze *And the Spring Comes* from the point of feminism. Perhaps, the theme of *And the Spring Comes* is mostly reflected in thinking about dreams and reality through the pursuit of art. But I think this movie also reflects feminism, which is a major theme. We can see from the movie that although Wang Cailing was rejected by love and dreams ... which reflects women's challenge to tradition. Moreover, in the film review, various kinds of women are depicted, such as the simple and lovely Song. When Hu Jinquan was insulted ... This shows that when men suffer setbacks, their revenge is always directed at innocent women, which shows that women are only appendages of men and the society. Through the description of women in the movie, we can see the unequal status of men and women, which is the basic resistance of feminism. When I was writing movie reviews, I mainly linked the two films through feminism. I think that through the common comparison between the two films, readers can understand the theme better.

写作者认为,对女权主义主题进行分析并不牵强,并举例进行了说明。但是美国同伴仍然坚持女权主义不是主要主题:

> Perhaps it is not far-fetched but it is simply just not the main theme ... I just believe you should state that initially. I think the idea of feminism as the connection between two movies is a great idea and allows you to analyze one central theme from two different viewpoints. This essentially allows you to connect the two movies (similarities) but also contrast them by culture and social background.

美国同伴认为,可以从两个不同角度来分析一个中心主题,将两部电影联系起来(相似之处),也可以从文化和社会背景两个视角对比两部电影。因此,写作者和同伴双方观点未达成一致,形成主导/主导型互动模式。

反思日志还呈现出学习者的批判意识和读者意识,它们是同伴互动的潜在结果。反思日志的数据表明,学习者对写作的整体反馈活动给予高度评价,部分被归因于他们的反馈体验。但是,很多学习者批评反馈活动的时间、形式和方式。下面举的例子节选自中国大学生的反思日志,提及了反馈互动可以增强批判思维:

> When I was communicating with American partners, we reached an agreement very smoothly, and we both thought the comments from each side were reasonable. However, my essay was greeted with more questions and disagreements when we were doing peer assessment with my classmates. Even though we tried to convince each other, we ended up with reservations. Anyway, I enjoyed the discussion with both sides of my partners, which allowed me to make improvement in different perspectives. Our thought can be different but in harmony. It is a very valuable experience for me to improve my English writing and critical thinking ability.

在这篇摘录中,中国大学生比较了与美国同伴和本国同伴进行互动的不同体验:与美国同伴沟通时,双方非常顺利地达成了协议,认为彼此的意见都是合理的。但是,与中国同伴进行反馈时,会遇到更多的问题和不同意见。尽管双方试图说服对方,但最后还是持保留意见。一方面,这说明中方反馈者倾向于给出指正性反馈,批判意识强;另一方面,不同的人对同一个问题的看法是不同的。在不同的社会环境下讨论相同的问题,可以碰撞出火花,不同的想法是可以协调的。这表明二语学习者已经形成了对写作的批判意识,意识到这只是看问题的视角不同,增强了从不同视角看问题的意识。

同伴互动增强了学习者的读者意识。美方反馈者在反思日志里提及了读者意识:

> Overall, I found the feedback very helpful, and it helped me to learn how to view my essay objectively and understand how the audience may view it. I feel the advice helped me structure my essay much better and create a more cohesive essay with a better flow. The

comments also led to some very interesting discussion about differences between the U. S. and Chinese cultures, and how they affected our views on these two films and the ideals the characters had.

美国大学生认为,在与不同文化的人进行交流时,应该考虑到对方文化,使用对方文化中同等的概念传达观点,以达到读者友好的目的;反馈互动可以帮助学习者从他人视角看待自己的写作,反馈互动让学习者增强读者意识。另外,美国大学生的读者意识强,在互动时会主动为对方考虑,让反馈更易于被对方理解和接受。下面中国大学生的反思日志也证实了这一点:

> From an e-mail, we can also tell a distinct difference between Chinese style and English style. When I was writing an e-mail to my American partner, I found it seemed that I was writing a note in TEM-4. I strictly obey the rules, from salution to signature, in a formal way. After receiving a reply from them, I made a comparison between two e-mails. I found that the e-mail from my American partner was written in a more casual and friendly way. They would use some sentences like, "please feel free to look at it", "but if is okay", or "but if it is convenient to you". It gives us a feeling that they are considerate of us. And my e-mail was written in a more direct way and completely took my own wishes into consideration, such as "expecting your early reply".

从中国大学生的反思日志可以看出,美国大学生会以随意和友好的方式达到读者友好的目的,说明美国大学生的读者意识强;中国大学生在这方面有所欠缺。

本研究中发现的跨洋互动写作混合小组的互动模式与之前在协同写作研究中确定的一对一/小组互动方式类似。具体来说,首先,本研究中偶尔出现的集体互动模式在某种程度上与 Donato(1994、2004)的集体模式、Storch(2002)的合作模式、Li & Zhu(2013)的集体支架相似。但是,本研究小组成员的集体互动模式并不像他们研究报告中的那样稳定。混合小组的集体互动模式具有动态性且与其他模式混合,与 Li & Kim

(2016) 的研究结果一致。例如，在第 20 轮第 2 篇中，写作者和中国同伴由协作互动模式转换为两位中国学生和美国同伴的集体互动模式。同时，本研究小组成员的集体互动模式出现的频率不像以往研究报告中那样频繁，仅有两例，这可以用写作者的读者报告中的观点来解释，"The one thing I would like to be changed would be that we should have been split into partners instead of groups. I feel that I would have had more of a conversation and learned more if I were with a partner instead of a group."，这表明学习者更倾向于配对的、两两双向的互动，而不是多人多向的集体互动模式。

其次，本研究中的合作互动模式和专家/新手互动模式，与 Unlu & Wharton（2015）的常规互动和从属互动模式、Storch（2002）和 Li & Kim（2016）的专家/新手模式及 Li & Zhu（2013）的权威/回应和主导/撤回模式类似。在这两种互动模式中，1 名或 2 名成员对写作任务有更多的控制权，对文本构建做出更大的贡献。不同的是，Storch（2002）中的专家和新手是根据学生的语言水平来定义的，Unlu & Wharton（2015）将教师定义为专家，将学生定义为新手；Li & Kim（2016）提出的专家和新手主要是根据学习者对研究课题的不同熟悉程度来定义的。反馈者在互动过程中起主导作用，写作者处于顺从地位。这一结果表明，除了语言能力和专业知识外，不同的反馈地位也可以体现在不同的层面上，并且能够产生最近发展区。

最后，本研究中协作模式的发现与 Unlu & Wharton（2015）提出的合作模式相呼应。在这种互动模式中，反馈者和写作者双方对书面文本都不拥有绝对的控制权，两两双向互动，主体间性的搭架策略明显。虽然双方在协作活动中可能发生认知冲突，但是小组成员在协商过程中形成了新的理解并达成共识。该模式不同于 Bradley 等（2010）和 Li & Kim（2016）的协作模式，这种模式中个体之间以平行的方式工作，很少为彼此写作做出贡献。

6.4 结语

本章基于社会文化理论，运用定量分析和定性分析相结合的研究方法，综合任务协商期间执行的语言功能、协作写作过程中的发起和响应功能、文本共建期间执行的修改功能3个方面考察跨洋互动写作中的同伴互动模式,并结合反思日志和在线讨论,分析同伴互动模式生成的影响因素。研究结果显示,写作者和中美同伴的语言贡献数量基本平衡,双方的互动具有一定的平等性。大量的他人修改亦说明写作者和同伴之间具有高相互性。但是,因每组同伴数量高于写作者数量,写作者未对同伴反馈做出一一响应。

互动小组形成集体、协作、合作、专家/新手和主导/主导5种互动模式。其中,协作型互动模式约占一半。中中小组的互动模式以协作型为主,以合作型和专家/新手型为辅;中美小组的互动模式集中于协作型。虽然双方互动出现认知冲突,但多数小组经过协商建立了理解并达成了新的共识,因此形成的互动以协作模式居多。有少量的集体型和主导/主导型互动模式。同伴互动模式受母语者/二语学习者的语言水平感知、参与动机和反馈经验与期望等个体因素,写作任务的性质、反馈出现频次和互动环境等情境因素,跨文化交际和思维方式等社会因素的影响。学习者具有批判意识和读者意识是同伴互动行为的结果。

本章探索同伴互评的互动模式,为探究在线同伴互动是否及如何促进学习和写作提供新的线索。部分小组因成员人数、时差、反馈周期和积极性不高等导致部分同伴评论未得到处理,互动变成单轮单向的交流。教师须控制小组成员人数,人数不对等不利于互动,一个二语写作者和两个母语者的人员配比更合理;教师须设置合理的反馈周期,充分考虑时差、节假日和其他学习任务等因素,给予学生足够的反馈时间,以便学生同伴更好地进行阐释和回应;教师还可以采取奖惩措施调动学生的积极性。了解不同互动模式的特点及其影响因素,有助于教师制定策略,帮助学生发展有利于成功写作的互动模式,以最大限度地提高网上同伴反馈的效果,增加协作写作的学习机会。

第七章 结论

随着"互联网+"时代的到来,跨洋互动写作已经成为一种常见的写作方式。本研究通过构建同伴互评理论框架,分析中美大学生在线跨洋互动写作过程中同伴互评的特点与规律,达到对比中美大学生同伴互评的异同和揭示中美同伴在线协同写作互动过程的目的,以支持合作性写作实践和研究的创新。本章首先总结了同伴互评、同伴互动和互动模式3个维度的研究成果,之后阐述了本研究的理论贡献,并提出了网络自然语境下混合小组进行合作写作的教学意义,最后总结了本研究的不足之处,并给未来基于网络平台的二语学习者和母语者协同写作研究提出了建议。

7.1 研究发现

在对同伴互评进行了理论上的重新界定和分类后,我们对中美跨洋互动写作项目的同伴互评类型和同伴互动展开讨论,采用多案例分析法从互动理论和最近发展区的角度揭示同伴互评和同伴互动背后反映出的中美文化和教育理念的差异。对第17轮、第18轮、第19轮和第20轮的在线写作、讨论、修改报告和后续访谈进行了比较系统和全面的对比分析,获得了一些有意义的发现,主要包括以下3个方面。

7.1.1 中美同伴互评特征的比较分析

(1) 中美同伴互评类型存在共性

中美大学生同伴互评的类型具有一致性,双方的同伴反馈都包括评价类反馈和情感反馈两种类型,且以评价类反馈为主;回评都包括接受性反馈、模糊性反馈和不接受性反馈3种类型,且以模糊性反馈为主。这表明中美大学生对同伴互评类型重要性次序的认识是一致的。

具体而言，第一，在中美大学生同伴反馈的评价类反馈中，指正性反馈数量最多，即同伴提供了大量的关于当前表现与期望表现之间差距的信息。一是因为双方在提供反馈方面具有相当丰富的经验，二是因为双方都有写作反馈的指导提纲，上面列有鉴析同伴写作的视角。第二，信息性反馈是最常见的评论形式。这意味着同伴反馈主要围绕着与写作内容相关的话题展开。这是因为该项目的活动初衷是通过网上互评，使二语学习者了解自己的二语水平与母语者之间的差距，并根据母语者提出的建议反思自己的二语学习，以期在后续学习中做出必要的调整，跨越互动中所发现的差距，加强沟通。第三，肯定性反馈，尤其是局部肯定性反馈所占比例很大。本研究中的局部肯定性反馈主要是针对文章的语篇组织、结构、连贯性和逻辑等写作方面做出的评价。第四，模糊性反馈以澄清为主，接受性反馈以局部接受为主。中美同伴反馈以指正性反馈为主，针对同伴对主题的不同理解和重读，中美写作者须阐释意图或者举例帮助同伴理解自己的观点，这导致澄清的数量最多。另外，无论是母语者还是二语学习者都认为同伴互动过程中双方需要部分接受同伴的观点，因此局部接受性反馈多。第五，中美大学生的同伴反馈和回评有相似的反馈模式。同伴反馈一般遵循以下模式：评价类反馈（验证性反馈→指正性反馈）→情感反馈。回评一般遵循以下模式：接受性反馈→模糊性反馈。

（2）中美同伴互评类型具有差异性

中美大学生的同伴反馈和回评类型及其子类的出现频次存在显著性差异。数据分析发现，双方的差异主要体现在批判意识与读者意识、权威对话与平等对话、静态文本与动态话语3个方面。

首先，中国大学生具有很强的批判性思维，体现在产生大量的辩护和局部接受性反馈。这个观点与以往研究的结论不同（中国学生倾向于维持和谐）。可能有以下几个原因：① 他们的二语语言能力有限；② 他们缺乏必要的二语语用语言知识，无法执行更复杂和巧妙的否定，缺乏表达不赞同的其他语言形式；③ 他们借鉴了自己的母语社交语用知识。美国大学生具有很强的读者意识，体现为错误分析和澄清反馈类型数量多。在同伴互评过程中，美国大学生会思考如何让说不同语言和来自不同文化的人理解自己的观点，也会关注二语学习者的语言问题，倾向于解决问题。尤其是美国大学生倾向于提供元语言解释，以帮助同伴理解复杂的词汇和语法结构。

其次,中美大学生具有权威对话意识和平等对话意识。对中美大学生的内容解释、澄清、回应、重述、经验求教、移情、整体肯定性评价和感谢等反馈类型出现频次差异的分析发现,中国大学生在陈述与写作内容(尤其是文化)相关的观点时倾向于将自己置于权威地位,注重表达自身观点,美国大学生则更关注意义协商;而在协商与语言使用相关的反馈内容时,中国大学生将美国大学生视为权威,而美国大学生则具有读者意识,产生重述反馈类型较多,以提高二语学习者使用目标语言的准确性。双方在交流写作主题和文章组织结构等方面时,却体现了合作立场。中美大学生在同伴互评过程中,其权威立场和合作立场呈现动态特征。

最后,在中美大学生的互动过程中,既有反馈者和写作者之间一对一的双向互动,也有多个反馈者之间的多向互动。反馈者在与写作者互动的过程中会引用其他反馈者的观点,出现中美大学生多个反馈者之间的互动。由此可见,中美大学生之间的同伴反馈是多向的、多轮的和动态的。从这个层面上说,中美大学生的交流和对话都具有动态的特征,他们利用对话来建立或维持同伴之间的一定程度的平等或平衡。

概括而言,二语学习者和母语者对同伴互评重要性次序的认识是一致的,有丰富的同伴互评经验的二语学习者和母语者的同伴互评类型之间具有一致性。但是互评类型出现频率的不同也反映出中美文化和中美教学理念的差异。中国大学生具有很强的批判性思维,倾向于表达自身观点,这可能是与汉语写作的传统目的"文以载道"有关,受"读者是被教育者"的教育理念的影响。美国大学生关注意义协商,他们的读者意识和平等对话意识强,体现了美国大学生写作的批评行为准则,这源于"写作为交际服务"的教育理念。在中美大学生同伴互评过程中,写作者和反馈者之间的关系是动态的,反馈者的态度会在权威立场和合作立场之间切换。

7.1.2 中美同伴互动行为的比较分析

(1)中美混合小组的互动行为存在共性

首先,中美写作者修改稿中作文修改的多少与反馈内容有关。如果反馈内容以中心思想、篇章组织与连贯性、语法、词汇和用法规范为主,则修改稿的修改多;如果修改意见以观点和内容为主,则修改少。其次,作文修改的多少还与反馈形式有关。对于笼统的反馈,写作者以自发修改或者不修改为主,双方缺少主体间性;对于具体的、详细的反馈,作者以他人修改为主,主体间性强。再次,中美大学生对于同伴反馈的接受和采纳建立在理解且易操作的基础上。中美大学生易于采纳关于文本结构的修改意见,不易采纳要求增加举例、具体阐释及大量内容的建议,因为这些建议要求写作者对论文的某些具体部分进行重写,这个在同伴反馈过程中操作性不强。多个同伴提出的相同的反馈意见易被采纳。最后,中美大学生和本国的反馈者的互动较少,缺乏主体间性,指导和激发兴趣等支架策略未得到回应,支架策略并不明显。

(2) 中美混合小组的互动行为具有差异性

首先,在作文修改方面,相对而言,中国大学生平均每人进行的作文修改数量多于美方写作组。中美大学生的修改方式也不同,中方以自发修改为主,美方的他人修改更多。美方写作者接收到的同伴反馈较多,但是被用于修改稿中的反馈意见不多;美方写作者尤其不易接受关于时态、词汇和写作技巧的建议。其次,中美大学生采纳的修改类型在数量排序上不同,既体现了双方对同伴反馈的接受度是不一致的,也说明反馈者对中美写作者给予的反馈的侧重点不同。反馈者对中国大学生提出的关于语法和结构的修改意见多,对美方写作者提出的修改意见主要集中于语篇结构。中国大学生采纳的反馈以语言形式和语篇结构方面的意见为主;而美方写作者更倾向于接受文本语篇层面的意见。最后,在中方写作组中,双方的互动涉及积极的指导、应急响应、热情的情感涉入和主动的兴趣激发,主体间性的支架策略明显;而在美方写作组中,双方的协商互动有时无法达成一致意见,缺少主体间性。

(3) 中美混合小组互动模式的异同

首先,中美写作组都以合作互动模式为主。中美大学生在文本结构和写作内容方面会存在认知冲突,但是双方通过互动协商建立了理解并达成了新的共识,形成的互动以合作模式居多。其次,在中方写作组中,常规互动模式最多;而在美方写作组中,出现一定数量的常规互动和从属互动模式。这说明中国大学生易于接受美国大学生的同伴反馈,尤其是与语言相关的反馈意见。美国大学生在处理与语言相关的反馈时会坚持自己的观点,不赞成同伴反馈,形成从属互动模式;会接受与写作文本结构相关的反馈,从而形成常规互动模式。另外,在协商写作文本的内容时,中方反馈者与其他反馈者之间偶尔互动，共同参与反馈任务。最后，反馈行为、互动行为、互动模式相互作用。同伴反馈的行为会促成某个互动行为，互动中行为的组合有助于形成在线互动中的某些关系模式；互动模式也会促进写作者的修改和采纳行为，形成多种类型的反馈和支架策略。同一个小组的互动模式也呈动态，前几轮互动可能形成从属模式，后几轮也可能又转换为合作互动模式。

7.1.3 二语写作中同伴互动模式的分析结果

（1）二语写作中同伴互动模式的共性

中中小组和中美小组都形成集体、协作、合作、专家/新手和主导/主导5种互动模式，以协作型居多。在二语写作小组中，虽然学习者在互动过程中会产生认知冲突，但是小组成员对不同观点进行协商，形成了新的理解并达成了新的共识，因此二语写作中同伴互动模式以协作模式居多。另外，在协商写作文本的内容时，二语学习者与其他反馈者之间偶尔出现互动，共同参与反馈任务，因此有少量的集体互动模式。也有个别跨文化交际中思维方式的差异导致双方观点无法达成一致的情况，形成主导/主导型互动模式。

（2）二语写作中同伴互动模式的差异性

中中小组互动以协作型为主，以合作型和专家/新手型为辅；中美小组主要集中于协作型。中中小组的专家/新手型和合作型互动模式多于中美小组，主要有以下3个原因：一是中国同伴的互动更侧重于修改作文，指出同伴写作中的问题、缺点和错误，提供负面反馈和批评，希望通过批评性和建设性的反馈帮助同伴提高文本质量。二是相较于中美小组，中中小组双方对文化差异的观点一致，相关交流较少；而文化差异的交流却是中美小组的协商重点。因此，协作型是中美小组主要的互动模式，而以平行的方式表达观点的合作模式在中中小组占有一定比例。三是部分美国同伴小组成员表现出个体能动性，但未表现出协作能动性。部分同伴只发布一次评论，可能只是为了满足课程要求，或者观察他人的合作进行间接参与，这降低了其他互动模式出现的可能性。

（3）同伴互动模式受个体、情境和社会因素的影响

英语母语者和二语学习者对自己和对方英语水平的认知、参与动机、反馈体验和反馈期望、互动环境、跨文化交流和思维方式差异等因素影响

学习者的语言中介功能、反馈的发起和响应及学生的修改行为,进而形成不同的互动模式。具体而言,英语母语者认为,英语写作对自身也不是容易之事,且他们肯定二语学习者的英语水平,这就使协作互动模式成为最常见的互动模式。中国大学生的参与动机是学习地道的英语表达方式,理解目标文化中的习语,了解不同的写作方式和技巧,与不同文化的人进行交流,因此中国大学生易于接受这些方面的反馈;而美国大学生的反馈期待是了解不同的文化和写作方式,因此出现一定数量的合作型和专家/新手型互动模式。

学习者的自我认知、对他人的认知、动机、反馈体验和期望、互动环境、跨文化思维等因素影响反馈互动行为;这些行为的组合有助于形成某些关系模式;学习者的批判意识和读者意识也由此发展起来。反过来,学习者在反馈互动中的行为和体验可能会影响个人的自我认知和学习目标;互动结果也会影响互动行为。因此,互动行为、互动模式、影响因素和互动结果之间的关系是非线性的,它们之间相互作用。

反馈互动是对话性质的。反馈不是反馈者传递信息给写作者的简单的、单向的行为,也不是反馈者和写作者之间的双向行为,而是一个多向的过程,反馈者和写作者既要面对其他约束和规范,也要面对其他权威。

7.2 研究启示

虽然国内外同伴反馈和同伴互动研究已经取得了丰硕的成果,但是国外同伴互评的相关术语众多且所指存在差异,分类存在重叠现象,国内同伴互评的相关理论研究较少。虽然部分研究已经关注合作写作中的群体动态和互动模式,但是对混合小组的互动行为和互动模式的研究较少,尤其鲜有研究对比混合小组里母语者和二语学习者同伴互评和同伴互动的异同。本研究从互动理论的视角对跨洋互动写作中同伴互评和同伴互动进行了较为全面和系统的对比分析。总的来说,本研究进一步丰富了同伴互评和互动的研究,拓宽了合作性写作研究的范围。本部分将分别从同伴互评和同伴互动两个方面阐释本研究的理论意义和教学启示。

7.2.1 理论启示

第一,本研究开发了可复制用于不同设置和研究目的的同伴反馈和回评编码方案,为同伴反馈的相关研究奠定了理论框架。该方案整合了以往学者们对于反馈内容和反馈功能的分类,解决了两种分类的重叠问题;修改了部分类别的定义、范畴;删除了一些类别,解决了以往分类中子类界限模糊的问题;将以往的一些子类别单独列为一类,使方案更加细化、操作性更强;增加了类别,反映出语料中出现的新的评论方式;整合了部分类别的定义和范畴,让方案的大类更具概括性。此外,本研究分别从反馈者和写作者视角对同伴反馈进行分类,总结同伴反馈和回评的一般性反馈模式,使同伴互评类型的研究更全面。

第二,本研究对中美同伴反馈类型的对比分析,进一步丰富了同伴反馈研究。作为二语写作研究的一个重要方面,国内一直没有给予同伴反馈类型的理论研究足够的重视。本研究从反馈的类型、分布和出现频次比较中美的同伴反馈,有助于找出中美同伴反馈类型的共性和差异性。中美同伴反馈类型的比较研究允许在给予和接收同伴反馈期间调查中西文化异同,并通过反馈现象探究其教学理念的异同。对比分析加深了我们对同伴反馈的认识,同时也有助于二语习得理论的完善和深入。

第三,本研究从互动理论的视角分析混合小组同伴反馈过程,进一步拓宽了合作性写作研究的范围。本研究重申了互动理论和最近发展区理论/支架在探索与解释在线混合小组协同写作活动中的作用,为如何探索和解释跨洋协同写作中的互动提供了一个新的观点。以前的研究从未从学习者互动行为(如采纳类型、作文修改和支架策略)的角度考察混合小组在线协同写作中的意义协商和文本共建过程,本研究提出了用于分析学习者的在线交流和文本共建的编码方案。本研究体现了小组互动的动态性和支架策略的灵活性,认为在线协同写作中的反馈互动是对话性质的,是一个多向多轮的互动过程。

第四,本研究为协同写作领域提供了方法论方面的帮助。通过完善多种编码方案来构建一个新的编码框架,开发了一种系统化方式来评估作文修改功能、采纳反馈类型和支架策略3个相关联的元素对于在线写作的作用,用于分析在线讨论、搭建活动和文本共建。

值得关注的是,本研究发现协作互动模式是最常见的模式。这一发现与预期不符。基于以往相关文献和常识推理,本研究的预期是当母语者成为反馈者时,会进行更多的专家/新手型互动,而不是协作型互动。同样,合作模式的出现也是在意料之外的。虽然学生有时会参与母语者关于写作技巧和语言适用性的辩论，特别是在他们有更多学科领域的知识（如语篇结构）时；然而，我们并未预料到这样的挑战可能预示着数据会凸显一种特定关系类型。

母语者和二语学习者都表现出对写作中的语言得体性的关注，并且承认关于语言表达得体性的知识是社交性的、构建性的和可变的（Lillis, 2003）。合作互动的优势是通过写作和阅读，不同群体的人展现出不同的知识储备，但是如果只有一方推动这种交流，有可能形成常规互动或从属互动。

7.2.2 教学启示

在教学上，随着计算机技术的发展，跨洋互动在线写作已经成为一种常见的写作方式，但本研究清楚地表明，该写作方式的协同性并不会自动导致参与者采取协作方式。在线同伴反馈不是面对面反馈的简单替代方案，需要精心组织才能最大限度地发挥其积极作用。撰写和组织连贯、和谐的反馈是一种有意义的交际写作实践。本研究提供了一些关于混合小组的同伴反馈和小组互动的数据，并在此基础上提出一些同伴反馈教学建议。在采用混合同伴小组形式时，写作教师须关注以下问题：

首先，对学生进行反馈培训是必须的。尽管本研究并没有关注培训效果，但参与者在进行在线讨论之前已有反馈清单并进行了面对面的同伴反馈培训，之后才进行在线讨论和文本修改。但是仅仅根据学生的反馈经验进行相关培训还远远不够，要鼓励教师组建有来自不同文化背景的学生的学生的学生群，对学生进行必要的培训，只有这样才能创造更多的任务和语言协商机会，帮助学生培养跨文化交流能力。文化价值在混合小组反馈活动中可能造成特殊挑战，因此二语写作教师在进行同伴反馈培训时，可以组织同伴之间的相互学习和讨论，以便来自不同文化、具有不同信念和反馈体验的学生定期分享他们的经验和观点，有助于以积极的方式改变同伴反馈行为。

其次，反馈培训需要培养和提高反馈者的读者意识与平等意识。以往关于同伴反馈培训的研究往往侧重于批评什么（如帮助学生专注于同伴反馈过程中的某些写作方面），以及如何传达同伴反馈（如帮助学生培养礼貌策略等）。本研究表明，培训需要让反馈者意识到与写作者交流和平等对话的重要性，让反馈者的观点更易于被写作者接受；同时为学生提供引导和指导，以便他们在参与同伴反馈时可以成为更平等的参与者。为了帮助学生更好地发挥写作者的角色，教师可考虑提供协助学生实践反馈策略的指导，指导他们阐明自己的意图并从同伴那里获得反馈。特别是可以帮助 ESL 学生在担任写作者角色时成为积极的参与者，以便他们能够在讨论自己的论文时发挥更重要的作用，并从同伴回应中获得更多益处。在混合群体中，轮流进行书面反馈可以促进同伴最大限度地平等参与反馈活动。

再次，教师需要控制混合小组的人数，设置合理的反馈时间。一个二语写作者和两个本族语反馈者或者一个母语写作者和两个二语反馈者的组合更适合，这样的组合设置和人数会更好地帮助母语者和二语学习者为同伴反馈做出贡献并从中受益。另外，设计同伴反馈交流时，要给予足够的时间让同伴考虑反馈的形式和内容，以便更好地做出阐释和回应。

最后，教师需要参与后续讨论。许多 ESL 学生认为教师是权威人士，教师的指导可以减轻 ESL 学生对同伴反馈质量的关注，增强他们在修改中有效地遵循反馈的信心。教师还可以通过指导学生反思个人贡献、共同努力和小组互动来促进写作文本的共建，完善协作式写作过程。在教师的指导和写作者与反馈者之间的协商互动下，网络上和面对面的同伴反馈相结合有助于提高学生作为反馈者和写作者的能力。

7.3 研究不足之处

由于语料来源受限和研究者自身知识水平有限，本研究难免存在一些不足，现总结如下：

第一，本研究语料是选自他人的跨洋互动写作项目，项目设计不能完全满足本研究的需要，存在搜集的符合要求的语料有限和缺少部分后期访谈材料的问题。研究目的不同，语料选择的标准不同，如同伴互评特征研究需要的语料既包括中美双方的反馈文本，也包括中美大学生的反思日志；而同伴互动行为和互动模式研究既需要中美双方的写作初稿、修改稿、双方的在线讨论，还需要双方的反思日志，而且每个小组里既要有中国反馈者也要有美国反馈者。本研究可以获取的符合这些标准的语料有限，尤其对于互动行为特征问题，因缺少充足的语料，我们只能采用多案例分析法而不是语料库法。因缺少美国学生后期访谈资料，本研究的美国大学生语料分析无法做到反馈数据、修改报告和访谈数据三方验证，只能采用以描述性分析为主、以推理性分析为辅的研究方法。

第二，本研究在中美同伴反馈类型的差异性分析过程中存在一定的主观性。目前的同伴反馈类型的识别仍然是综合运用文献回顾和人工识别两种方法，无法实现计算机自动标注，在具体识别过程中，难免存在研究者个人的主观判断。

7.4 对未来研究的建议

网络科技快速发展，国际合作课程越来越多，在线协同写作将成为各种二语背景下的常见教学活动，同伴反馈中的母语者和二语学习者的互动和反馈值得进一步研究。未来的研究可以使用本研究中建立的编码框架，进一步探索用更大的样本和/或不同的方法来研究相关问题。具体可以探讨以下方面：① 中介因素（如性别、情感，语言熟练程度和技术使用）对在线写作环境中同伴互动行为和策略的影响。来自混合人口背景的学生在在线协同写作环境中的跨文化交流值得进一步研究。② 互动模式对小组写作产出及个人学习的影响。可通过数据分析协同写作过程中个体发展与互动事件之间的联系，特别是在通过支架产生最近发展区的情况下。③ 教师在混合小组协同写作活动中的积极作用，以及教师如何在网络环境中支持学生的学习。一些学生在报告中陈述了自己对教师互动的积极态度，但是该项目活动期间中美双方教师没有参与项目，只关注活动进展并提供技术支持，而且本研究的重点是同伴互动而不是师生互动。此外，由于 CMC 技术的发展，在线模式下的协作式写作正在蓬勃发展。当前，维基是二语课堂合作写作的主要在线平台，谷歌文档（Google File）被认为是二语语言中合作写作的良好工具；而本研究涉及的跨洋互动写作的在线平台存在很多技术问题，需要更新。因此，未来的研究可以使用谷歌文档和维基考察学生在混合小组协作式书写任务中的互动，阐明维基和谷歌文档等 Web 2.0 工具在二语互动写作中的作用。

随着新技术的不断发展，在线协作写作将成为各种二语语境下的共同学习活动，而且会有越来越多的研究提供更多关于计算机媒介协作写作中的互动和二语学习技术的可行性见解。随着对这些问题的理解深入，写作教师能够更好地帮助母语者和二语学习者成为同伴反馈的有效参与者，并通过同伴反馈促进二语学习。

参考文献

[1] ADAMS, R., 2007. *Do second language learners benefit from interacting with each other*? [C] // MACKEY A. Conversational interaction in second language acquisition: A collection of empirical studies. Oxford: Oxford University Press: 29—51.

[2] ALJAAFREH, A. & LANTOLF, J. P., 1994. Negative feedback as regulation and second language learning in the zone of proximal development [J]. *The Modern Language Journal*, 78: 465—483.

[3] ALLEN, D. & KATAYAMA, A., 2016. Relative second language proficiency and the giving and receiving of written peer feedback [J]. *System*, 56: 96—106.

[4] ALLEN, D. & MILLS, A., 2014. The impact of second language proficiency in dyadic peer feedback [J]. *Language Teaching Research*, 20(4): 1—16.

[5] ALLWRIGHT, R. L., 1984. The importance of interaction in classroom language learning [J]. *Applied Linguistics*, 5(2): 156—171.

[6] ANGELOVA, M. & ZHAO, Y., 2016. Using an online collaborative project between American and Chinese students to develop ESL teaching skills, cross-cultural awareness and language skills [J]. *Computer Assisted Language Learning*, 29(1): 167—185.

[7] ARNOLD, N., DUCATE, L. & KOST, C., 2012. Collaboration or cooperation? Analyzing group dynamics and revision processes in wikis [J]. *CALICO Journal*, 29: 431—448.

[8] BAKHTIN, M. M., 1981. *The dialogic imagination: Four*

essays [M]. Austin, TX: University of Texas Press.

[9] BAKHTIN, M. M., 1986. *Speech genres and other late essays* [M]. Austin, TX: University of Texas Press.

[10] BAKHTIN, M. M., 1994. *The Bakhtin reader: Selected writings of Bakhtin, Medvedev, and Voloshinov* [C]. New York: Bloomsbury Academic.

[11] BARGH, J. A., MCKENNA, K. Y. A. & FITZSIMONS, G. M., 2002. Can you see the real me? Activation and expression of the "true self" on the Internet [J]. *Journal of Social Issues*, 58: 33—48.

[12] BELZ, J. A., 2003. Linguistic perspectives on the development of intercultural competence in telecollaboration [J]. *Language Learning & Technology*, 7(2): 68—117.

[13] BERG, E. C., 1999. The effects of trained peer response on ESL students' revision types and writing quality [J]. *Journal of Second Language Writing*, 8(3): 215—241.

[14] BOUD, D., KEOGH, R. & WALKER, D., 1985. *Reflection: Turning experience into learning* [M]. London: Kogan, Page, Nichols.

[15] BRADLEY, L., 2014. Peer-reviewing in an intercultural wiki environment-student interaction and reflections [J]. *Computers and Compositions*, 34: 80—95.

[16] BRADLEY, L., LINSTROM, B. & RYSTEDT, H., 2010. Rationalities of collaboration for language learning in a wiki [J]. *ReCALL*, 22(2): 247—265.

[17] BRAIDI, S. M., 2002. Re-examining the role of recasts in native-speaker/nonnative-speaker interactions [J]. *Language Learning*, 52(1): 1—42.

[18] BRYAN, S., 2005. The relationship between negotiated interaction, learner uptake, and lexical acquisition in task-based computer-mediated communication [J]. *TESOL Quarterly*, 39(1): 33—58.

[19] BUCKWALTER, P., 2001. Repair sequences in Spanish L2 dyadic discourse: A descriptive study [J]. *Modern Language Journal*, 85

(3): 380—397.

[20] CAPLAN, S. E. & TURNER, J. S., 2007. Bringing theory to research on computer-mediated comforting communication [J]. *Computers in Human Behavior*, 23(2): 985—998.

[21] CARLESS, D., SALTER D., YANG, M., et al., 2011. Developing sustainable feedback practices [J]. *Studies in Higher Education*, 36(4): 395—407.

[22] CARSON, J. G. & NELSON, G. L., 1996. Chinese students' perceptions of ESL peer response group interaction [J]. *Journal of Second Language Writing*, 5(1): 1—19.

[23] CASTANEDA, D. A, & CHO, M. H., 2013. The role of wiki writing in learning Spanish grammar [J]. *Computer Assisted Language Learning*, 26(4): 334—349.

[24] CHENG, K. H., LIANG, J. C. & TSAI, C. C., 2015. Examining the role of feedback messages in undergraduate students' writing performance during an online peer assessment activity [J]. *The Internet and Higher Education*, 25: 78—84.

[25] CHO, H., 2017. Synchronous web-based collaborative writing: Factors mediating interaction among second-language writers [J]. *Journal of Second Language Writing*, 36: 37—51.

[26] CHO, Y. H. & CHO, K., 2011. Peer reviewers learn from giving comments [J]. *Instructional Science*, 39: 629—643.

[27] CHO, K. & MACARTHUR, C., 2010. Student revision with peer and expert reviewing [J]. *Learning and Instruction*, 20(4): 328—338.

[28] CHO, K. & SCHUNN, C. D., 2004. *The SWoRD is mightier than the pen: Scaffolded writing and rewriting in the discipline* [Z]. In Proceedings of IEEE International Conference on Advanced Learning Technologies: 545—549.

[29] CHO, K. & SCHUNN, C. D., 2007. Scaffolded writing and rewriting in the discipline: A web-based reciprocal peer review system [J].

Computers & Education, 48(3): 409—426.

[30] CHO, K., SCHUNN, C. D. & CHARNEY, D., 2006. Commenting on writing: Typology and perceived helpfulness of comments from novice peer reviewers and subject matter experts [J]. *Written Communication*, 23(3): 260—294.

[31] CHONG, K., 2010. Investigating the perception of student teachers in Hong Kong towards peer-editing [J]. *English Language Teaching*, 3 (1): 53—59.

[32] COLLIS, B., DEBOER, W. & SLOTMAN, K., 2001. Feedback for web-based assignments [J]. *Journal of Computer Assisted Learning*, 17: 306—313.

[33] CUMMING, A., 1989. Writing expertise and second language proficiency [J]. *Language Learning*, 39: 81—141.

[34] DAMON, W. & PHELPS, E., 1989. Critical distinctions among three approaches to peer education [J]. *International Journal of Educational Research*, 13(1): 9—19.

[35] DE GUERRERO, M. C. M. & VILLAMIL, O. S., 2000. Activating the ZPD: Mutual scaffolding in L2 peer revision [J]. *The Modern Language Journal*, 84: 51—68.

[36] DIAB, N. M., 2016. A comparison of peer, teacher and self-feedback on the reduction of language errors in student essays [J]. *System*, 57: 55—65.

[37] DONATO, R., 1994. *Collective scaffolding in second language learning* [C]. // LANTOLF J. P. & APPEL G. Vygotskian approaches to second language research. Norwood, NJ: Ablex: 33—56.

[38] DONATO, R., 2004. Aspects of collaboration in pedagogical discourse [J]. *Annual Review of Applied Linguistics*, 24: 284—302.

[39] DOUGHTY, C. & PICA, T., 1986. "Information gap" tasks: Do they facilitate second language acquisition? [J]. *TESOL Quarterly*, 20 (2): 305—325.

[40] DUFF, P., 1986. *Another look at interlanguage talk: Talking*

task to task [C]. // DAY, R. Talking to learn: Conversation in second language acquisition. Rowley, MA: Newbury House: 147—181.

[41] DUSSIAS, P. E., 2006. *Morphological development in Spanish-American telecollaboration* [C]. // BELZ, J. & THORNE, S. Internet-mediated intercultural foreign language education. Boston: Heinle & Heinle: 121—146.

[42] EDASAWA, Y. & KABATA, K., 2007. An ethnographic study of a keypal project: Learning a foreign language through bilingual communication [J]. *Computer Assisted Language Learning*, 20(3): 189—207.

[43] ELLIS, R., 2010. Epilogue: A frame work for investigating oral and written corrective feedback [J]. *Studies in Second Language Acquisition*, 32(2): 335—349.

[44] ELLIS, R., BASTURKMEN, H. & LOEWEN, S., 2001. Preemptive focus on form in the ESL classroom [J]. *TESOL Quarterly*, 35(3): 407—432.

[45] ELOLA, I. & OSKOZ, A., 2010. Collaborative writing: Fostering foreign language and writing conventions development [J]. *Language Learning & Technology*, 14(3): 51—71.

[46] ENE, E. & UPTON, T. A., 2014. Learner uptake of teacher electronic feedback in ESL composition [J]. *System*, 46: 80—95.

[47] FALCHIKOV, N., 1986. Product comparisons and process benefits of collaborative peer group and self-assessment [J]. *Assessment & Evaluation in Higher Education*, 11(2): 146—166.

[48] FERRIS, D. R., 2010. Second language writing research and written corrective feedback in SLA: Intersections and practical applications [J]. *Studies in Second Language Acquisition*, 32: 181—201.

[49] FISHER, E., 1997. *Developments in exploratory talk and academic argument* [C]. // WEGERIF, R. & SCHRIMSHAW, P. Computers and talk in the primary classroom. Clevedon: Multilingual Matters Ltd: 38—48.

[50] FOSTER, P., 1998. A classroom perspective on the negotiation

of meaning [J]. *Applied Linguistics*, 19(1): 1—23.

[51] FOSTER, P. & OHTA, A., 2005. Negotiation for meaning and peer assistance in second language classrooms [J]. *Applied Linguistic*, 26(3): 402—430.

[52] GAN, Z. D., DAVISON, C. & HAMP-LYONS, L., 2009. Topic negotiation in peer oral assessment situation: A conversation analytic approach [J]. *Applied Linguistics*, 30(3): 315—334.

[53] GASS, S. M. & VARONIS, E. M., 1985. Variation in native speaker speech modification to non-native speakers [J]. *Studies in Second Language Acquisition*, 7(1): 37—57.

[54] GERE, A. & ABBOTT, R., 1985. Talking about writing: The language of writing groups [J]. *Research in the Teaching of English*, 19: 362—385.

[55] GIELEN, M. & DE WEVER, B., 2015. Structuring peer assessment: Comparing the impact of the degree of structure on peer feedback content [J]. *Computers in Human Behavior*, 52: 315—325.

[56] GILLIES, R. M., 2006. Teachers' and students' verbal behaviours during cooperative and small-group learning [J]. *British Journal of Educational Psychology*, 76(2): 271—87.

[57] GOLDSTEIN, L. M., 2006. *Feedback and revision in second language writing: Contextual, teacher, and student variables* [C]. // HYLAND, K. & HYLAND, F. Feedback in second language writing: Contexts and issues. New York: Cambridge University Press: 185—205.

[58] GUARDADO, M. & SHI, L., 2007. ESL students' experiences of online peer feedback [J]. *Computers and Composition*, 24(4): 443—461.

[59] GUTH, S. & HELM, F., 2010. *Telecollaboration 2.0: Language, literacies and intercultural learning in the 21st century* [M]. Frankfurt: Peter Lang.

[60] HART-DAVIDSON, W., MCLEOD, M., KLERKX, C., et al., 2010. *A method for measuring helpfulness in online peer review* [Z].

// In Proceedings of the 28th ACM International Conference on Design of Communication. ACM: 115—121.

[61] HATTIE, J. & TIMPERLEY, H., 2007. The power of feedback [J]. *Review of Educational Research*, 77(1): 81—112.

[62] HELM, F. & GUTH, S., 2010. *The multifarious goals of telecollaboration* 2.0 [C]. // Guth, S. & Helm, F. Telecollaboration 2.0: Telecollaboration in education. Bern, Switzerland: Peter Lang: 69—106.

[63] HIRVELA, A., 1999, Collaborative writing instruction and communities of readers and writers [J]. *TESOL Journal*, 8(2): 7—12.

[64] HISLOP, J. & STRACKE, E., 2017. ESL students in peer review: An action research study in a university English for academic purposes course [J]. *University of Sydney Papers in TESOL*, 12: 9—44.

[65] HSU, H. C., 2020. The impact of task complexity on patterns of interaction during web-based asynchronous collaborative writing tasks [J]. *System*, 93: 1—13.

[66] HU, G. W., 2005. Using peer review with Chinese ESL student writers [J]. *Language Teaching Research*, 9(3): 321—342.

[67] HU, G. W. & LAM, S. T. E., 2010. Issues of cultural appropriateness and pedagogical efficacy: Exploring peer review in a second language writing class [J]. *Instructional Science*, 38: 371—394.

[68] HUANG, C. Q., HAN, Z. M., LI, M. X., et al., 2019. Investigating students' interaction patterns and dynamic learning sentiments in online discussions [J]. *Computers & Education*, 140: 103589.

[69] HUISMAN, B., SAAB, N., VAN DRIEL, J., et al., 2018. Peer feedback on academic writing: Undergraduate students' peer feedback role, peer feedback perceptions and essay performance [J]. *Assessment & Evaluation in Higher Education*, 43: 955—968.

[70] HUTCHBY, I. & WOOFFITT, R., 1998. *Conversation analysis: Principles, practices and applications* [M]. Oxford: Polity Press.

[71] HYLAND, K. & HYLAND, F., 2006 Feedback on second language students' writing [J]. *Language Teaching*, 39(2): 83—101.

[72] JEFFREY, R., 2015. Using feedback comments to develop a rating scale for a written coursework assessment [J]. *Journal of English for Academic Purposes*, 18: 51—63.

[73] JORDAN-HENLEY, J. & MAID, B. M., 1995. Tutoring in cyberspace: Student impact and college/university collaboration [J]. *Computers and Composition*, 12(2): 211—218.

[74] KEH, C. L., 1990. Feedback in the writing process: A model and methods for implementation [J]. *ELT Journal*, 44(4): 294—394.

[75] KESSLER, G., 2009. Student-initiated attention to form in wiki-based collaborative writing [J]. *Language Learning & Technology*, 13(1): 79—95.

[76] KESSLER, G. & BIKOWSKI, D., 2010. Developing collaborative autonomous learning abilities in computer mediated language learning: Attention to meaning among students in wiki space [J]. *Computer Assisted Language Learning*, 23(1): 41—58.

[77] KORMOS, J., 2006. *Speech production and second language acquisition* [M]. Mahwah, NJ: Erlbaum.

[78] KOST, C., 2011. Investigating writing strategies and revision behavior in collaborative wiki projects [J]. *CALICO Journal*, 28(3): 606—620.

[79] KRAMSCH, C., 2008. Ecological perspectives on foreign language education [J]. *Language Teaching*, 41(3): 389—408.

[80] KRASHEN, S. D., 1985. *The input hypothesis: Issues and implications* [M]. New York: Longman Inc.

[81] LANTOLF, J. P., 2000. A century of language teaching and research: Looking back and looking ahead [J]. *The Modern Language Journal*, 84(4): 467—471.

[82] LANTOLF, J. P. & PAVLENKO, A., 2001. (S)econd (L)anguage (A)ctivity theory: Understanding second language learners as people [C]. // Breen, M. Learner contributions to language learning: New

directions in research. London: Longman: 141—158.

[83] LANTOLF, J. P. & THORNE, S. L., 2006. *Sociocultural theory and the genesis of second language development* [M]. Oxford: Oxford University Press.

[84] LEE, I., 2014. Revisiting teacher feedback in EFL writing from sociocultural perspectives [J]. *TESOL Quarterly*, 48(1): 201—213.

[85] LEE, L., 2010. Exploring wiki-mediated collaborative writing: A case study in an elementary Spanish course [J]. *Calico Journal*, 27 (2): 260—276.

[86] LEE, L. & MARKEY, A., 2014. A study of learners' perceptions of online intercultural exchange through Web 2.0 technologies [J]. *ReCALL*, 26 (3): 281—297.

[87] LEIJEN, D. A. J., 2017. A novel approach to examine the impact of web-based peer review on the revisions of L2 writers [J]. *Computers & Composition*, 43: 35—54.

[88] LI, M., 2013. Individual novices and collective experts: Collective scaffolding in wiki-based small group writing [J]. *System*, 41 (3): 752—769.

[89] LI, M. & KIM, D., 2016. One wiki, two groups: Dynamic interactions across ESL collaborative writing tasks [J]. *Journal of Second Language Writing*, 31: 25—42.

[90] LI, M. & ZHU, W., 2013. Patterns of computer-mediated interaction in small writing groups using wikis [J]. *Computer Assisted Language Learning*, 26(1): 61—82.

[91] LI, M. & ZHU, W., 2017a. Explaining dynamic interactions in wiki-based collaborative writing [J]. *Language Learning and Technology*, 21(2): 96—120.

[92] LI, M. & ZHU, W., 2017b. Good or bad collaborative wiki writing: Exploring links between group interactions and writing products [J]. *Journal of Second Language Writing*, 35: 38—53.

[93] LIAW, M. L., 2006. E-learning and the development of

intercultural competence [J]. *Language Learning & Technology*, 10(3): 49—64.

[94] LILLIS, T., 2003. Student writing as "academic literacies": Drawing on Bakhtin to move from "critique" to "design" [J]. *Language and Education*, 17(3): 192—207.

[95] LIU, N. F. & CARLESS, D., 2006. Peer feedback: The learning element of peer assessment [J]. *Teaching in Higher Education*, 11(3): 279—290.

[96] LIU, J. & HANSEN, J., 2002. *Peer response in second language writing classrooms* [M]. Ann Arbor: University of Michigan Press.

[97] LIU, J. & SADLER, R. W., 2003. The effect and affect of peer review in electronic versus traditional modes on L2 writing [J]. *Journal of English for Academic Purposes*, 2(3): 193—227.

[98] LOCKHART, C. & NG, P., 1995. Analyzing talk in peer response groups: Stances, functions, and content [J]. *Language Learning*, 45(4): 605—655.

[99] LONG, M. H., 1981. Input, interaction and second-language acquisition [J]. *Annals of the New York Academy of Sciences*, 379(1): 259—278.

[100] LONG, M. H., 1983. Linguistic and conversational adjustments to nonnative speakers [J]. *Studies in Second Language Acquisition*, 5(2): 177—193.

[101] LONG, M. H., 1985. *A role for instruction in second language acquisition: Task-based language teaching* [C]. // HYLTENSTAM, K. & PIENEMANN, M. Modeling and assessing second language development. Clevedon, Avon: Multilingual Matters: 77—99.

[102] LONG, M. H., 1996. *The role of the linguistic environment in second language acquisition* [C]. // RITCHIE R. & BHATIA, T. Handbook of second language acquisition. San Diego, CA: Edward Arnold: 413—468.

[103] LONG, M., INAGAKI, S. & ORTEGA, L., 1998. The role of implicit negative feedback in SLA: Models and recasts in Japanese and Spanish [J]. *The Modern Language Journal*, 82(3): 357—371.

[104] LU, J. Y. & LAW, N., 2012. Online peer assessment: Effects of cognitive and affective feedback [J]. *Instructional Science*, 40(2): 257—275.

[105] LUDEMANN, P. M. & MCMAKIN, D., 2014. Perceived helpfulness of peer editing activities: First-year students' views and writing performance outcomes [J]. *Psychology Learning and Teaching*, 13(2): 129—136.

[106] LUNDSTROM, K. & BAKER, W., 2009. To give is better than to receive: The benefits of peer review to the reviewer's own writing [J]. *Journal of Second Language Writing*, 18(1): 30—43.

[107] LUO, T., 2016. Enabling microblogging based peer feedback in face to face classrooms [J]. *Innovations in Education and Teaching International*, 53(2): 156—166.

[108] LYSTER, R. & RANTA, L., 1997. Corrective feedback and learner uptake: Negotiation of form in communicative classrooms [J]. *Studies in Second Language Acquisition*, 19(1): 37—66.

[109] MABRITO, M., 1991. Electronic mail as a vehicle for peer response: Conversations of high-and low-apprehensive writers [J]. *Written Communication*, 8(4): 509—532.

[110] MACKEY, A., GASS, S. M. & MCDONOUGH, K., 2000. How do learners perceive interactional feedback? [J]. *Studies in Second Language Acquisition*, 22(4): 471—497.

[111] MAK, B. & CONIAM, D., 2008. Using wikis to enhance and develop writing skills among secondary school students in Hong Kong [J]. *System*, 36(3): 437—455.

[112] MASON, J. B. & BRUNING, R., 2001. *Providing feedback in computer-based instruction: What the research tells us* [R]. In Center for instructional innovation. University of Nebraska-Lincoln.

[113] MAYO, M. D. P. G. & PICA, T., 2000. Interaction among

proficient learners: Are input, feedback and output needs addressed in a foreign language context? [J]. *Studia Linguistica*, 54(2): 272—279.

[114] MCGROARTY, M. E. & ZHU, W., 1997. Triangulation in classroom research: A study of peer revision [J]. *Language Learning*, 47(1): 1—43.

[115] MENDONCA, C. & JOHNSON, K. E., 1994. Peer review negotiations: Revision activities in ESL writing instruction [J]. *TESOL Quarterly*, 28(4): 745—769.

[116] MERCER, N., 1996. The quality of talk in children's collaborative activity in the classroom [J]. *Learning and Instruction*, 6(4): 359—377.

[117] MERKEL, W., 2018. Role reversals: A case study of dialogic interactions and feedback on L2 writing [J]. *Journal of Second Language Writing*, 39: 16—28.

[118] MIN, H. T., 2006. The effects of trained peer review on EFL students' revision types and writing quality [J]. *Journal of Second Language Writing*, 15(2): 118—141.

[119] MOXLEY, J. M., 2012. *Aggregated assessment and objectivity* 2.0. [Z]. //In Proceedings of the Second Workshop on Computational Linguistics and Writing (CLW 2012): Linguistic and Cognitive Aspects of Document Creation and Document Engineering: 19—26.

[120] MURPHY, B. & NEU, J., 1996. *My grade's too low: The speech act set of complaining* [C]. // GASS, S. M. & NEU, J. Speech acts across cultures: Challenges to communication in a second language. Berlin/New York: Mouton de Gruyter: 191—216.

[121] NAKAHAMA, Y., TYLER, A. & LIER, V. L., 2001. Negotiation of meaning in conversational and information gap activities: A comparative discourse analysis [J]. *TESOL Quarterly*, 35(3): 377—405.

[122] NARCISS, S., 2008. *Feedback strategies for interactive learning tasks* [C]. //Spector, J. M., Merrill, M. D., Merrienboer, V. J. J. G., et al. Handbook of research on educational communications and

technology (3rd ed.). Mahwah, NJ: Erlbaum: 125—143.

[123] NARCISS, S. & HUTH, K., 2004. *How to design informative tutoring feedback for multi-media learning* [C]. // Niegemann, H. M., Leutner, D. & Brünken, R. Instructional design for multimedia learning. Münster: Waxmann: 181—195.

[124] NELSON, G. L. & CARSON, J. G., 2006. *Cultural issues in peer response: Revisiting "culture"* [C]. // Hyland, K. & Hyland, F. Feedback in second language writing: Contexts and issues. New York: Cambridge University Press: 42—59.

[125] NELSON, G. L. & MURPHY, J. M., 1992. An L2 writing group: Task and social dimensions [J]. *Journal of Second Language Writing*, 1(3): 171—193.

[126] NELSON, G. L. & MURPHY, J. M., 1993. Peer response groups: Do L2 writers use peer comments in revising their drafts? [J] *TESOL Quarterly*, 27(1): 135—141.

[127] NELSON, M. M. & SCHUNN, C. D., 2009. The nature of feedback: How different types of peer feedback affect writing performance [J]. *Instructional Science*, 37(4): 375—401.

[128] NICOL, D., THOMSON, A. & BRESLIN, C., 2014. Rethinking feedback practices in higher education: A peer review perspective [J]. *Assessment & Evaluation in Higher Education*, 39(1):102—122.

[129] NGUYEN, T. T. M., 2008. Criticizing in an L2: Pragmatic strategies used by Vietnamese EFL learners [J]. *Intercultural Pragmatics*, 5(1): 41—66.

[130] OHTA, A. S., 2001. *A longitudinal study of the development of expression of alignment in Japanese as a foreign language* [C]. Rose, K. & Kasper, G. Pragmatics in Language Teaching. Cambridge: Cambridge University: 103—120.

[131] OLIVER, R., 2002. Age differences in negotiation and feedback in classroom and pairwork [J]. *Language Learning*, 50(1): 119—151.

[132] PARKER, K. R. & CHAO, J. T., 2007. Wiki as a teaching tool [J]. *Interdisciplinary Journal of e-Skills and Lifelong Learning*, 3(3): 57—72.

[133] PAULUS, T. M., 1999. The effect of peer and teacher feedback on student writing [J]. *Journal of Second Language Writing*, 8(3): 265—289.

[134] PERPIGNAN, H., 2003. Exploring the written feedback dialogue: A research, learning and teaching practice [J]. *Language Teaching Research*, 7(2): 259—278.

[135] PICA, T., 1994. Research on negotiation: What does it reveal about second language learning conditions, processes, outcomes? [J]. *Language Learning*, 44(3): 493—527.

[136] PREECE, J., 1998. Empathic communities: Reaching out across the web [J]. *Interactions*, 5(2): 32—43.

[137] RICHARDS, I., PLATT, J. & WEBER, H., 1985. *Longman Dictionary of Applied Linguistics* [M]. Harlow: Longman.

[138] RICHARDS, J. C. & SCHMIDT, R. W., 2010. *Longman dictionary of language teaching and applied linguistics* [M]. Longman: Pearson Education Limited.

[139] ROBINSON, P., 2001. Task complexity, task difficulty, and task production: Exploring interactions in a componential framework [J]. *Applied Linguistics*, 22(1): 27—57.

[140] ROMMETVEIT, R., 1985. *Language acquisition as increasing linguistic structuring of experience and symbolic behavior control* [C]. // WERTSCH J. Culture, communication and cognition: Vygotskyan perspectives. Cambridge: Cambridge University Press: 183—204.

[141] ROSALIA, C., 2010. *EFL students as peer advisors in an online writing center* [M]. NY: New York University.

[142] RULON, K. & MCCREARY, J., 1986. *Negotiation of content: Teacher-fronted and small-group interaction* [C]. // DAY, R.

Talking to learn: Conversation in second language acquisition. Rowley, MA.: Newbury House: 182—199.

[143] RUSSELL, A. A., 2004. *Calibrated Peer Review—a writing and critical thinking instructional tool* [Z]. // In Proceedings of the AAAS Conference on Invention and Impact: Building Excellence in Undergraduate Science, Technology, Engineering and Mathematics (STEM) Education: 67-71.

[144] SATO, M., 2007. Social relationships in conversational interaction: A comparison between learner-learner and learner-NS dyads [J]. *JALT Journal*, 29: 183—208.

[145] SATO, M. & LYSTER, R., 2012. Peer interaction and corrective feedback for accuracy and fluency development [J]. *Studies in Second Language Acquisition*, 34(4): 591—626.

[146] SATO, M., 2017. Interaction mindsets, interactional behaviors, and L2 development: An affective-social-cognitive model [J]. *Language Learning*, 67(2): 249—283.

[147] SCHMIDT, R.W., 1990. The role of consciousness in second language learning [J]. *Applied Linguistics*, 11(2): 129—158.

[148] SCHUNN, C. D., 2017. *Writing to learn and learning to write through SWoRD* [C]. // CROSSLEY, S. A. & MCNAMARA, D. S. Adaptive educational technologies for literacy instruction. New York: Routledge: 243—259.

[149] SHUTE, V. J., 2008. Focus on formative feedback [J]. *Review of Educational Research*, 78: 153—189.

[150] SOLER, E. A., 2002. Relationship between teacher-led versus learners' interaction and the development of pragmatics in the EFL classroom [J]. *International Journal of Educational Research*, 37: 359—377.

[151] SOMMERS, E. & LAWRENCE, S., 1992. Women's ways of talking in teacher-directed and student-directed peer response group [J]. *Linguistics and Education*, 4(1): 1—36.

[152] SOTILLO, S., 2005. Corrective feedback via Instant

Messenger learning activities in NS-NNS and NNS-NNS Dyads [J]. *CALICO Journal*, 22(3): 467—496.

[153] STANLEY, J., 1992. Coaching student writers to be effective peer evaluators [J]. *Journal of Second Language Writing*, 1(3): 217—233.

[154] STEVENSON, M. & PHAKITI, A., 2014. The effects of computer-generated feedback on the quality of writing [J]. *Assessing Writing*, 19: 51—65.

[155] STORCH, N., 2002. Patterns of interaction in ESL pair work [J]. *Language Learning*, 52(1): 119—158.

[156] STORCH, N., 2004. Using activity theory to explain differences in patterns of dyadic interactions in an ESL class [J]. *Canadian Modern Language Review*, 60(4): 457—480.

[157] STORCH, N., 2005. Collaborative writing: Product, process, and students' reflections [J]. *Journal of Second Language Writing*, 14(3): 153—173.

[158] STORCH, N., 2012. *Collaborative writing as a site for L2 learning in face-to-face and online modes* [C]. // KESSLER, G., OSKOZ, A. & ELOLA, I. Technology across writing contexts and tasks. CALICO, Texas: Texas State University: 113—129.

[159] STORCH, N., 2013. *Collaborative Writing in L2 Classrooms* [M]. Bristol: Multilingual Matters.

[160] STRENSKI, E., FEAGIN, C. O. & SINGER, J. A., 2005. Email small group peer review revisited [J]. *Computers and Composition*, 22(2): 191—208.

[161] STRIJBOS, J. W., MARTENS, R. L., PRINS, F. J., et al., 2006. Content analysis: What are they talking about? [J]. *Computers & Education*, 46(1): 29—48.

[162] SUSSER, B., 1994. Process approaches in ESL/EFL writing instruction [J]. *Journal of Second Language Writing*, 3(1): 31-47.

[163] SWAIN, M., 1985. *Communicative competence: Some roles of*

comprehensible input and comprehensible output in its development [C]. // GASS, S. & MADDEN C. Input in second language acquisition. Rowley, MA: Newbury House: 235—252.

[164] SWAIN, M., 1995. *Three functions of output in second language learning* [C]. // COOK, G. & SEIDLHOFER, B. Principle and practice in applied linguistics: Studies in honor of H. G. Widdowson. Oxford: Oxford University Press: 125—144.

[165] SWAIN, M., 2000. *The output hypothesis and beyond* [C]. // LANTOLF, J. P. Sociocultural theory and second language learning. Oxford: Oxford University Press: 97—114.

[166] SWAIN, M., 2001. Integrating language and content teaching through collaborative tasks [J]. *Canadian Modern Language Review*, 58(1): 44—63.

[167] SWAIN, M., 2013. The inseparability of cognition and emotion in second language learning [J]. *Language Teaching*, 46(2): 1—13.

[168] SWAIN, M. & LAPKIN, S., 1998. Interaction and second language learning: Two adolescent French immersion students working together [J]. *The Modern Language Journal*, 82(3): 320—337.

[169] TARDY, C., 2006. *Appropriation, ownership, and agency: Negotiating teacher feedback in academic settings* [C]. // HYLAND, K. & HYLAND, F. Feedback in second language writing. USA: Cambridge University Press: 60—78.

[170] THONUS, T., 2004. What are the differences? Tutor interactions with first-and second-language writers [J]. *Journal of Second Language Writing*, 13(3): 227—242.

[171] THORNE, S. L., 2003. Artifacts and cultures-of-use in intercultural communication [J]. *Language Learning & Technology*, 7(2): 38—67.

[172] THORNE, S. L. & BLACK, R. W., 2007. Language and literacy development in computer-mediated contexts and communities [J]. *Annual Review of Applied Linguistics*, 27(1): 133—160.

[173] TOCALLI-BELLER, A. & SWAIN, M., 2005. Reformulation: The cognitive conflict and L2 learning it generates [J]. *International Journal of Applied Linguistics*, 15(1): 5−28.

[174] TOPPING, K. J., 2010. Methodological quandaries in studying process and outcomes in peer assessment [J]. *Learning and Instruction*, 20(4): 339−343.

[175] TRAUTMANNN, N. M., 2006. *Is it better to give or to receive? Insights into collaborative learning through web-mediated peer feedback* [D]. Ithaca: Cornell University.

[176] TSENG, S.C. & TSAI, C.C., 2007. Online peer assessment and the role of the peer feedback: A study of high school computer course [J]. *Computers & Education*, 49(4): 1161−1174.

[177] TSUI, A. B., 2001. *Classroom interaction* [C]. // CARTER, R. & NUNAN, D. The Cambridge guide to teaching English to speakers of other languages. Cambridge: Cambridge University Press: 120−179.

[178] TSUI, A. B.M. & NG, M., 2000. Do secondary L2 writers benefit from peer comments? [J]. *Journal of Second Language Writing*, 9(2): 147−170.

[179] TUDGE, J. R. H., 1992. Processes and consequences of peer collaborations: A Vygotskian analysis [J]. *Child Development*, 63(6): 1364−1379.

[180] UNLU, Z. & WHARTON, S. M., 2015. Exploring classroom feedback interactions around EAP writing: A data based model [J]. *Journal of English for Academic Purposes*, 17: 24−36.

[181] VAN DEN BERG, I., ADMIRAAL, W. & PILOT, A., 2006. Design principles and outcomes of peer assessment in higher education [J]. *Studies in Higher Education*, 31(3): 341−356.

[182] VAN DEN BRANDEN, K., 1997. Effects of negotiation on language learners' output [J]. *Language Learning*, 47(4): 589−636.

[183] VILLAMIL, O. S. & DE GUERRERO, M. C. M., 1996. Peer revision in the L2 classroom: Socio-cognitive activities, mediating

strategies, and aspects of social behavior [J]. *Journal of Second Language Writing*, 5: 51—75.

[184] VILLAMIL, O. S. & DE GUERRERO, M. C. M., 2006. *Socio-cultural theory: A framework for understanding the socio-cognitive dimensions of peer feedback* [C]. // HYLAND, K. & HYLAND, F. Feedback in second language writing: Contexts and issues. New York: Cambridge University Press: 23—42.

[185] VYGOTSKY, L.S., 1978. *Mind in society: The development of higher psychological processes* [M]. Cambridge, MA: Harvard University Press.

[186] VYGOTSKY, L. S., 1986. *Thought and language* [M]. Cambridge, MA: MIT Press.

[187] WAGER, W. & WAGER, S., 1985. Presenting questions, processing responses, and providing feedback in CAI [J]. *Journal of Instructional Development*, 8(4): 2—8.

[188] WARE, P. D. & O'DOWD, R., 2008. Peer feedback on language form in telecollaboration [J]. *Language Learning & Technology*, 12(1): 43—63.

[189] WHITE, T. L.& KIRBY, B. J., 2005. It is better to give than to receive: An undergraduate peer review process [J]. *Teaching of Psychology*, 32(4): 259—261.

[190] WIENE, N., 1954. *The human use of human beings: Cybernetics and society* [M]. Oxford, England: Houghton Mifflin.

[191] WIENE, P. H. & BUTLER, D. J., 1994. *Student cognitive processing and learning* [C]. // HUSEN, T. & POSTLETHWAITE, T. N. The international encyclopedia of education (Vol.10). Oxford: Pergamon: 5738—5745.

[192] WOOD, D., BRUNER, J.S. & Ross, G., 1976. The role of tutoring in problem-solving [J]. *Journal of Child Psychology and Psychiatry and Allied Disciplines*, 17: 89—100.

[193] YANG, M., BADGER, R. & YU, Z., 2006. A comparative

study of peer and teacher feedback in a Chinese EFL writing class [J]. *Journal of Second Language Writing*, 15(3): 179−200.

[194] YU, S., 2019. Learning from giving peer feedback on postgraduate theses: Voices from Master's students in the Macau EFL context [J]. *Assessing Writing*, 40: 42−52.

[195] YU, S. L. & LEE, I., 2014. An analysis of Chinese EFL students' use of first and second language in peer feedback of L2 writing [J]. *System*, 47: 28−38.

[196] YU, S. L & LEE, I., 2016a. Exploring Chinese students' strategy use in a cooperative peer feedback writing group [J]. *System*, 58: 1−11.

[197] YU, S. L & LEE, I., 2016b. Peer feedback in second language writing (2005—2014) [J]. *Language Teaching*, 49(4): 461−493.

[198] YU, S. L, ZHANG, Y. R., ZHENG, Y., et al., 2019. Understanding student engagement with peer feedback on master's theses: A Macau study [J]. *Assessment & Evaluation in Higher Education*, 44(1): 50−65.

[199] YULE, G. & MACDONALD, D., 1990. Resolving referential conflicts in L2 interaction: The effect of proficiency and interactive role [J]. *Language Learning*, 40(4): 539−556.

[200] ZAMEL, V., 1983. The Composing processes of advanced ESL students: Six case studies [J]. *TESOL Quarterly*, 17(2): 165−187.

[201] ZHANG, Z., 2017. Student engagement with computer-generated feedback: A case study [J]. *ELT Journal*, 71(3): 317−328.

[202] ZHANG, Y. R., YU, S. L. & YUAN, K. H., 2018. Understanding master's students' peer feedback practices from the academic discourse community perspective: A rethinking of postgraduate pedagogies [J]. *Teaching in Higher Education*, 25(1): 1−15.

[203] ZHAO, H. H., 2010. Investigating learners' use and understanding of peer and teacher feedback on writing: A comparative study in a Chinese English writing classroom [J]. *Assessing Writing*, 15

(1): 3—17.

[204] ZHAO, H. H., 2014. Investigating teacher-supported peer assessment for EFL writing [J]. *ELT Journal*, 68(2): 155—168.

[205] ZHU, W., 2001. Interaction and feedback in mixed peer response groups [J]. *Journal of Second Language Writing*, 10(4): 251—276.

[206] ZHU, W. & MITCHELL, D. A., 2012. Participation in peer response as activity: An examination of peer response stances from an activity theory perspective [J]. *TESOL Quarterly*, 46(2): 362—386.

[207] 蔡基刚, 2011. 中国大学生英语写作在线同伴反馈和教师反馈对比研究 [J]. 外语界 (2): 65—72.

[208] 高歌, 2010. 不同分组条件下同侪反馈对学生英语写作的影响 [J]. 外语学刊 (6): 93—97.

[209] 高瑛, 汪溢, Christian D. Schun, 2019. 英语写作同伴反馈评语采纳及其影响因素研究 [J]. 外语电化教学 (2): 17—24.

[210] 韩晔, 杨鲁新, 2021. 非英语专业硕士生对多稿多轮同伴反馈认知投入的个案研究 [J]. 外语与外语教学 (3): 92—101.

[211] 蒋宇红, 2005. 在线同伴评价在写作能力发展中的作用 [J]. 外语教学与研究 (外国语文双月刊) (3): 226—230.

[212] 寇金南, 2016. 我国大学英语课堂不同小组互动模式的特征研究 [J]. 外语与外语教学 (1): 24—32.

[213] 刘立新, 游晓晔, 2018. 基于跨文化修辞学视角的跨洋互动写作教学活动设计 [J]. 现代外语 (2): 257—267.

[214] 刘永厚, 2015. 英语专业写作小组同伴反馈和教师反馈效果研究 [J]. 外语界 (1): 48—55.

[215] 马广惠, 2002. 中美大学生英语作文语言特征的对比分析 [J]. 外语教学与研究 (5): 345—349.

[216] 孟晓, 2009. 同伴反馈在英语写作教学中的应用研究 [J]. 山东外语教学 (4): 59—62.

[217] 庞继贤, 吴薇薇, 2000. 英语课堂小组活动实证研究 [J]. 外语教学与研究 (6): 424—430.

[218] 裘莹莹,马广惠,游晓晔,2019. 中美跨洋写作互动中同伴反馈类型的对比研究 [J]. 外语教学理论与实践(2):69—76.

[219] 邵名莉,2009. 同伴评价在英语专业写作教学中的运用研究 [J]. 外语教学理论与实践(2):47—53.

[220] 孙亚玲,莱斯莉·格兰特,徐娴轩,等,2015. 中美优秀教师教学理念及行为比较 [J]. 教育科学研究(2):65—72.

[221] 汪清,谢元花,2011. 外语环境下任务类型、水平配对与意义协商研究 [J]. 现代外语(1):75—82.

[222] 王颖,李振阳,2012. 国外二语写作中电子反馈模式的研究评述 [J]. 外语电化教学(7):11—16.

[223] 翁克山,李青,2013. ACMC环境下英语写作同侪互评质量与效能研究 [J]. 解放军外国语学院学报(4):62—67.

[224] 伍志伟,2018. 外语写作跨洋互动研究二十载:成果、问题与展望 [J]. 现代外语(2):235—245.

[225] 项茂英,2003. 情感因素对大学英语教学的影响:理论与实证研究 [J]. 外语与外语教学(3):23—26.

[226] 解冰,高瑛,贺文婧,等,2020. 英语写作同伴互评感知量表的编制与探索性应用 [J]. 外语教学,41(3):67—72.

[227] 徐锦芬,寇金南,2017. 大学英语课堂小组互动模式研究 [J]. 外语教学(2):65—69.

[228] 徐锦芬,寇金南,2018. 任务类型对大学英语课堂小组互动的影响 [J]. 外语与外语教学(1):29—38.

[229] 徐锦芬,舒静,2020. 我国大学英语课堂同伴协商互动实证研究 [J]. 外语教学与研究,52(6):868—879.

[230] 徐锦芬,朱茜,2019. 基于Peerceptiv互评系统的英语在线同伴互评研究 [J]. 外语电化教学(2):10—16.

[231] 许春燕,张军,2018. 跨洋互动在线写作教学对中国学生英语书面语的影响 [J]. 现代外语(2):246—256.

[232] 许春燕,张军,战菊,2017. 动态系统论视角下跨洋互动写作课程学生英语作文的复杂度、准确度和流利度研究 [J]. 中国外语(6):53—61.

[233] 薛红果, 2011. 网络环境下美国同伴的反馈对中国学生英语写作能力影响的个案研究 [J]. 外语电化教学 (1): 33—37.

[234] 杨丽娟, 杨曼君, 张阳, 2013. 我国英语写作教学三种反馈方式的对比研究 [J]. 外语教学 (3): 63—67.

[235] 杨苗, 2006. 中国英语写作课教师反馈和同侪反馈对比研究 [J]. 现代外语 (3): 293—301.

[236] 于书林, Icy Lee, 2013. 基于社会文化活动理论的二语写作同伴反馈系统模型构建 [J]. 山东外语教学 (5): 24—29.

[237] 赵国霞, 2002. 课堂师生言语互动及其对学生英语口语的影响 [D]. 南京: 南京师范大学.

[238] 赵雷, 2015. 任务型口语课堂汉语学习者协商互动研究 [J]. 世界汉语教学 (3): 362—376.

[239] 郑超, 杜寅寅, 伍志伟, 2013. 中美学生英语"跨洋互动"行动研究与语料分析 [M]. 北京: 科学出版社.

[240] 周一书, 2013. 大学英语写作反馈方式的对比研究 [J]. 外语界 (3): 87—96.

附 录

附录1：中国写作者的同伴反馈语料

【写作原稿】

Self-awareness & Collective Unconsciousness

In the movies, *And the Spring Comes*, and *Mona Lisa Smile*, both protagonists, Kathrine and Wang Cailing, were confronted with great obstacles, but they all try to attain their goals. But differently, the strong self-awareness buried in Wang's mind urges her to fulfill her own dream at all costs. However, Kathrine, who has high education, regards the emancipation of women's minds and help the independent and complete personality of students as her hope. On account of various factors, they have different destinies.

Wang lives in a remote, small town, and she has the longing for her singing career and passion for love. However, this young dreamer, surrounded by people that are stubborn, boring, and are biased against art and the dreamers' attitude, behavior, the road to Wang's success is quite tough. Kathrine has a close affinity to Wang here, whose idea collides with the traditional view that "women will eventually return to their families". There, in the two films, exists collective unconscious in the society, which means that the prejudice towards women, hipsters or arts is in the

---

① 此处保留原稿原状，包括其不规范表达。

soul of human race. Namely, the vast majority of people accept something true unconsciously though they do not have a clear understanding. This is a tragedy of times and is awfully hard to change.

In such position, to be honest, Kathrine is luckier than Wang, she grows and lives in a transition age where a group of women have broken the shackles of conventions and can manifest their capacity in the society, which let her be free and active. Meanwhile, with Kathrine's encouragement and support, some female students gradually realize their identity, and have the self-awareness to pursue emancipation. At the end of the film, Joan chooses to step into marriage, which makes me wonder Katherine's challenge to those impartiality towards women is failed, but Joan's explanation let me realize that the core of the movie is not enable women to absolutely emancipate from the restrictions of family, or choose one between career success and academic mastery to manifest their independence, but to live the way they want and keep their thoughts free.

As for Wang Cailing, she lives in a small town where the minds of the residents have been solidified permanently. For those old fogies, Wang Cailing's dream is a negligible and impractical joke. Wang Cailing even made the residents look up to her by over beautifying her experience. However, what she got was endless ridicule. They even scorn Wang's life style, and persuade her to marry. Even though Wang has a strong self-awareness, within question, she compromises to reality.

From the two movies, we see a gap between self-awareness and collective unconscious. Someone wins in the battle, and someone fails. Regardless the results, we should show our appreciation to those who stand in the front line fighting against authority and old-fashioned customs, for the reason that their actions may affect or correct people's misbelief in a degree. Most importantly, what can we do when a collision between self-awareness and collective unconscious happens? Firstly, so as to acquire true liberation, people should be loyalty to themselves. Besides, remember that escapism will not solve any problems. The key is that people have the capacity, firmness, determination and bravery to do their own decisions, to achieve ambition and to fight against those inequitable conventions. What's more, since the process is quite tough, those who attain their goal are always persevering, patient and diligent. So even if the reality has also been consistently disappointed, just take them in your stride. And remember in your mind, there is nothing insurmountable. With such determination, your dream and hope are sure to wait you at the end of tunnel.

However, sometimes we feel that it is impossible to cross thorough the collective unconscious. If so, you can learn to reconcile with reality and adversity by employing the forbearing and liberal nature that buried in your soul. For instance, Wang not attain her goal at last, so she adopts a girl and starts selling meats, which can be seen as concession. However, we also notice that she does not marry a man that she dislikes. Meanwhile, she teaches her daughter to sing and smiles a lot than before. We can assume that she wants to cultivate her daughter to be a singer. In this way, she finds the approach to satisfy the need of self-actualization. This is her uncompromising posture. In doing so, we are likely to find a way out of confusion and frustration.

Cao Biqin

【反馈与回评】

Wed., Apr. 15, 2020 2:50 p.m.

Dear Cao,

We have read your article in detail. This film review takes two protagonists as representatives of self-consciousness and collective unconsciousness. The theme is very profound, and this entry point is also very good. The article talks about the performance of the two protagonists' self-consciousness and collective unconsciousness, and the question of what we should do when the two conflict, which also leads to our thinking.

However, there is a problem in the article. Perhaps we do not know much about the words "self-consciousness" and "collective unconsciousness", and the discussion in the article is somewhat empty and difficult to understand. So you can explain the two words to us, and it might be better to use the examples in the films to prove it.

If you have any questions about the review, you can tell me!

Guoliang

Tue., Apr. 17, 2020   1:36 a.m.

Dear Cao,

Your essay has a very interesting analysis! I like the reflection on self-awareness and collective unconsciousness. I agree that these movies show self-awareness and the collective unconsciousness of their different countries and communities. I think this essay does a great job of explaining how difficult it is to overcome hardships, but overcoming hardships is possible. I would suggest using a few more specific movie scenes to demonstrate your points. For example, in the fourth paragraph, the point "They even scorn Wang's lifestyle, and persuade her to marry. Even though Wang has a strong self-awareness, within the question, she compromises to reality" could be more concise. I wonder in what specific scene does Wang compromise with reality, and who "they" is. I remember Wang's parents question her about marriage. Is that the scene you were thinking of? When your points are backed up with specific movie scenes, they will be even stronger!

Let me know if you have questions about my suggestion!

Megan

Fri., Apr. 17, 2020   9:39 a.m.

Dear Guoliang,

I have gotten your comments. Thanks for the advice. Here I want to share with you the idea of us about the collective unconscious.

Collective unconscious refers to structures of the unconscious mind which are shared among beings of the same species. Namely, sometimes human beings have a consistent attitude and recognition that are populated by instincts towards something.

We can see the collective unconscious in the two movies from many details. For example, in the movie *And the Spring Comes*, Hu Jinquan, a young man who loves ballet deeply, does ballet on the ground. However, residents around Hu do not understand him, even laugh at his action, and doubt how can a man dance. Similarly, when Wang starts singing, people leave quickly. The arts are strange to most people which Hu and Wang devote themselves. These people look down upon arts, and they cannot figure out a rational reason why they dislike arts because this kind of thinking about the collective unconscious is buried in the soul of the human race. Though a few people can break the shackles of the collective unconscious, most people are still susceptible to the collective unconscious. Besides, those people who are out of collective control are hard to realize their dream because they are not able to get people to understand them. In the movie *Mona Lisa Smile*, Wesley College, its education that spreads to students is the idea that "women should serve men" and that schools do not teach them how to get knowledge and wisdom, but how to be a "qualified wife". All the efforts that female students make is to pave the way for marrying a good husband. The school even treats marriage as the standard of educational success. This is a kind of collective unconscious. People who no matter men or women, think that women have no place in politics or business and should stay home. Though this idea is ridiculous in a contemporary's mind, people in that times value it.

I am going to end my explanation here. If you have any questions about my explanations, please tell me.

Cao Biqin

Fri. Apr. 17, 2020　9:43 a.m.

Dear Megan,

　　Thanks for the advice. I will try to answer your questions.

　　In the movie, we can see that some people persuade Wang to marry. For example, Zhou Yu said, "Tsai-ling, come to live with me. I will take care of you ... And you are not getting any younger, share life in earnest." Besides, when Hu Jinquan could not bear people's comments, he asked Wang to marry him. When Wang went home, her mother asked her whether she can get married this year. What is more, Miss Zhang also went to Wang's home, and she said, "You really should find a husband." In the sentence "They even scorn Wang's lifestyle", "They" indicates Miss Wang and many residents in that small town. Have you ever noticed that Wang is always alone? Whether she walked in the street or she was accused by Huang Sibao, nobody talked to her or tried to help her. So, I believe residents in the town scorn and dislike her.

　　After experiencing the swindling of Gao Beibei, Wang went to Dating Agency. I do not know if there is a Dating Agency in America that is an organization aiming at helping people to find a partner. I think Wang's act that she went to Dating Agency is a kind of compromise since she wanted to get rid of rumors. However, she failed.

　　I am going to end my explanation here. I really appreciate your advice. It will help me improve my article. If you have any questions about my explanations, just tell me.

Cao Biqin

Mon. Apr. 20, 2020　7:00 a.m.

　　Hello, Cao,

　　I really liked the theme of your essay. It was interesting how you compared Wang Cailing's and Katherine's stories by acknowledging how their environment influenced their destinies, as you put it. I also liked your idea of emphasizing these women's struggle with self-awareness versus the collective unconscious. I grasped what you were trying to say, but maybe you can provide more examples from the films to demonstrate this further. I think you have a strong theme here, but I think you should dive deeper into talking about your idea of the collective unconscious.

   Thanks for working with me!

Heidi

Mon., Apr. 20, 2020   7:49 a.m.

   Hello, Cao,

   Thank you for your careful contact with the plot in the movie to explain to us the meaning of self-consciousness and the collective unconsciousness. I think I can understand the theme of your film review now, which is very profound.

   But I just want to mention some minor problems in the article. Firstly, at the end of the first paragraph, for various reasons, they have different destinies. You can say something briefly and let us know what you think. Secondly, I think in the fifth paragraph, you can add some plots in the film to your views on what to do when self-consciousness and collective unconsciousness collide so that we can understand it more intuitively. Finally, some sentences in this article are too long, which may lead to some grammatical errors. For example, the last sentence of the third paragraph is so long that it may take us a long time to understand.

   Look forward to your reply!

Guoliang

Tue. Apr. 21, 2020   12:22 p.m.

Dear Cao,

   Thank you for your elaborations and specific movie scene additions. I understand which scenes you were referring to and where you were getting your ideas from better. I think those quotes and scenes from the movie will be a great addition to your essay! I agree that the evidence from the movie supports your claims. I notice that Heidi made a similar comment. So I think adding the scenes that you explained to me will improve your essay from both Heidi's and my own suggestions.

I've enjoyed working with you so far!

Megan

Wed. Apr. 22, 2020　2:54 p.m.

Dear Heidi,

Thank you for the comments. Actually, I have also noticed that there exists ambiguity about self-awareness and collective unconsciousness in my article. Megan, and Guoliang also point out this problem. I have explained this to them. You can read my reply to them. Hopefully that help.

If you have other questions and suggestions after reading my explanations, please let me know.

Thank you again for your advice.

Cao Biqin

Thu. Apr. 23, 2020　6:24 p.m.

Dear Megan,

Thank you again for your suggestions! It really helps me improve my article. I will continue to revise the article. After revising it, we will post it on the website. If you have time, you can give us other suggestions.

It is nice to work with you!

Cao Biqin

Thu. Apr. 23, 2020　6:26 p.m.

Dear Guoliang,

Thank you for the comments.

"Different destinies", I think it is inappropriate there because it is irrelevant to the context. I have also noticed that the first paragraph needs improvements. However, I do not work out a start so far. If you have some idea, just tell me. Besides, I like the idea of adding some plots in the fifth paragraph because it seems so empty without plots. Do you think it is suitable if I add the scene where Professor Watson choose to leave after being cheated? In addition, I will try to make modifications to sentence length.

Looking forward to your reply.

Cao Biqin

Sun. Apr. 26, 2020 8:29 a.m.

Hi, Cao,

I think the opening paragraph of the essay is suitable. It is to the point that you draw out the theme you want to express through the two protagonists. Maybe you can delete the last sentence, because "on account of different factors, they have different destinies" requires you to continue to explain why, which may conflict with the meaning you are expressing.

I think the fifth paragraph can first add how the two protagonists are loyal to themselves in order to gain freedom, and then add how the protagonists face up to difficulties and do not escape. Adding a certain plot of the film together with your explanation will be more convincing.

Guoliang

【修改稿】

Wed. Apr. 29, 2020 7:07 a.m.

Self-awareness & Collective Unconsciousness

After watching the two movies, *Mona Lisa Smile*, *And the Spring Comes*, we learn that Wang Cailing and Waston are alienated from most people in the society. This article will focus on the relationship of self-awareness and collective unconsciousness to illustrate the two films.

Wang lives in a remote, small town, and she has the longing for her singing career and passion for love. However, it is quite tough for Wang to achieve her dream, because she is surrounded by stubborn people who have strong prejudice against art and the dreamers' attitude, behavior. Kathrine has a close affinity to Wang here, whose idea collides with the traditional view that "women will eventually return to their families". There, in the two films, exists collective unconscious in the society, which refers to structures of the unconscious mind and is shared among beings of the same species. Namely, sometimes human beings have a consistent attitude and recognition that are populated by instincts towards something, and they also accept something true unconsciously though they do not have a clear understanding. We can see collective unconscious in the two movies from many details. For example, in the movie *And the Spring Comes*, Hu Jinquan, a young man who loves ballet deeply, does ballet in the ground. However, residents around Hu do not understand him, even laugh at his action, and doubt how can a man dance. Similarly, when Professor Wang starts singing, people leave quickly. The arts are strange to most people which Hu and Wang devote themselves to. These people look down upon arts, and they cannot figure out a rational reason they dislike arts, because this kind of thinking about art is buried in the soul of residents who do not really understand art. In the movie *Mona Lisa Smile*, Wesley College, its education does not teach student how to get knowledge and wisdom, but teaches that "women should serve men" and how to be a "qualified wife". All the efforts that female students make is to pave the way for marrying a good husband. The school even treat marriage as the standard of educational success. This is a kind of collective unconscious. People, no matter men or women, think that women have no place in politic or business and should stay home. Though this idea is ridiculous in a contemporary's mind, people at that times value it.

  A few people can break the shackles of collective unconscious. However, the reason Wang and Watson can break loose from collective unconscious is that they are women with a heightened degree of self-awareness which means that they have the capacity for introspection and the ability to recognize themselves as an individual separate from the environment and other individuals. In the two movies, both protagonists, Kathrine and Wang Cailing, were confronted with great obstacles, but they all try to attain their goals. But differently, the strong self-awareness buried in Wang's mind urges her to fulfill her own dream at all costs. However, Kathrine, who has high education, regards the emancipation of women's minds and help the independent and complete personality of students as her hope.

Nevertheless, most people are still susceptible by collective unconscious. Besides, those people who are out of collective control are hard to realize their dream, because they are not able to get people to understand them. This is a tragedy of times and is hard to change.

In such position, to be honest, Kathrine is luckier than Wang, she grows and lives in a transition age where a group of women have broken the shackles of conventions and can manifest their capacity in the society, which let her be free and active. Meanwhile, with Kathrine's encouragement and support, some female students gradually realize their identity, and have the self-awareness to pursue emancipation. As the end of the film, Joan choose to step into marriage, which makes me wonder Katherine's challenge to those impartiality towards women is failed, but Joan's explanation let me realize that the core of the movie is not enable women to absolutely emancipate from the restrictions of family, or choose one between career success and academic mastery to manifest their independence, but to live the way they want and keep their thoughts free.

As for Wang Cailing, she lives in a small town where the minds of the residents have been solidified permanently. For those old fogies, Wang Cailing's dream is a negligible and impractical joke. Wang Cailing even make the residents look up to her by over beautifying her experience. However, what she got was endless ridicule. They, Miss Wang, and many residents in that small town, even scorn Wang's lifestyle. Whether she walks in the street or she is hit by Huang Sibao, nobody talks to her or tries to help her. They also persuade her to marry. For example, Zhou Yu says:"Tsai-ling, come to live with me. I will take care of you ... And you are not getting any younger, share life in earnest." Besides, when Hu Jinquan could not bear people's comments, he asks Wang to marry him. When Wang goes home, her mother asks her whether she can get married this year. What is more, Miss Zhang also goes to Wang's home, and she says:"You really should find a husband." Even though Wang has a strong self-awareness, within question, she compromises to reality. After experiencing the swindle of Gao Beibei, Wang goes to Dating Agency, trying to live like a "normal" girl. I think Wang's act is a kind of compromise since she wants to get rid of rumors. However, she fails.

From the two movies, we see a gap between self-awareness and collective unconscious. Someone wins in the battle, and someone fails. Regardless the results, we should show our appreciation to those who stand in the front line fighting against authority and old-fashioned customs, since their actions may affect or correct people's misbelief in a degree. Most importantly, what can we do when a collision between self-awareness and collective unconscious happens? Firstly, to acquire true liberation, people should be loyal to themselves. Besides, remember that escapism will not solve any problems. The key is that people have the capacity, firmness, determination, and bravery to do their own decisions, to achieve ambition and to fight against those inequitable conventions. What's more, since the process is quite tough, those who attain their goal are always persevering, patient and diligent. So even if the reality has also been consistently disappointed, just take them in your stride. And remember in your mind, there is nothing insurmountable. With such determination, your dream and hope are sure to wait you at the end of tunnel.

However, sometimes we feel that it is impossible to cross thorough the collective unconscious. If so, you can learn to reconcile with reality and adversity by employing the forbearing and liberal nature that buried in your soul. For instance, Wang does not attain her goal at last, so she adopts a girl and starts selling meats, which is a concession. However, we also notice that she does not marry a man that she dislikes. Meanwhile, she teaches her daughter to sing and smiles a lot than before. We can assume that she wants to cultivate her daughter to be a singer. In this way, she finds the approach to satisfy the need of self-actualization. This is her uncompromising posture. In doing so, we are likely to find a way out of confusion and frustration.

【反思】

Wed. Apr. 29, 2020   7:17 a.m.

We benefit a lot from this trans-oceanic interactive activity. Firstly, it is a great opportunity for us to communicate with native speakers. Through this activity, we learn the American students' writing style and see that the words and expressions of their article are more natural and adequate than ours. So we need to take consideration about how to improve our grammar, Chinglish language, fluency of sentence, etc. Secondly, the comments to our article from Chinese students and American students are from two perspectives. It helps us to know the readers' feelings about America and China when they read our movie review. Thirdly, this activity helps us know the difference of thinking mode in Chinese and American students. It is a true reflection of the different characteristics of communication between the two in English. Fourthly, after two weeks of cross-border communication, we also know our problems. Through the communication with Megan, Heidi, Guoliang, we find that the ignorance of film plots in our writing is inadequate.

It is important to use language when we learn it. If learners can learn more and write more and have frequent interaction with native speakers in specific situations, students can learn language structure and vocabulary. This activity helps us to think in English when communicating with a native speaker.

Thank again for Megan, Heidi, Guoliang's advice.

附录 2：美国写作者的同伴反馈语料

【写作原稿】

Movie Essay

After watching both films, it was easy to see the immediate difference in culture. Chinese culture and American culture are very different, yet they hold some similarities. It was interesting to follow Cailing Wang's story because of these stark differences in culture. I have never watched a movie with this kind of storyline. As a music school teacher, Wang dreams of being an opera singer and of using her talent to stand out from the crowd. What *And the Spring Comes* tries to convey are the hopes of artists, misfits, and visionaries alike, all stuck in hopelessly dead-end situations, especially considering women's empowerment. A story very bleak, the movie offers the occasional light-hearted moment (Wang shown with a cast after surviving her fall) to break the heaviness of the main story. With several roadblocks and emotional ties to people who do not particularly respect her in the way she respects them, she gets caught on several occasions where she ends up disappointed. The man she thought she loved, the painter, uses her for the trip to Beijing. The way that she gets treated because of her looks stood out to me because it made people disregard her.

I would say one aspect of Chinese culture that stood out to me is the way this movie is filmed. It uses several different camera angles to capture different well put together scenes. Chinese film culture uses different techniques I have never seen before. For example, the representations are mostly dark to emphasize Wang's unhappiness with her seeking surroundings. I also noticed some scenes are filmed from lower points, closer to the ground, and some are further far away, creating a different mood. Another aspect of cultural difference I noticed was food. There were several scenes where food was a way of forgiveness or a stage of togetherness. Food is integrated into the daily life and culture of Chinese people. They celebrate festivals by food and offer sacrifices to ancestors with delicious meals. Food is present in American culture, of course, but Americans do not value the gesture or importance as much as Chinese people.

In the American movie, *Mona Lisa Smile*, Julia Roberts portrays an art history professor teaching at the all-female Wellesley College in 1953. She is not an obvious choice as Wellesley is an exclusive institution where its faculty, students, and alumni are generally snobby. Katherine Ann Watson tries to teach her students to have a mind of their own and inspires them to reach their full potential. This film uses the past as an emphasis on Katherine's modernized character for her time. This modernism is present in both films to portray the problematic pursuit of these women's dreams. I am used to American movies, so it was easy to see the clear difference between them. This kind of American film always seems to follow along the same plotline, a beautiful woman working hard, inspiring others, and she finds someone to fall in love with, conflict, then leading to a happy ending.

Heidi Gogel

【反馈与回应】

Wed. Apr. 15, 2020 1:06 p.m.

Dear Heidi,

　　Hello. Nice to meet you!

　　We have read your article in great detail. To be honest, you make wonderful work. This is a multi-angle film review. In your article, you mentioned a variety of perspectives, such as cultural differences, the shooting angle of the film, and the wonderful culture of food. In the comparison, you choose the comparison method of object-object. The advantage of this method of comparison is that it can describe the characteristics of each comparative thing in detail. We also see that you wrote about the unprecedented shooting angle of *And the Spring Comes* and started to write about cultural differences from the image of food, which is a very novel point of view! Chinese people have a very deep emotion for food, and it is also an important part of Chinese culture. (We can communicate later.)

But the deficiency is that the points you write are scattered, and the structure of the article is not very clear. The comparison of this kind of film review between the two films is more suitable to use the subject-subject comparison method, which makes the comparison more obvious and the point of view more concentrated. There is also a point we think that this article lacks a summary end! If there is a conclusion, it will be even more perfect!

In addition, do you have a personal e-mail address or WeChat? We can continue to communicate in the future!

Guoliang(This review is written by my companion and me.)

Thu. Apr. 16, 2020   5:28 a.m.

Hi, Heidi,

I am glad to read your article. You say that the storyline of the two films is quite different. I feel the same. *And the Spring Comes* is a typical Chinese art cinema that needs audiences' patience to learn the connotation. You notice that the way the movie is filmed is different. Besides, you have mentioned Chinese film techniques. I think it would be better if you can figure out the American film techniques.

Then in your first and last paragraphs, you mention the plot of the two films, but you separate the two films. You can try to make some comparisons in the plot. By reading this article, I know a lot of details that I ignored before. For example, in *And the Spring Comes*, the emergence of food also has something that filmmakers want to express to us. In addition, you also have a strong ability to grasp the theme. I really appreciate this point.

If you have any questions, please let me know.

Cao Biqin

Mon. Apr. 20, 2020 5:15 a.m.

Hello, Guoliang,

Nice to meet you too. Thank you for your thoughtful comments! I appreciate your comments on my views on the way the movie was filmed and the cultural aspects of the movies. This was an interesting assignment to complete and your input will help me greatly with the revision of this essay. I realize I have to fix the format, write a better summary, and provide a clearer theme to my paper. Also, my e-mail is *heidigogel@gmail.com*!

Thank you, and it was nice working with you!

Heidi Gogel

Mon. Apr. 20, 2020 5:25 a.m.

Hello, Cao,

Thanks for your comments! I thought it was interesting how you mentioned *And The Spring Comes* needs the audience's patience to learn the connotations. This is an interesting concept that I haven't thought about and agree with. The movie brings us along with Wang Cailing's life and lets us experience her frustrations along with her road to success. I think you're right that I should also include American film techniques to compare the two.

Thank you for working with me!

Heidi Gogel

Mon. Apr. 20, 2020   8:26 a.m.

Hello, Heidi,

   Thank you for your affirmation of our comments. Reading your article again, we think it is good to compare the two films from the perspective of Chinese and American culture.

   Here, we would like to make two suggestions. On the one hand, maybe your space design is a little unreasonable. The first one and second paragraphs are about *And the Spring Comes*, and the third paragraph is about *Mona Lisa Smile*. For example, in the third paragraph, "so it was easy to see the clear difference between them", you can introduce some differences for us in detail. On the other hand, in the second paragraph, you mentioned the shooting techniques and Chinese food of Chinese culture. I think you can start from these two aspects, compare some of the differences between Chinese and American cultures in these two aspects, and give us an intuitive and in-depth understanding of American culture.

   Look forward to your reply!

Guoliang

Wed. Apr. 22, 2020   5:11 a.m.

Hello, Guoliang,

   Again, thank you for your comments! I realize my essay seems a little rushed, and my structure is not organized well. I appreciate your feedback and will try to edit my essay accordingly to make it easier to read and more enjoyable. I will also try to include more of a comparison between American and Chinese cultures to strengthen an understanding of American culture.

   Thank you!

Heidi Gogel

Wed. Apr. 22, 2020   2:29 p.m.

Dear Heidi,

　　Thank you for the messages. I read your article again. Here, I would like to make another suggestion.

　　In the third paragraph, you mention that "this modernism is present in both films to portray the problematic pursuit of these women's dream". To avoid any ambiguity, maybe you can give some explanations about how the two movies display "modernism". You also can employ some plots to strengthen your idea. In doing so, your article will be more persuasive.

　　Please let me know if you have any questions.

Cao Biqin

Thu. Apr. 23, 2020   1:31 p.m.

Hi, Heidi,

　　We are glad to have your feedback on our suggestion. After reading your article again, we think that there is one more point that you can improve, that is, when you comment on the Chinese film *And the Spring Comes*, you can not only summarize the plot but also write about the shooting techniques and the Chinese culture shown in the film. We think that if you can also describe the way the film was made in the *Mona Lisa Smile* comments, it will make the article more perfect. And if you can connect American culture with shooting techniques like the description of *And the Spring Comes*, it is also in line with the content of the cultural exchange between China and America that you mentioned at the beginning of the article.

　　Look forward to hearing from you again!

Guoliang

【修改稿】

Wed. Apr. 29, 2020　4:07 a.m.

Cultural Essay

After watching the Chinese film *And the Spring Comes*, and the American film *Mona Lisa Smile*, it was easy to spot the differences in not only culture but the visual techniques used in the movies. It was interesting to follow each woman's story, and it was clear to see their similar positions as aspiring women in their societies. Striving for success and seeking to achieve their dreams is what these women are motivated by throughout their unique stories. What these movies try to convey are the hopes of artists, misfits, and visionaries alike, and are all "stuck" in hopelessly dead-end situations, especially from a woman's perspective. With their journeys, women's empowerment is what I will be focusing on for this analysis to emphasize the struggles both women faced in entirely different cultures.

After watching American movies, naturally, I took notice that color signifies what mood a scene is trying to portray and what it wants the audience to feel. For example, warm colors usually represent a happier setting, while darker colors depict a more ominous, sadder mood. This is seen throughout both movies. In *Mona Lisa Smile*, Katherine Ann Watson is starting a new job at the prestigious all-girls school Wellesley College, and the scenes are mostly bright and ironically welcoming. I think this represents the false welcome the college instills while it encourages old views and mindsets, leading to the oppression of women not knowing how to use their voice. Watson is a modernized woman for her time, and she tries to teach her students to have a mind of their own and inspires them to reach their full potential. She faces several obstacles that steer her from this notion, but she remains consistent with her beliefs. Modernism is present in both films to portray the problematic pursuit of these women's dreams.

As a music school teacher, Wang Cailing dreams of being an opera singer and yearns to stand out from the crowd. She is a woman who, like Watson, faces several roadblocks that keep her from reaching her dreams, leaving her repeatedly disappointed from failure. Wang's story is bleak because of the way people treat Wang, and this is shown by the way this movie was filmed. I found this movie particularly interesting because of the scenes themselves as they were different from what I have seen. The representations are mostly dark to emphasize Wang's unhappiness with her seeking surroundings. Some sad scenes are filmed from lower points, closer to the ground, and some are further far away, creating a different distant mood. Another aspect of cultural difference I noticed was food. There were several scenes where food was a way of forgiveness or a stage of togetherness. Food is integrated into the daily life and culture of Chinese people. They celebrate festivals by food and offer sacrifices to ancestors with delicious meals. Food is present in American culture, of course, but Americans do not value the gesture or importance as much as the Chinese. Both movies successfully portrayed strong characters with determination to complete their goals and unique storylines to go along with them, while also providing a look into cultural differences.

【反思】

Thu. Apr. 30, 2020   3:12 a.m.

The Border-Crossing Activity was a unique and enjoyable experience, very different from a lecture setting. It was nice to be able to connect with people of my age across the world, studying in college just like me. I worked with students named Cao, and Guo, and as for expectations, I was not sure what to expect. I was nervous in the beginning, but the students I worked with were friendly and thoughtful when it came to revision suggestions, so I would say my expectations were exceeded. They helped me understand where I was not able to successfully describe American culture, which would help them learn more about it. One thing that struck me most about this assignment was how well their English was written. They were responding to me with no problem, and I thought that was very impressive because English is a hard language to learn if it is foreign to you, and it's so different from Chinese.

Another thing I found that struck me was how well their analyses were formed. I thought some of theirs were written well because they went into a lot of details I hadn't considered, such as the Chinese culture present that I hadn't noticed in *And the Spring Comes*. Something that struck me was how long their essays had been compared to ours. They went into explicit details and used language that portrayed a lot of abstract ideas, and I appreciated this. It helped with my writing because it helped me understand a lot of ideas that I would not be able to put into words otherwise. While rewriting my draft, I considered their words and tried to provide a more distinct comparison between American and Chinese cultures. The comments from Guoliang persuaded me to do this because they couldn't grasp the contrast I was trying to make because of my lack of input from *Mona Lisa Smile*. They also suggested I strengthen my argument by providing more examples from the films, and considering the lacking structure of my essay, I thought this activity helped me to be more open-minded when it comes to working with bigger groups of people, especially with people so far away. Working with these students also helped me with my writing skills as they taught me that abstraction works if you have enough evidence to support it. Finally, three adjectives I would use to describe this activity would be enjoyable, challenging (in a good way) and rewarding because of the results.

附录3：中国写作者后续访谈转录

采访者：游晓晔老师和一名硕士生
被访谈者：五位中方写作者

问1：反馈时为什么要注重组织、构思和主题句？

学生根据老师提供的反馈清单，并结合写作课堂教师给予的反馈框架，进行同伴反馈。反馈清单和反馈框架都关注写作文本的组织、结构和主题句。此外，同伴反馈还特别关注与社会问题相关的内容的观点交流。

问2：中国学生提供同伴反馈的关注点是语言、内容还是结构？

中国学生对同伴作文的语言、内容和结构都很关注。整体而言，中国学生先关注内容，后关注语言。双方注重对对方写作内容和观点的理解，尤其是文化讨论，因为美国同伴对中国影片中体现的文化了解有限。同伴是英语母语者，因此中国学生不是侧重于关注对方的语言错误，而是学习地道的语言表达；偶尔也关注对方的语言表达，譬如重复用词，因为即使是母语者也会犯语言方面的错误。

问3：中国学生更希望美国同伴提出语言问题还是与内容相关的建议？

中国学生希望对方关注语言。比如，美国同伴提出语言和内容两方面的反馈时，中国学生一直就语言问题做出回应和交流，忽略关于内容的意见。对于美国同伴提出的语言问题，中国学生会先考证，会接受大多数。

问4：在交流过程中，中国学生会模仿美国同伴的语言吗？

尤其在互动过程中，中国学生会模仿美国同伴的语言；在通过电子邮件沟通的过程中，中国学生也会模仿美国同伴的语言。

问5：在同伴反馈过程中，中国学生对写作内容、语言和结构等方面进行评价时，对哪部分最有信心？

中国学生对写作内容进行评价时最有信心，尤其是中国文化方面的评价。中国学生在大一下学期学习了议论文篇章结构知识，因此对结构方面的评价也比较有信心。中国学生对语言方面的评价没有信心，会在做出评论之前，与本国同学商讨。

问6：美国学生的写作符合中国学生的期望/想象吗？

中国学生原以为美国学生的写作有非常严谨的结构，而实际上美国学生的文章篇章结构松散，但中心集中，连贯性很好，做到了"形散神不散"。

中国学生原以为美国学生对中国文化了解有限，但出乎意料的是部分美国学生很了解中国文化，接受文化差异，有较强的文化包容性，其与同伴讨论的范围更广，包括社会、文化和哲学；但有的美国学生不接受文化差异。

问7：美国学生基于电影对中西文化进行对比；而中国学生则关注对社会问题的讨论，认为只有关注社会问题并对讨论进行升华，才能使文章更深刻。中国学生的写作思维与英语写作教学是否相关，是受汉语写作课教学的影响吗？

中国学生的写作受中学语文写作教学的影响，教师们强调通过素材、社会热点问题、名人名言等，丰富学生的写作内容，提高学生的写作水平。中国学生在交流互动过程中引入社会热点，因为他们将此活动不仅仅看成是一项学习任务，更将其看成是一次中西观点交流的宝贵经历。因此，中国学生投入大量的时间和精力，将交流的内容和自己的兴趣紧密联系起来，而不是像对待应试作文一样完成写作任务。

问8：中国学生对美国学生文章的组织和构思等提出不同意见，部分美国学生认为与文章组织结构相关的评论是低年级学生的需求，高年级的学生不需要这样的评论；也有美国学生的写作任务是写一篇影评。中国学生对此有何看法？

美国学生对于"没有回到影片"等反馈，没有做出回应，原因是虽然美国学生在修改过程中没有做出改动，但是双方在交流互动中已经解释了该问题，双方的关注点不同，切入角度不同。中国学生认为美国学生的回应可以被理解，可能是写作要求的传达和理解的不同导致的。

中国学生的写作也有"形散神不散"的类型，形式不是评判写作的唯一标准，有些名篇已经打破了写作的固有形式。学术写作不一定每段和每篇都有主题句，但是文章的逻辑一定要好。美国学生的文章也出现过句与句之间没有任何连接、没有逻辑关系的情况。中国学生认为跨洋互动活动增强了自身对写作结构的意识。

问9：在交流过程中，是维持和谐关系更重要，还是做出批判性评论帮助对方修改文章从而提高对方写作质量更重要呢？参与者们会不会为了维持和谐关系而避免一些尖锐的评论？

在网上交流过程中，同伴用礼貌的方式提出建议，意见不同时也会注意措辞，未出现为了维持和谐关系而避免尖锐评论的情况。

问10：从这次活动中，中国学生发现了哪些中美写作的差异？

美国学生很少指出中国学生的语言问题，对中国文化感兴趣；中国学生的修改主要集中在语言方面，较少改动内容。

美国学生更像侦探，把影片中的情节用到写作中，电影分析很透彻。美国学生的写法方法多样，因为有的学生认为自己是高年级学生，不用低年级的方法写；有的学生认为课程的性质是修辞课，只需要讨论修辞问题，不需要探讨电影之外的问题。中国学生的论文与社会现象结合紧密。

美国学生的"读者意识"强，知道读者是谁，以及应该给予什么样的回应或持什么样的态度（譬如，给学生发邮件与给朋友发邮件的形式不同），也会对语言做出相应的调整。

附录 4：第 18 轮跨洋互动写作项目活动说明（美国学生）

Border-crossing activity is an attempt to improve students' communication ability and cultural sensitivity by encouraging them to communicate across national, language, and cultural boundaries.

In this particular activity, eighteen of the Pennsylvania State University undergraduate students are paired up with nine students from Nanjing University and nine students from Guangdong University of Foreign Studies. All participants watched two movies and wrote an essay of about 500 words. Students are asked to make one or two observations/arguments on the two movies (See the Movie Essay Prompts). The students' essays are made available on ×××××× at midnight on April 10(noon on April 11 in China). The essays are numbered and each essay leads a thread. Free exchange is encouraged between the students underneath the original essay. Students are also encouraged to exchange ideas through e-mail or WeChat. Hopefully, mutual understanding will be fostered, and sensitivity to English styles used in different contexts will be cultivated. To post comments, one will need to login in first. The user's name and password will be provided by the professor.

Students will work in groups. Every group consists of two Chinese students and two American students. When you read an essay, you can analyze both its content and form, discussing cultural, rhetorical, and linguistic issues. You may use the reader response guide attached here to organize your comments. You make comments and suggestions in these areas in the hope of improving each other's essays and enhancing mutual understanding. When you comment, please be sure to offer a brief explanation in your post. When you make a suggestion, please be sure to describe the essay in a way to help the student see the purpose of this writing; evaluate the student's progress towards the goals of the movie essay assignment; suggest specific advice that the student can follow in his or her revisions.

Please go back to your post in a day or two to read and respond to any follow-ups from other students. When someone responds to your essay, you will receive an e-mail alert. Make sure that you exchange with a student for his or her essay three times within two weeks (by April 25). Then you revise your essay based on the feedback received (by April 28). You post your revised essay and your reflections (See the Reflection Prompts) in the same thread where your original essay is posted.

At the end of the activity, your performance will be assessed in the following three areas: attitudes, knowledge, and skills. See the evaluation criteria attached.

Please save all your postings and your ensuing e-mail correspondence, and turn them in for grading at the end of the semester.

Instructions on Accessing the Website

The URL for the forum: forum/index. php.

Please take the following steps to fully establish your presence in this online space:

(1) The forum for the exchange is called PSU-NJU/GDUFS EXCHANGE. To enter this exchange, click the name of the exchange and enter the password: April 2018.

(2) To post on this exchange, you will need to log in. Click "Log in" in the upper right corner, and you will be prompted to enter your user's name and password.

(3) After you've logged in, please update your profile. Click your user's name in the upper right corner arrow, then the user's control panel, and then your profile.

(4) If you have not sent me your essay, you can post it on the site yourself. Underneath the list of groups, you will see "New Topic". Click it and then you will be able to post the essay. I will then place the essay in a certain group.

Your User's Name and Password

Please note that the user's name contains the blank space and the dot after the family name initial, and the password is the one after the ">" symbol.

After login, you can (and should) change your password. The change password function is located at:

(1) Click your user's name in upper right corner after loging in.

(2) Click "User Control Panel" after clicking the drop-down arrow.

(3) Click "Profile".

(4) Click "Edit Account Setting".

(5) Change password (you will need their current password to do this).

Movie Essay Prompts

Please write an essay in at least 500 words to discuss the two movies *Mona Lisa Smile* and *And the Spring Comes*. You are expected to examine any aspects of Chinese and American culture represented and non-verbal strategies used in both movies. Choose one or two cultural aspects or communicative strategies as the focus of your essay and express your opinions by drawing examples from the movies as evidence.

Cultural representations include, but are not limited to:

- Women's empowerment
- Social and physical mobility
- Personal development and growth
- Success and the means to achieve it

Verbal strategies include, but are not limited to:

- ethos, pathos, logos
- 义(yi), 礼(li), 智(zhi), 信(xin), 言(yan)

Non-verbal strategies include, but are not limited to:

- Camera shots, movements, angles
- Framing, cuts

- Lighting
- Characters' clothes, make-up, accessories, gestures, etc.

The American movie *Mona Lisa Smile* is on reserve in the Music and Media Library on the second floor of West Pattee Library. You can check it out for two hours (and to watch it in the library). The Chinese movie *And the Spring Comes* can be watched for free at ××××××.

The movie essay will be due on April 10, on which day we will conduct a peer review to improve your essay. Soon after that, we will post your essay on a web platform to initiate the border-crossing activity with students at Nanjing University, China.

Reader Response Guide

- Overall response (State your general reaction to the text; your main observation)
- Focus (State what you think the focus statement is; indicate whether all sections of the text fit the focus)
- Development for readers (State what reader position you see, if any; indicate whether the text supplies enough or too much, or too few details for the reader position)
- Organization and coherence (State what organization you see; identify what parts fit and which don't; comment on coherence—how helpful or not helpful the transitions are between sections)
- Design (Comment on the overall visual effect of the text; indicate whether the layout of the page is consistent with the audience, genre, and purpose of the text)
- Language, grammar, and conventions (Point out significant or repeated errors in these categories)
- Main emphasis for revision (State the most important thing to change for the next version)

Reflection Prompts

When the online exchange is over, you are expected to revise your movie review and reflect upon the exchange activity. To guide your reflection, please refer to the following questions. Please share your thoughts on questions (1)(2)(3)(7)(8) and answer one more question out of the rest. Thank you.

(1) What were your expectations for the border-crossing activity? Are your expectations being met? Why or why not?

(2) Please name three things that struck you most when you interacted with your Chinese peers, and explain why. (You may comment on the differences and/or similarities in lexical choice, writing style, idea presentation, rhetorical preference, cultural convention, etc.)

(3) Did you incorporate what had been discussed into the revised draft? If so, please elaborate on how the discussion led to the revisions you made. If not, please explain why.

(4) Do you think the activity is beneficial to you in terms of knowledge gains or skill enhancement? If so, please elaborate. If not, please explain why.

(5) What kinds of persona did you create and present in this activity? How about your Chinese peer's persona? Do you notice any differences and/or similarities? Are there any textual evidence to support your claims?

(6) Could you provide three adjectives to describe the activity? Please explain your choice.

(7) Could you provide three adjectives to describe your feelings about the activity? Please explain your choice.

(8) Are there additional comments, suggestions, and observations you would like to make to better help us assess your performance in this activity?

Performance Assessment Criteria

Your performance in the border-crossing activity (20 points) is represented in the portfolio of the first draft of the movie essay, online forum posts, the revised movie essay, and your reflections. Your performance will be assessed in the following three areas: attitudes, knowledge, and skills.

1. Attitudes

- Your drafts and reflection are handed in on time, and your forum posts are prompt.
- You keep an open mind throughout the activity.
- You are eager to engage in the discussion of a variety of issues (language, social, cultural, etc.).

2. Knowledge

- You demonstrate (increased) knowledge of your home culture/society.
- You demonstrate increased knowledge of the other culture/society.
- You demonstrate linguistic, stylistic, and generic knowledge in writing.
- You demonstrate digital literacy (e. g. emoji, external links, cross-reference, etc.) throughout the activity.

3. Skills

- You make constructive and critical (not condescending or overrated) comments when discussing with your peers.
- You engage your peers in an in-depth discussion on a variety of issues (linguistic, social, cultural, etc.).
- You can draw upon a variety of communicative resources throughout the activity.
- You can make informed decisions in choosing the appropriate communication tools and strategies to get your messages across.